Voices Prophesying War 1763–1984

Voices Prophesying War 1763–1984

I. F. CLARKE

LONDON
OXFORD UNIVERSITY PRESS
NEW YORK TORONTO
1966

Oxford University Press, Ely House, London W.1
GLASGOW NEW YORK TORONTO MELBOURNE WELLINGTON
CAPE TOWN SALISBURY IBADAN NAIROBI LUSAKA ADDIS ABABA
BOMBAY CALCUTTA MADRAS KARACHI LAHORE DACCA
KUALA LUMPUR HONG KONG

Printed in Great Britain by
W. & J. Mackay & Co Ltd, Chatham, Kent

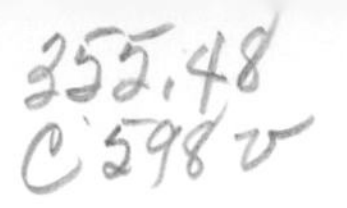

Contents

List of Illustrations

Acknowledgements

This book owes much to the help and advice of many persons and of many institutions.

I wish to express my grateful thanks to the staff of the Andersonian Library, the University of Strathclyde, for their unfailing help. I am particularly indebted to my kind friend and colleague, Geoffrey Wood, F.L.A., Librarian of the Andersonian Library. He has been most generous in the time he has spent in solving the many bibliographical and historical problems that have arisen in the course of my work. I thank him for his great willingness to assist and advise at all times.

Two of my colleagues have helped me at various stages in my researches. Dr John Butt has given excellent advice on aspects of nineteenth-century history; and Mr Donald Gordon found time to read the manuscript and raised many valuable points that have undoubtedly improved the book. I must thank Mrs Barr, who typed the final draft and helped in organizing the bibliographies. Most of all I have to thank my wife. This book would never have been completed if it had not been for her constant help.

A work of this kind has to depend on the willing collaboration of librarians in many lands. It gives me particular pleasure to record that I have always been fortunate in the prompt and valuable assistance from many libraries. I wish to thank the following: Abteilung Auskunft, Deutsche Bücherei, Leipzig; The Librarian, Bayerische Staatsbibliothek, Munich; The Director, Biblioteca Naçional, Madrid; The Chief Librarian, General Assembly Library, New Zealand; Reference Department, The Hoover Institution; The Librarian, Imperial War Museum; Katalogabteilung, Deutsche Staatsbibliothek; The Kriegsarchiv, Oesterreichisches Staatsarchiv; Bibliography Division, Library of Congress; The Librarian, National Library of Australia; Reference Division, National Library of Canada; The City Librarian, City of Portsmouth Central Library; The Librarian, The Prince Consort's Library; The Secretary, Private Libraries Association; Service Historique, Ministère des Armées, Paris.

I must record my lasting debt to the staff of the Reading Room of the British Museum and the Bodleian Library. And finally, I wish to acknowledge the help, book lists and suggestions sent by three friends: Jakob Bleymehl of Saarland, Dr Kremzow of Vienna, and Pierre Versins of Lausanne. My grateful thanks to them and to all who have assisted me in my work during the past three years.

UNIVERSITY OF STRATHCLYDE *May*, 1966

Chapter One

The Warfare of the Future: The Opening Phase, 1763–1871

IN the early summer of 1871 an anonymous story about a successful German invasion of the United Kingdom alarmed the nation and astounded many readers throughout Europe. This story was the *Battle of Dorking*, which came out in the May issue of *Blackwood's Magazine*; and its tale of disaster and defeat had such an effect that the Prime Minister felt it necessary to speak out against what he called the alarmism of a clever magazine article. Before the end of the year many other pamphlets and short stories had appeared to support or to deny the possibility of an invasion as the author had described it; and by the April of 1872 the fortunate author, Lieutenant-Colonel Sir George Tomkyns Chesney, had received a handsome sum from *Blackwood's* in final settlement of the large profit made from the many reprints.

The *Battle of Dorking* episode was much more than a major publishing event of 1871. It was undoubtedly the most remarkable propaganda piece that had appeared since the time of the Junius Letters. It had a dominant effect on the course and pattern of the new fiction of futuristic warfare, since Chesney's story provided both the form and the technique for most of the tales about imaginary wars of the future that began to appear throughout Europe after 1871. French, German, Italian, and American writers were glad to acknowledge their indebtedness to a story they considered the wonder of its day and the perfect prototype of its kind. And later on, although the demands of nationalism and the taste for romance among the new literate masses of the eighteen-nineties caused some changes in the pattern established by Chesney, the *Battle of Dorking* continued to exert its influence as late as the First World War. Then it was the turn of American patriots to use fiction as a means of warning their countrymen about the dangers of remaining unprepared in a warring world. In 1914 George

Putnam, the American publisher, bought the copyright of Chesney's story for publication in the United States; and in the introduction he wrote for *America Fallen*, an imaginary invasion published in 1915, Putnam devoted several paragraphs to a commentary on Chesney's *Battle of Dorking*, 'the work of a man who was a great staff officer and an accomplished student of military history'.

And yet Chesney was certainly not the first writer to describe an imaginary war of the future nor even an imaginary invasion of the British Isles. Long before 1871 there had been a succession of occasional pamphlets and satires that had used the description of future wars as a means of propaganda. Few of these, however, attracted more than a passing interest; and not one of them ever enjoyed success on a scale that could bear any comparison with the European reputation of the *Battle of Dorking*. The fact is that before Chesney the tale of the war-to-come was generally presented in political rather than in military terms. Writers looked on war as a customary process of European society. In their imagination they projected the weapons and tactics of their own day into a future that was simply the old world reshaped to suit their individual purposes. Before the *Battle of Dorking* no author of an imaginary war of the future ever suggested that the deliberate use of new weapons could have a decisive effect on the outcome of a battle.

It will be evident, therefore, that any account of the origin and development of these imaginary wars will also be a history of the various European attitudes to war itself. These stories show in an often striking manner all those moods and habits of mind that range from the nationalistic, often aggressive, and generally epic descriptions of future battles in the period before 1914 to the present-day forecasts of the horror that threatens mankind in tales like *Ape and Essence* and *On the Beach*. So, in one sense, all that follows will relate the rise and decline of the idea of armed conflict as a traditional practice readily accepted by Western industrial societies.

During the first main period in the course of the new fiction between 1871 and 1914 the decisive factors were the effect of technology on the conduct of war and the coming of universal literacy. After the Franco-German War of 1870 had changed the power system in Europe, and after the first ironclads and the first breech-loaders had started off the arms race, the fiction of imaginary warfare developed very rapidly. It became standard practice for writers in the major European countries to describe the shape of the war-to-come in order to demonstrate the need for bigger armies or better warships. As the new elementary schools taught the masses of the great industrial nations to read, the numbers of these imaginary wars increased, until by the eighteen-nineties they became a feature of the popular Press. Almost all of them took it for granted that the next war would be fought more or less after the style of the last, and that war would continue to be conducted in a relatively restrained and humane manner. This was a consequence of the time-lag, then for the most part unrecognized, between traditional attitudes to war and the rapid development of increasingly destructive weapons. Not a single writer—not even H. G. Wells—ever guessed that industrialism plus mass conscription would make it possible for a Falkenhayn to plan the Battle of Verdun with the intention of bleeding the French armies to death.

Today there is no comparable failure of the imagination. The world knows only too well what the effects of another total war could be. Special studies like the Rand Corporation *Report on non-military defense* have made everyone familiar with the jargon of Overkill, of nuclear and thermonuclear explosions, of bonus kills and exposure over the 200 *r* level. The brutal facts of the new military technologies describe the disaster of nuclear warfare in terms that fiction cannot better. Indeed, one expert in this field has claimed that 'even writers of fiction have failed to give us a deep impression of the nature and the extent of this catastrophe. Perhaps even they cannot truly visualize what it would mean to the survivors to see fifty, eighty, or a hundred million people killed within a few days or hours and tens of millions grievously ill, living without hope in hovels amidst poisonous radio-active debris.'[1]

Once, and it is difficult to realize it was only a hundred years ago, many men believed that the advance of science would provide the supreme deterrent. In 1864 Victor Hugo wrote in joyful phrases to the French balloonist, Nadar, that the invention of aircraft would mean the end of warfare. Out of science would come peace, since aircraft would bring about 'the immediate, absolute, instantaneous, universal and perpetual abolition of frontiers. Armies would vanish, and with them the whole business of war, exploitation and subjugation. It would be an immense peaceful revolution. It would mean the liberation of mankind.'[2]

Two world wars changed that simple faith. It was shattered in the First World War, when the great artillery battles and the grinding attrition of trench warfare demonstrated the powers of science in the *Materialschlacht*—the new kind of conflict that killed men and squandered material at a rate and on a scale never known before. But it took another world war and the invention of nuclear weapons before men finally gave up hoping that the advance of science would bring on the millennium. A fact central to human experience today is that, although a nuclear war would be the most terrible war ever fought, it would be the first in which there would be no real fighting. The struggle of man against man, of battery against battery, could never take place. After the last bombs had fallen, and after the survivors had waited ninety days in their shelters to escape the worst dangers of local fall-out, they would emerge into a blasted world, a desolate planet inherited by the insects and bacteria. Possibilities of this magnitude make it futile to describe the shape of a nuclear war. Today the image of the future is a shattered world seen through the periscope of the last submarine as it roves the seas in search of survivors from the last war upon the planet Earth. The paradox running through the whole literature of the imaginary wars of the future is that they begin as an argument on the need to prepare for the next war and they end on the Huxleyan theme of the need to prepare against the possibility of another war.

All this has come about in no more than two centuries. The earliest account of a future war appeared in an anonymous story of 1763, *The Reign of George VI, 1900–1925*, which was one of the earliest tales of the future and the first to project an ideal state into the centuries to come. The author had turned to the vacant area of the future in order to demonstrate a perfect Patriot King at work. The hero of the action is King George VI, who restores the greatness of his country and conquers all before him in the manner of an ideal eighteenth-century monarch. There is a curious prophetic irony about the description of the many marches and battles that make George VI master of Europe and King of France; for the narration is so much taken up with the best possible eighteenth-century system that time has not moved on. All the battles in the European War of 1917–20 are old-style affairs of infantry advancing in the oblique order of Frederick the Great and of naval battles hammered out by frigates and ships of the line. The kings of Europe still lead their troops into battle and at sea the secret weapon is the fire-ship. This the Duke of Grafton uses with devastating effect in 1920, when he discovers a Russian fleet in Stockholm: 'On a dark night he sent in six fire-ships among their squadron; eleven ships of the line were burnt and seven frigates, four sunk and seven taken.'

The unconscious irony of this history appears even more strikingly in the account of George VI's greatest victory before the gates of Vienna in May 1918, at a time when—in the real course of history—millions of men were in action along the Western Front and the Ludendorff Offensive was coming to a halt before the Americans at Château-Thierry. Contrast the scale of those facts in 1918 with the fiction of 1763:

> The Russian army had a superiority of above sixty thousand men, consequently their numbers were two to one; but no dangers could depress the heart of George. Having, with moving batteries, secured the rear and wings of his army from being surrounded, he placed his artillery in the most advantageous manner; and dividing his front into two lines, at the head of the first he began the attack, after his artillery had played on the enemy an hour, with great success. The Russian infantry, animated by the presence of their Czar under whom they had so often conquered, repulsed him with some loss. . . . George flew like lightning to his weakened troops; and, placing himself at the head of six regiments of dragoons, made such a furious attack on the eager Russians as threw them into disorder with great success.[3]

It is easy enough to find something quaint—even comic—in the contrast between the unprecedented scale of operations during the First World War and this would-be prophet's total failure to anticipate any change whatever in the nature of warfare. In projecting the battles of the eighteenth century into the year 1918 he had, however, been as true to the expectations of his times as so many later writers were to be true to nineteenth-century intimations of future aeronautical developments in their descriptions of air attacks by enormous airships propelled by steam, or electricity, or by more mysterious sources of power. In fact, the principal weakness in the *Reign of George VI* is that it had appeared during the closing phase of an ancient way of life, on the eve of momentous developments that were to alter the pattern of civilization as decisively and as completely as the discovery of agriculture and the domestication of animals had begun the process of civilization.

By an odd chance this first English historian of time-to-come had published his prediction during the last decades when it was still possible to expect that there would not be any extraordinary changes in the centuries ahead. A natural ignorance of the world-changing powers of technology had prevented the writer from having any idea that the tactics and weapons of his own time might not continue into the twentieth century. But, even as his book was being read, many factors were already at work that were soon to change the European attitude to time and in consequence would introduce a new dimension into the imagination. The change begins with the rapid success of the first balloon ascents, which date from the spectacular triumphs of the Montgolfier brothers and of Jacques Charles during the second half of 1783. These public demonstrations of the results of the new laboratory science, especially in the work of Jacques Charles, were a most powerful stimulant to the imagination. They helped to develop the sense of a human capacity for great achievements; and this growing awareness of the power of technology was still further enlarged by the enthusiasm that followed on the increasing use of the Watt steam engine during the closing decades of the eighteenth century. Changes of this order had a decisive effect on the development of that singular Western sense of the future as a distinct and desirable period of time. And out of the growing sharpness of the new vision of the future there came the new habit of predicting the shape of things to come.

This distinctive Western attitude to time made its first major appearance in the visual fantasies of the numerous prints that followed on the early balloon ascents. The imagination of many engravers had made the leap from the fact of flight by balloon in the seventeen-eighties to the possibility of balloon battles and balloon journeys to the moon in the future. The results of this shift in the imagination came out in many prints produced throughout Europe that showed vast Charlières with several decks of cannon sailing majestically through the clouds to bombard helpless ground troops from the air. And these appeared some twenty years before Robert Fulton made the first attempt to apply the new science to the art of war, when he demonstrated his 'plunging boat' to the French in 1803. Already the sense of the new potential in science had begun to act upon the imagination. Men were beginning to see that warfare might one day be very different from the tight squares and charging cavalry of their times. In this way the first rudimentary impressions of future wars had outrun the course of development years before Admiral

St. Vincent declared that Fulton's invention of the submarine and the torpedo 'was laying the foundation for doing away with the Navy on which depended the strength and prestige of Great Britain'.

The emergent technology of the industrial revolution was one factor that helped to establish the tale of imaginary warfare as a political and literary device. This joined with the anxieties aroused by the dangers of an invasion during the war against Napoleon to produce the earliest English war fantasics in print and prose. The prints began in the last years of the eighteenth century and they continued until Nelson's victory at Trafalgar ended the Great Terror caused by fears for the safety of Britain in the event of a French invasion. The purpose of the engravers was to attack Napoleon and to stiffen the British will to resist by showing the horrors to be expected from a French conquest. And in like manner on the French side there were plays and prints to encourage the nation in its efforts against the perfidious islanders. Some of these prints showed extraordinary contrivances reputed to have been designed for the invasion of England: large rafts, capable of transporting thousands of men and their equipment, with a windmill to provide motive power. Others displayed troop-carrying Montgolfières loaded with infantry and cavalry in the act of passing over Dover Castle; and some engravers bent hopeful fantasy to its limit in visions of a French army on the march through a newly constructed Channel Tunnel whilst up above a fleet of Charlières moved towards England.

In poetry and the drama writers on both sides of the Channel produced visions of a triumphant Britain repelling the invader or of the invading French triumphing over the British. The *Anti-Jacobin* for 1798 gave excerpts from a play then running at the Théâtre des Variétés in Paris. This was *La Descente en Angleterre: Prophétie en deux actes*, an interesting piece which already contained many of the stock characters and incidents that were to be a feature of the imaginary war fiction of the eighteen-nineties. The scene is Dover and the hero is that well-known figure of chauvinistic literature—the enemy citizen whose passion for a just cause makes him work for the other side. The part is played by Fergusson, a tavern-keeper, who organizes a group of conspirators to seize Dover Castle in order to assist a French landing. But the course of a patriotic drama can never run smoothly, and the author brings on a useful means of suspense in the person of 'a traitor sold to the

Combat Aërien: A French print captioned 'Aerial combat between two vessels, each of 100 pieces of artillery with steel bows in place of gunpowder, and with crews of 1,000 men, in the year 100 of the invention of aerostatic [i.e. lighter-than-air] machines'. The original has a key explaining the letters A (100-foot

vessels), B (balloons giving buoyancy—in practice more than can be shown in the drawing would be used), C (sails), D (rudders), E (chaloupe or aerial launch carrying a few men), etc. From François-Louis Bruel, *Histoire Aéronautique* (Paris, 1909), No. 146.

The Brig *Dorothea* blown up in one of Robert Fulton's demonstrations of his newly invented torpedo. Plate I from Fulton's book *Torpedo War and Submarine Explosions* published at New York in 1810.

party of Pitt'. He reveals all. The conspirators are apprehended by the Governor of Dover Castle and condemned to death, but at the last moment the French land, save their friends from the scaffold, and set off at the double for London, the general officer in command crying out: 'Englishmen! Now is your time to destroy the British Government which has caused all your misfortunes, desolated your neighbours, and set Europe on fire. It is time that the fate of the people should no longer depend on the caprice of an individual.'

These sentiments have nothing to do with the fantastic technology of the invasion rafts and the projects for invading Britain by balloon. They spring from the universal desire to see the enemy as contemptible, inferior, and already defeated. As the course of these imaginary wars unfolds it becomes clear that, no matter who

'AN ACCURATE REPRESENTATION of the FLOATING MACHINE Invented by the FRENCH for INVADING ENGLAND. and Acts on the principals of both Wind & Water Mills. carries 60,000 Men & 600 Cannon' [*sic*]. Engraving described in MS. note as 'from a drawing by Monsieur Freville —just arriv'd'; from a copy in the National Maritime Museum, Greenwich, by permission of the Trustees.

is the author and no matter what is the period of the story, these great wars of fiction are invariably directed by the internal principle that the greater the passion the greater is the element of nationalistic fantasy. An indication of this can be seen from the dialogue of the conspirators in the first act of the *Descente en Angleterre*. The chief conspirator begins:

Gordon: My friends, I will not remind you of the crimes of the English Government: the long tyranny which it has exercised upon the seas; the disasters which it has carried into the Colonies; the perfidiousness which it employs to perpetuate the scourge of war. I will not talk of Pitt. You all know that cunning is his instrument, deception his element, and that his infernal policy would sacrifice all the belligerent nations to his ambition.

'*La Thilorière, ou Descente en Angleterre:* Project for a Montgolfière capable of lifting 3,000 men, and costing only 300,000 francs!!!!! [*sic*] It will have suspended from it a lamp which will provide a jet of flame sufficient to prevent it from cooling down!!!' From *Le Publiciste*, Thursday 13 Prairial, Year XI [1805]. By permission of the Director of the Science Museum, London.

Fergusson: Yes, it is time to put a stop to the murderous plots of that destroyer of the human race.

A Conspirator: Philosophy has already devoted him to the execration of the people.

Gordon: English Patriots, you have already heard the thundering eloquence of Fox. He summons you to assert your rights.

Fergusson: We shall know how to defend them.

Gordon: His voice invokes liberty.

Fergusson: We will gain it at the expense of our lives.

Gordon: But let us not stop for idle talk; let us think of carrying out our plan. You are all decided in favour of a French descent that will shatter your chains, and bring freedom to your degraded country?

Conspirators: Yes! Yes!

Fergusson: We swear it.

Gordon: The guarantees of victory are Fox and his friends; our courage and Buonaparte. The genius of liberty watches over the people, and will soon crush their tyrants. [*He unfolds a large piece of paper*] In two hours the descent will be made. The regiment in this town is commanded by the brave Houssey. We can count on him; but we have everything to fear from the Commander of the Port; he is sold to Pitt and his infamous agents. We must anticipate him and strike the first blow.[4]

There is little difference between this fantasy of the Napoleonic period and the mass production of British and German visions of future wars in the years before 1914. What the dramatist had written in *La Descente en Angleterre* would be repeated in the new setting of cruisers and torpedo boats in a tale like Karl Bleibtreu's *Die "Offensiv-Invasion" gegen England* of 1907. Hope and fear, a desire to teach and to warn, are behind all these tales of future warfare. The French in 1803 look to a successful invasion of Great Britain; and on the other side of the Channel equally sturdy patriots foresee a total defeat for the French. One anti-French forecast appeared in a play of 1803, *The Invasion of England.* The author's purpose was quite simple: he wanted to show how British courage, resolution, and soldierly ability would triumph over the dastard French invaders. The theme of the play was to become very familiar in the imaginary wars published between 1871 and 1914: 'Better for us to fall than our country.' It had all the trappings of patriotism and sentiment. A young mother laments over her innocent children and a handsome 'Lieutenant of the Navy' comes in with the news that the main French invasion forces had been defeated: 'They had slipt out of Boulogne, with a parcel of their

Result of the invention of aerostatic machines. Engraving by J. M. Will, with captions in German and French referring to the great advantage that will be attributable to the inventor of aerostatic [lighter-than-air] machines which

will be able to intervene in great battles by aerial bombardment. From F.-L. Bruel, op. cit., No. 145.

flat boats full of troops, in a dark night—they had given our sloops of war the slip; but on daylight, being half-channel over, some of our frigates fell in with them.' That vision of future victory sprang from the mood of anger and alarm that had swept the country in 1803, when it was learnt that the First Consul had ordered the construction of invasion craft at Dunkirk and Cherbourg.

When the thousands of pinnaces, sloops, gunboats and other craft were ready, the scheme was for the flotillas to assemble at Boulogne. From there, weather and the Royal Navy permitting, they would transport the invasion force across the Channel for the great task of stamping out British resistance to the French domination of Europe. The menace of a French invasion produced attitudes and responses that recall the more recent mood of 1940.

'Divers Projets de Descente en Angleterre.' '. . . French army on the march through a newly-constructed Channel Tunnel whilst up above a fleet of Charlières moved towards England.' Engraving after a print in F.-L. Bruel, op. cit., No. 158.

'Does haughty Gaul invasion threat?' wrote Robert Burns. 'Then let the louns beware, Sir!' As the rumours of dead Germans and wrecked invasion barges had produced an imagined victory out of real anxieties in 1940, so the comparable situation during the time of the expected French invasion had fathered similar fantasies of a British victory in verse, in engravings, and in the drama. Here, for instance, is the comforting vision of victory as it was reported in *The Armed Briton* by William Burke. A dragoon enters with the news for the heroine:

Dragoon: The enemy, madam, after their landing, having pushed on and taken possession of this place, halted to arrange themselves for further operations—but our generals, aware of the intention and that this was only a division of the enemy, resolved to attack without

> delay, and by that means prevent their being joined by any other bodies of the invading force. With this view, they lost not a moment, but collecting and forming the troops as they arrived, led them bravely on, the officers pointing out to the men [*imitating with his sword*] with their swords the enemy entrenched in front, and reminding them that in all probability the events of that day would give forever their country a prize to the conquerors. Four times our brave soldiers assaulted the enemy's works, but were as often compelled to retreat before a tremendous fire of grape-shot from their batteries. [*Georgiana appears terrified*] The carnage was now becoming dreadful —the ardour for attack slackened for the moment—but 'British courage was not to be subdued'. [*Looking fierce*] A few heroes were seen everywhere, flying sword in hand through the broken ranks, exhorting Britons 'not to abandon tamely their country.' In an instant the fatigued troops became re-animated—the unjust attack and danger of their country filled them with fresh indignation; and nobly rallying in the midst of the enemy's shot and shells, those brave men once more rushed furiously on to the assault, over heaps of their slain countrymen.[5]

More striking than this, however, were the prints and caricatures that poured out during the period of the war against Napoleon. It was a time of intense patriotic activity for the many outstanding artists who regularly turned out satirical prints against the hated Bonaparte. One of the first of these anti-French prints appeared in 1796, the work of the brilliant caricaturist, James Gillray. It was called the 'Promised Horrors of the French Invasion'; and it showed what many people were already forecasting: French troops barbarously slaughtering the inhabitants of London, and Pitt bound ready for execution.

The engravings produced by Gillray and his contemporaries reveal the other point of origin for the new habit of showing the dangers of the day fully developed in a future time of terror. Between Gillray in 1796 and Saki's *When William Came* of 1913 there is little real difference. Indeed, only a different enemy and different circumstances distinguish the purpose behind Gillray's picture of the French in London from the purpose that shaped Saki's account of the German occupation of London. Both men in their different ways were using the art at their command to warn their countrymen to prepare, whilst they still had time, against the dangers that might come. But before the prose fiction of the imaginary war could begin to attract the attention of a nation or of an entire continent, as the *Battle of Dorking* was to do in 1871, new literary habits had still to emerge. The *Anti-Gallican*, for instance, which was constant in its attacks on the French, gave most of the space to addresses by bishops, generals, and gentlemen on the perils of invasion, and to poems that breathed defiance to the enemy. It was unusual to find in one number[6] a brief sketch of London under French occupation:

An Invasion Sketch

London, 10 Thermidor, year – –

General Bonaparte made his public entrance into the Capital over London Bridge, upon a charger from HIS BRITANNIC MAJESTY'S stables at Hanover, preceded by a detachment of Mamelukes. He stopped upon the bridge a few seconds to survey the number of ships in the river; and beckoning to one of his Aid-de-camps ordered the French flag to be hoisted above the English—the English sailors on board, who attempted to resist the execution of this order, were bayonetted, and thrown overboard. When he came to the Bank, he smiled with complaisance upon a detachment of French grenadiers who had been sent to load the bullion in waggons, which had been previously put in requisition by the prefect of London, Citizen MENGAUD, for the purpose of being conveyed to France.

But propaganda forecasts of this type were very brief and appeared very rarely before the *Battle of Dorking* and the beginnings of the arms race altered matters in Europe. Until 1871, and certainly during the first half of the nineteenth century, the anxieties of the nation still found their usual means of expression in satirical prints as well as through the customary channels of the public oration, the tracts against the peril of the day, and especially through the traditional medium of poetry. Burns, Coleridge, and Scott all wrote verses on the theme of the invasion danger. In 1803, when Napoleon was assembling his Armée de l'Angleterre across the Channel, Wordsworth wrote a prophetic poem of rejoicing over the destruction of the French invasion force that never appeared. Very appropriately it was called 'Anticipation':

Shout, for a mighty Victory is won!
On British ground the Invaders are laid low;
The breath of Heaven has drifted them like snow,
And left them lying in the silent sun,
Never to rise again! The work is done.

There is no fundamental distinction between anxieties at a possible French invasion in 1803 and the detection of similar

This day was published,

AN

ADDRESS to the PEOPLE

OF THE UNITED KINGDOM OF

Great Britain and Ireland,

ON THE THREATENED

INVASION.

EXTRACTS FROM THE ABOVE WORK.

AMONG the inexpressibly dreadful consequences which are sure to attend the conquest of your Island by the French, there is one of so horrible a nature, as to deserve distinct notice. This barbarous, but most artful people, when first they invade a country in the conquest of which they apprehend any difficulty, in order to obtain the confidence of the people, compel their troops to observe the strictest discipline, and often put a soldier to death for stealing the most trifling article. Like spiders they artfully weave a web round their victim, before they begin to prey upon it. But when their success is complete they then let loose their troops, with resistless fury, to commit the most horrible excesses, and to pillage, burn, and desolate, without mercy, and without distinction. But the practice to which I particularly allude will make your blood freeze in your veins. These wretches are accustomed, whenever they prevail, to subject the women to the most brutal violence, which they perpetrate with an insulting ferocity, of which the wildest savages would be incapable. To gratify their furious passions is not however their chief object in these atrocities. Their principal delight is to shock the feelings of fathers and brothers, and husbands! Will you, my Countrymen, while you can draw a trigger, or handle a pike, suffer your daughters, your sisters, and wives, to fall into the power of such monsters?

Specimens of French Ferocity and Brutality in Wales.

It is well known that in the last War some French troops succeeded in effecting a landing in Wales. They were greatly superior to the regular force which happened to be in the part of the country where they landed: but, upon seeing, at a distance, a number of Welsh women with red cloaks, whom they mistook for soldiers, they surrendered! The following proofs of their ferocity and brutality are well attested.

A peasant whom they had compelled to assist them in landing their stores, presumed to ask for some compensation, upon which the commanding Officer drew a pistol, and SHOT THE POOR FELLOW THROUGH THE HEART.

Two Officers went to a house, in which was a woman in child-bed, attended by her mother, who was upwards of Seventy Years old. The French brutes tied the husband with cords, and, in his presence, defiled both the wife and the mother!!!

LONDON

Printed by H. Bryer, Bridewell Hospital, Bridge Street.

The Address is sold by J. DOWNES, Temple Bar; J. SPRAGG, King Street Covent Garden; J. ASPERNE, Cornhill; and J. HATCHARD, Piccadilly.

Price Two-pence each, or Twelve Shillings the Hundred, and Eighteen-pence per Dozen.

Advertisement, with hair-raising extracts from the text, of a twopenny booklet 'Address to the People of . . . Great Britain and Ireland on the Threatened Invasion', published by four London booksellers in 1803.

German plans in Erskine Childers's admirable *Riddle of the Sands* in 1903. Armaments, the size of populations, and the power of European countries had all changed beyond precedent since Wellington's 70,000 troops had formed square and prepared to receive cavalry at Waterloo. In the space of one hundred years the population of the United Kingdom had come close to trebling itself and the British people had employed all the contrivances of the new technology to establish an immense empire throughout the world. But no matter how great had been the change in circumstances, the situation of the island race remained unchanged. From Cecil to Marlborough, from Pitt to Asquith, the national policy had been grounded on the principle that the United Kingdom could never allow any single nation to be predominant in Europe, and that in all operations affecting the security of the British Isles the Royal Navy had to have decisive superiority. From Shakespeare to Churchill it had been the constant refrain of poets and politicians that the narrow seas served the country in the office of 'a moat defensive to a house'. As Coleridge put it:

> And Ocean, 'mid his uproar wild,
> Speaks safety to his Island child!
> Hence for many a fearless age
> Has social Quiet loved thy shore;
> Nor ever proud Invader's rage
> Or sacked thy towers, or stained thy fields with gore.

But that was in the days of sail, when it was easy to maintain British naval superiority. In an epoch of wooden ships there was little to fear until steam and armour-plating revolutionized the nature of naval warfare, and conscription plus railways did the same for land warfare. Out of these developments came a central paradox of the nineteenth century. Whilst a poet like Tennyson could find reasons for immense hope in 'the ringing grooves of change', the admirals and the generals only too often could see nothing but disaster in the invention of the steamship. As discovery followed on discovery in that hectic epoch, from the first screw propeller to the devastating use of the shell projectile at the Battle of Sinope in 1853, the exuberant delight in the new myth of progress covered a multitude of anxieties about the future of an island people in a time of unending technological advance. The generation of the Reform Bill and the Great Exhibition had been born under the twin sign of Watt and Napoleon. Steam power and continental militarism appeared to make a nightmare of the future for many thoughtful people—especially for the military. Some felt that the recent invention of the steamship had made the war against Napoleon a very close-run affair. That was the view of Robert Southey, the poet and the biographer of Nelson. He observed in 1829 that it was 'worthy of especial remark, and more especial gratitude that if steam ships had been rendered manageable only ten years earlier—nay, even a less time—our deadly struggle with Buonaparte must have been decided upon our own soil; and in that case London might easily have shared the same fate as Moscow'.[7]

Southey's remarks throw light on the process that finally triggered off the explosion of imaginary wars in 1871. He had seen how warfare had ceased to be a traditional business; and he seems to have guessed how military preparedness would become a balancing act on the edge of technological development. His views on the changes made by steam anticipated the invasion scare of the eighteen-forties when it was widely assumed that the new steamships had put an end to British naval supremacy. This scare, the first of many invasion scares, was largely provoked by the Prince de Joinville's pamphlet of May 1844. The Prince was a son of Louis Philippe and an ardent supporter of French naval development. In his *Note sur les Forces Navales de la France* he sought to drive home the importance of the French fleet by describing how France could use the new steamships to reduce Britain's naval lead. Since the imagination had not yet mastered the scale of the changes then taking place at sea, de Joinville's account of the damage that could be done to British commerce and his indication of the way the steamship could facilitate operations against Britain were together responsible for a major panic over the possibility of invasion. The danger had been stated all too clearly by de Joinville: 'With a steam navy an aggressive war of the most audacious nature may be carried on at sea. We are then certain of our movements, at liberty in our actions; the weather, the wind, the tides will no longer interfere with us.' In consequence, the nation began to lose faith in the abiding principle, so well put in Blackstone's famous dictum, that 'the royal navy of England hath ever been its greatest defence and ornament'. Thus, in 1845 Palmerston was for a time ready to believe it possible for the French to convey a large force across the Channel on a favourable night. He told the Commons: '. . . the Channel is no longer a barrier. Steam navigation has rendered that which was before impassable by a military force nothing more than a river passable by a steam bridge.'[8] And in 1848 Wellington himself unwittingly added to the general anxiety when a letter of his on national defence to Sir John Burgoyne, Inspector-General of Fortifications, was published in the *Morning Chronicle* without his knowledge. The letter was a considerable shock, since the public for the most part ignored the limiting conditions Wellington had been careful to write into his opinion. They forgot his point that 'if it be true that the exertions of the fleet alone are not sufficient to provide for our defence', and they saw only the terrible warning that 'we are not safe for a week after the declaration of war'.

The many profound changes in the pattern of warfare since 1847 make it difficult for us to appreciate the full extent of the shock caused by Wellington's letter. His great prestige only served to confirm the worst fears that the days of Britain's insular security were over; for the Duke had said that, apart from the Dover area, there was 'not a spot on the coast on which infantry might not be thrown on shore at any time of the tide, with any wind, and in any weather'. The characteristically blunt statement from Wellington caused a major panic in many papers. It seemed to deny many accepted ideas consecrated by centuries of repetition. The poet Campbell had boasted in some famous lines that Britannia required no bulwarks—'no towers along the steep'. But the new steamships seemed to destroy this natural order of society; and for this reason many found it difficult to make the necessary mental adjustment from the traditional picture of Nelson's weather-beaten ships on perpetual watch outside the French ports to the new era of steamships and possible invasions.

It was certainly no simple matter of steamships moving secretly by night across the Channel. And the Prince Consort was only revealing half the story when he announced in 1850 that 'nobody who has paid any attention to the peculiar features of our present era will doubt for a moment that we are living at a period of most wonderful transition'. For the steamship panic of the eighteen-forties marked the beginnings of a process of transition and rapid development in every aspect of warfare that has not yet ended. One immediate effect was that naval tactics of a sudden became a matter of guesswork and the signal books had to be rewritten. Technology had come bearing many gifts that were to prove dangerous, and already in the eighteen-forties anxious questions were being asked about the state of the national defences and about the best equipment for the armed forces. At times even the Duke of Wellington did not know the right answer, as Lord Hardinge discovered in 1851, when he argued in favour of issuing the new Minié rifle to the infantry. The Duke would not consent. The arms race had started and Hardinge feared that in the course of the next three or four years there would be a general war in Europe: 'we shall be involved in it, and we shall be beaten unless we have a rifle'.[9]

From the steamship episode of the eighteen-forties to the many alarms in the years before 1914 not a decade passed without a national commotion of some kind. At times the alarm would sound on an incident like the engagement between the ironclad *Monitor* and the Confederate *Merrimac* during the American Civil War. According to *The Times*, it meant the end of British naval supremacy, since the performance of the new ironclad had made all but the *Warrior* and the *Ironside* obsolete. And at once the Press began to cry: 'We are actually without a war fleet. We shall be outstripped to a certainty by America, and possibly by France, if we do not move at once. Already America is preparing to finish her Stevens battery, which promises to be to the *Monitor* what that was to the *Merrimac*.'[10]

On other occasions the panic would start from a political development like the *coup d'état* by Louis Napoleon in December 1851. This made him dictator of France and at once all the worst memories of the first Napoleon revived to make the year 1852 another time of anxiety. In the January of that year the Prince Consort told Prince William of Prussia that the public was 'occupied and bothered by the idea of a possible French invasion'. Then, in the May of the same year Queen Victoria wrote to the Earl of Derby that 'all the Foreign Powers have to be careful about is to receive an assurance that the *Empire* does *not* mean *a return to the policy of the Empire*, but that existing treaties will be acknowledged and adhered to'.[11] Month by month there was an unbroken series of pamphlets, books, and articles in the Press which anxiously examined the state of the national defences. One of these was an anonymous prediction of twenty-three pages, *A History of the sudden and terrible invasion of England by the French in the month of May, 1852*. It foretold how 'that little Corsican, Louis Napoleon Bonaparte', improved on his uncle by launching a successful invasion of Britain.* The point of the story was the danger of not being prepared for the new style of warfare. National indolence and the inadequate equipment of the troops brought on the disaster when 'the whole of the English army was annihilated before they could come within shot of the enemy'.

The French invasion follows the pattern of contemporary fears. Louis Napoleon makes secret preparations to attack Britain, and when all is ready a French fleet of fourteen steamers crosses the Channel and lands the advance guard on the Sussex coast. In little more than a fortnight the French have crushed all opposition, seized London, and imposed an enormous indemnity. The author mixes anger with ridicule in order to make the reader see the dangers threatening the country:

When Parliament met, some talked like old women of the Law of Nations, and Declarations of War; forgetting that he who had stolen the liberties of his country, like a thief in the night, would not be very likely to hesitate where only his enemies were concerned; others, no less like old women, vaunted the courage of the people, and spoke in the true Bobadil style of swallowing a disciplined army of Frenchmen like so many oysters, forgetting that an English mob, which is all that could be raised at a short notice, and which may easily be repulsed by half-a-dozen policemen, was not likely to stand firm very long against the deadly fire of the Tirailleurs de Vincennes; while a third party, more foolish than either, pointed triumphantly to the fortifications of Portsmouth, and hinted historically at Tilbury and the Spanish Armada, just as if the French generals knew nothing of the science of war, and would invade England through a strong fortress or by a dangerous river, rather than, as they actually did, force the position in the centre, whence the road to London was the shortest, and where the people were utterly and entirely destitute of the means of defence.[12]

The chief device for commenting on a crisis, however, was still the book, the pamphlet, and the article in the monthly or quarterly journals. They poured from the presses year by year: *Thoughts on National Defence, The Defensive Position of England, On National Defence in England, A Memoir on the Defence of East Suffolk, System of National Defence, Measures for the Defence of England, The National*

* Two French imaginary wars, published about this time, were devoted to very different ends. Louis Geoffrey in his *Napoléon Apocryphe, 1812–1832* (1841) described an imaginary conquest of the world by Napoleon. In *Hurrah! ou la revolution par les Cosaques* (1854) the Socialist writer, Ernest Coeurderoy, wrote of a Slav invasion that destroyed the decadent bourgeois society of the West.

Defences, The Invasions and Projected Invasions of England, A French Officer's Ideas upon the Defence of England, Political and Legislative Considerations on National Defence, On the Defence of England: Naval, Littoral and Internal, The Defences of London, The Perils of Portsmouth, The Fleet of the Future, National Defences: the Great Question of the Day.

These and hundreds like them filled the decades between 1840 and 1880 with their forecasts of disaster, with complaints, denunciations, plans, and counter-plans for the defence of the British Isles. All of them were variations on the Prince Consort's theme of 'most wonderful transition', and all of them were trying to find some effective and final answer to the problem of adapting the armed forces and their equipment to the new dynamics of warfare. For one writer the only hopeful fact in a gloomy future was that 'if scientific discoveries have increased the faculty of attack, and diminished that of defence in general, exception has to be made in reference to the attack of maritime fortresses by floating vessels'.[13] Here at least the invention of hollow shot gave the shore batteries every advantage. The guessing game had begun. Would new weapons have a decisive effect in the next war? Would the advantage lie with the attack or the defence? One distinguished officer thought that the odds were certainly on the side of the invader:

It is a question that has been considered, whether the introduction of more rapid means of locomotion through the adoption of steam, and of more speedy methods of the communication of information through the adoption of electricity, will be more favourable in future wars to the attack or the defence. Both will no doubt to a certain extent be benefited, but as the essence of the success of an attack in most cases depends upon surprise, and in all cases on rapidity of action, it appears certain that the assailant will derive more advantage from these improvements than those who have to resist his assault. In case of an invasion being at a future time directed against our shores, it will not now be necessary that the transports or the armed vessels that are to convey them should be assembled in any particular port, or collected beneath some well-marked feature of the shore where their concentration must be known to the cruisers of the enemy. It will be only necessary that a certain point should be fixed upon the chart as the rendezvous for their flotilla, and only known to the commanders who have to direct the operations. These, too, would not necessarily be acquainted with the spot, until they had already left their ports, and were out of sight of land. The power of steam would allow these vessels to be collected at a certain point without danger of delay, or of being blown back to friendly harbours by unfavourable breezes. The introduction of the electric telegraph would allow various descents to be made on different parts of the coasts simultaneously, and would thus prevent the great advantage which has hitherto accrued to the defence of acting on interior lines in such a manner as to allow different parts of an assailant force, attacking at intervals to be overwhelmed by the superior force of the defendant thrown judiciously on particular points, while other points of assault were watched and defended by weak detachments.[14]

For many of these writers the problem resolved itself into the facile solution of new ships for the navy, or new weapons for the army, or new fortifications along the coast from Plymouth to the Thames. But these did not answer the really crucial question of what was to be done if great continental armies did manage to establish a bridgehead on this side of the English Channel. How was an island nation to defend itself against the danger of attack by immensely superior land forces? As Sir John Burgoyne had pointed out to the Master-General of the Ordnance in his memorandum, *Observations on the possible Results of a War with France, under our present system of Military Preparation*, there were in 1846 some 30,000 regular troops in the whole of the United Kingdom; and that, when the troops needed for reserves and for garrisoning Ireland had been subtracted, there were at the most perhaps 10,000 left to face an invading force ten times their number. The point was developed by the Royal Commission on national defence of 1859. As the Commissioners saw the matter, the great danger was that if the Fleet, 'from whatever cause, be unable to keep the command of the Channel, it appears to your Commissioners that the insular position of the kingdom, so far from being an advantage, might prove a disadvantage for defensive purposes, in as much as it would enable any superior Naval Power or Powers to concentrate a larger body of troops on any part of our coasts, and more rapidly and secretly than could be done against any neighbouring country having only a land frontier; and an army so placed could maintain its base, and be reinforced, and supplied with more facility than if dependent on land communications'.[15]

One solution much favoured at this time was to establish special fortifications in such vital areas as Portsmouth and Plymouth. Some of them are still there, close to the anti-tank ditches and air-landing obstacles devised against another threat of invasion. But, in fact, there were only two possible answers to the problem. One way was for Britain to find some acceptable means of increasing the number of trained men available for home defence. The other way was to choose between the advantages of following the Prussian system of universal military service or the more distasteful French practice of using a ballot system to augment their large regular forces. The one was unthinkable and the other was impossible. And so a temporary answer was found in the expedient of directing the Lords-Lieutenant to establish formations of Volunteers, when there were fears of a French invasion in 1859. They were to consist mainly of artillery batteries and engineers for coastal defence, as well as infantry battalions organized in brigades for home defence. The First Lord of the Admiralty called on the Commons 'to restore the naval supremacy of England'; and in the debate on the National Defences Lord Lyndhurst warned the country of French intentions: '. . . the French are at the present moment building steamers for the purpose of transporting troops, each of which is being constructed to carry 2,500 men with all the necessary stores'.[16] The Poet Laureate rose to the occasion with a special poem on the Volunteer movement for *The Times* of 9th May:

The War

There is sound of thunder afar,
Storm in the south that darkens the day,
Storm of battle and thunder of war,
Well, if it do not roll our way.
Storm! storm! Riflemen form!
Ready, be ready to meet the storm!
Riflemen, riflemen, riflemen form!

Let your reforms for a moment go,
Look to your butts and take good aims
Better a rotten borough or so
Than a rotten fleet or a city in flames!
Form! form! Riflemen form!
Ready, be ready to meet the storm!
Riflemen, riflemen, riflemen form!

The Volunteer system, however, in spite of all the rhetoric and the fashions it generated, could not be the final answer, since the role of the Volunteers was to supplement but not to replace the regular forces. What these part-time troops might have to face was revealed in a succession of wars that suddenly flared up in Europe. For the Italian campaign of 1859 the French mobilized an army of 120,000. In the wars against Denmark in 1864 and against Austria in 1866 the Prussian General Staff showed a formidable capacity for using the railway, the telegraph, and the mass forces of their conscript system to make the change from peace establishments to large armies in a brief space of time. Then came the war of 1870 and the stupefaction that followed on the rapidity and completeness of the German victories. For most observers would have agreed with Matthew Arnold, Professor of Poetry in the University of Oxford and Inspector of Schools, in his 'conviction as to the French always beating any number of Germans who come into the field against them. They will never be beaten by any nation but the English, for to every other nation they are, in efficiency and intelligence, decidedly superior'.[17] Convictions of this kind explain the astonishment of all who watched the rapid progress of the Franco-German War. What everyone had imagined to be the greatest military power in Europe had been crushed in a series of dazzling victories. The speed and scale of the operations seemed so unprecedented that the *Annual Register* for 1870 was at a loss for comparisons: 'Only by becoming, in imagination, the readers of some future historical work, and comparing it with any or all of the histories that now stand upon our shelves, can we form an idea of the place that must be found in the world's annals for the catastrophe of Sedan and the siege of Paris.'

But suppose the Fleet were absent one day, and suppose that the Prussian General Staff had secretly concentrated several armies close to railheads and North Sea ports, what could the Volunteers do when the German veterans stormed ashore somewhere on the South Coast? That was a hidden fear after 1870; and it was the starting-point for a sudden run of imaginary wars that followed on the warning vision at the end of Chesney's *Battle of Dorking*. It had happened to France and it could happen to Britain. But, Chesney wrote, the consequences would be even more terrible: 'When I look at my country as it is now—its trade gone, its factories silent, its harbours empty, a prey to pauperism and decay—when I see all this and think what Great Britain was in my youth, I ask myself whether I have really a heart or any sense of patriotism that I should have witnessed such degradation and still care to live.'

Chapter Two

The Break-in Phase: The Battle of Dorking Episode

ON 18th January 1871 the Hohenzollerns took over the palace of the Bourbons and in the Galerie des Glaces at Versailles the German princes hailed the King of Prussia as the first Emperor of the new German Reich. The splendid ceremonies and the sonorous proclamations marked the end of French military dominance in Europe and the emergence of a new political power. There was already a suggestion of coming changes in the Emperor's declaration: 'We undertake the Imperial dignity, conscious of the duty to protect with German loyalty the rights of the Empire and its members, to preserve peace, to maintain the independence of Germany, and to strengthen the power of the people.'

Ten days later at the German Headquarters one of the French delegates, General de Valdan, signed the articles of an armistice between the two nations. And eleven days after that a distinguished officer of the Royal Engineers, writing from the India Office, sent John Blackwood the outline of a short story. He believed that if *Blackwood's Magazine* published his story it would drive home the need for a complete reorganization of the British military system. It was the starting-point for 'that wonderful and stirring romance', as Admiral Colomb called the *Battle of Dorking*. The would-be contributor was Sir George Tomkyns Chesney, who had begun his military career as a second-lieutenant in the Bengal Engineers and after outstanding service in India had been recalled to establish the Royal Indian Civil Engineering College at Staines. Chesney, a colonel at this time, was an enterprising and energetic man, one of the new race of educated soldiers to be found in a specialist branch like the Royal Engineers. He had first written for *Blackwood's* in 1867; and on his return from India in 1870 he renewed his connexion with the magazine in a letter in which he offered to review the second volume of Kaye's *History of India*.

The Battle of Dorking: Reminiscences of a Volunteer. Mag. J.B.

You ask me to tell you, my grandchildren, something about my own share in the great events that happened fifty years ago. 'Tis sad work ~~calling up~~ turning back to that bitter page in our history, but you may perhaps take profit in your new homes from the lesson it teaches. For us in England it came too late. And yet we had plenty of warnings if we had only made use of them. The danger did not come on us unawares. It burst on us suddenly, 'tis true, but its coming was foreshadowed plainly enough to open our eyes, if we had not been wilfully blind. We English have only ourselves to blame for the humiliation which has been brought on the land. Venerable old age! Dishonourable old age, I say, when it follows a manhood dishonoured as ours has been. I declare even now though fifty years have passed, I can hardly look a young man in the face when I think

First page of Chesney's MS. of *The Battle of Dorking* written for *Blackwood's Magazine* (and annotated 'Mag.-J.B.' by John Blackwood) in 1871. (By permission of Mr. Douglas Blackwood.)

This made him a regular contributor and led to his suggestion for a story 'describing a successful invasion of England, and the collapse of our power and commerce in consequence'.

Chesney was fortunate enough to have found the right moment for discharging his frightening forecast upon the British people, since most of the year 1871 was passed in a mood of foreboding and anxiety for the future. In fact, Chesney's success owed everything to the moment and to his capacity for showing contemporary fears fully realized in an imaginary future. The accident of an effective style and the fact that the *Battle of Dorking* had appeared in a widely read magazine made Chesney the true begetter of the new fiction of imaginary warfare, although he was not the first in the field. His immediate predecessor was Alfred Bates Richards, the editor of the *Morning Advertiser*, who had long campaigned for an improved system of national defence and had played a leading part in the establishment of the Volunteers in 1859.[1] In the August of 1870 Richards had a pamphlet printed for private circulation, *The Invasion of England* (*A possible tale of future times*). It described an enemy invasion in which incompetent regulars and heroic Volunteers die in familiar English surroundings. It is possible that Chesney may have seen the pamphlet; but since he denied that he had copied from Richards, and since he had sent his sketch of an imaginary invasion to Blackwood twelve days before Richards printed his own story in the *Morning Advertiser*, it is unlikely that Richards' story had any influence on Chesney. He had nothing to learn from Richards. He was a far better writer and had an unusual imaginative capacity for transforming the facts of a military situation into an alarmingly realistic narrative. No matter who was first in time, there is no doubt at all that the whole of Europe considered that Chesney's *Battle of Dorking* had introduced a new type of purposive fiction. French, German, Dutch, Scandinavian, and Italian writers paid him the compliment of applying to their own countries the techniques Chesney had so successfully employed in Britain.

The nation was a ready victim for a tale of terror that would realize its fears and the ominous predictions then being made. According to the *Pall Mall Gazette* of 9th January, 'most Englishmen believe that at present the country is not properly secured against attack, that its purely defensive forces are not sufficiently large or sufficiently organized to make invasion virtually impossible'. On 21st January Lord John Russell bore out this claim in a letter to *The Times* in which he recommended that a force of 200,000 troops, regulars and militia, should be retained in the United Kingdom. Once again the general alarm began to sound throughout the Press; and then, as news arrived of the entry of the German troops into Paris, the sense of anxiety increased markedly. Many feared that the event was symbolic—even prophetic—of what might yet happen to the British people. They thought that, but for good luck and the English Channel, those long lines of German infantry might have been moving through London on that grey and cheerless morning of 1st March, instead of parading past the veiled statues in the Place de la Concorde. The alarm even penetrated to the usually placid pages of *All the Year Round*: 'Half a million men, who have trodden down France and threatened England, may pine for fresh conquests. It may suddenly appear necessary for United Germany to win colonies, and a foothold in Central Asia, Persia or India.'[2] That was the mood of the year 1871. The *Annual Register* looking back on the events of the year saw it as a time of chronic anxiety, when Britain 'was in one of her fits of periodical alarm about herself, and to believe those who should know best, she was never in so fatally unprepared a condition as now, at a moment when the Prussian armaments were secretly gathering against her, if indeed the French war, as some of our journals more than insinuated, had not been undertaken chiefly as a prelude to the working-out of some sinister design upon ourselves'.[3]

Chesney was indeed fortunate in the timing of the *Battle of Dorking*; he was still more fortunate in his gift for writing a vigorous narrative and in his experience as a military specialist. He followed in the tradition of the numerous army and navy officers who had been turning out pamphlets on the problems of national defence ever since the appearance of the steamship had revolutionized the conduct of warfare. But he broke with this tradition by presenting his arguments in fictional form. Moreover, although precedents for the story of imaginary warfare had existed long before Chesney, he owed little to them—despite many obvious affinities of mood and intention. His effectiveness as a writer owed everything to the new realistic technique he had borrowed deliberately from the stories of Erckmann-Chatrian as well as to the imaginative procedure of attempting to assess the intentions of an enemy. In this sense the imaginary war is older than Alexander and Hannibal. Soldiers have always had to plan their campaigns on the basis of what they considered the enemy would do in certain circumstances. Add the methods of the realistic narrative to the practice of the military assessment and the product is a full-scale story of imaginary warfare.

Chesney's most telling contrivance, however, was to transform the old-style military tract into a vivid narrative by presenting all his propaganda through the experiences of the Volunteer who tells the story. Chesney begins: 'You ask me to tell you, my grandchildren, something about my own share in the great events that happened fifty years ago. 'Tis sad work turning back to that bitter page in our history, but you may perhaps take profit in your new homes from the lesson it teaches. For us in England it came too late.' From that ominous start the narrative goes on its way, as the Volunteer tells of one disaster after another. He represents the well-intentioned Volunteer, the typical middle-class gentleman who meant well to his country, provided that he was not asked to pay what he thought was too high a price for national safety. In this way Chesney contrives to condemn both the nation and the system of defence. He achieves a double take, since the Volunteer stands for and comments on the follies that have allowed the enemy to invade and conquer. The story opens with his bitter reflections on what might have been—the 'if only' gambit of the purposive writer; and it advances from the first moments of apprehension through rising anxieties to the final terror and despair of total defeat.

The Volunteer is certainly not the hero of the story. His sole function is to play the part of narrator and lamenting chorus. The tragic hero is the nation itself, and in the manner of high tragedy the nation brings on its own doom; for, being neither completely good nor totally evil, it provokes the final disaster by an error of collective folly. It is a tragedy of them and us, set in black and white, a political myth for a period of nationalism, designed to excite feelings of pity and terror. As an unhappy Britain makes the swift change from apparent security and happiness to defeat and humiliation, the moral and military purpose of the story comes out in the lamentation of the closing lines: 'The rich were idle and luxurious; the poor grudged the cost of defence. Politics had become a mere bidding for Radical votes, and those who should have led the nation stooped rather to pander to the selfishness of the day, and humoured the popular cry which denounced those who would secure the defence of the nation by enforced arming of its manhood, as interfering with the liberties of the people. Truly the nation was ripe for a fall.' The disaster was complete. There was no hope for a revival of national greatness, whereas a poem on similar themes, published anonymously in 1871, found consolation in the certainty of an ultimate victory for Britain:

> The German and the Muscovite
> Shall rule the narrow seas;
> Old England's flag shall cease to float
> In triumph on the breeze.

The footstep of the invader
Then England's shore shall know,
While home-bred traitors give the hand
To England's every foe.

Disarmed before the foreigner,
The knee shall humbly bend,
And yield the treasures that she lacked
The wisdom to defend.

But not for aye—yet once again,
When purged by fire and sword,
The land her freedom shall regain,
To manlier thoughts restored.

Taught wisdom by disaster,
England shall learn to know
That trade is not the only gain
Heaven gives to man below.[4]

Chesney was too good a soldier and too sensible a writer to make the mistake of weakening his story with the anticlimax of producing hope out of disaster. In fact, the only weakness in the story is the device he uses to get rid of the Royal Navy and so arrange for the Germans to land their invasion forces without hindrance. He introduces an ingenious variation on the doctrine of 'the absence of the Fleet', which had dominated military thinking on home defence ever since the Duke of Wellington had written his famous letter to Sir John Burgoyne. The fear was that some accident—a storm or a naval war overseas—might lead to the dispersal of the Fleet; and this Chesney arranged to demonstrate in his prologue to the invasion:

I need hardly tell you how the crash came about. First, the rising in India drew away a part of our small army; then came the difficulty with America, which had been threatening for years, and we sent off ten thousand men to defend Canada—a handful which did not go far to strengthen the real defences of that country, but formed an irresistible temptation to the Americans to try and take them prisoners, especially as the contingent included three battalions of the Guards. Thus the regular army at home was even smaller than usual, and nearly half of it was in Ireland to check the talked-of Fenian invasion fitting out in the West. Worse still—though I do not know it would really have mattered as things turned out—the fleet was scattered abroad; some ships to guard the West Indies, others to check privateering in the China Seas, and a large part to try and protect our colonies on the Northern Pacific shore of America, where, with incredible folly, we continued to retain possessions which we could not possibly defend.[5]

The Germans seize the moment of our maximum weakness to launch the war they had been secretly planning for many years. Chesney shows in so many words how the new forces of the centralized nation state and of modern technology had made possible a sudden and overwhelming attack. It is a restatement of that War of Surprises in 1870. Telegraphic communications are suddenly cut off; embassies and legations are sent packing at an hour's notice. But the difference is that in the ports from the Baltic to Ostend troops hurry aboard the waiting transports. The Volunteer reports the preparations for war and in his other role as commentator directs the devastating cannonade of Chesney's criticism upon the frightened reader: 'But everything had been arranged beforehand; nor ought we to have been surprised, for we had seen the same Power, only a few months before, move down half a million men on a few days' notice, to conquer the greatest military nation in Europe, with no more fuss than our War Office used to make over the transport of a brigade from Aldershot to Brighton.'

This is the strategy of Chesney's military moralizing on the duty of national defence. They show enterprise, discipline, and exceptional military abilities: we are feckless, unprepared, and have been imprudent enough to send off the best part of the Fleet on a fool's errand to the Dardanelles. There are even secret weapons to change the course of European history and allow the author to bring the enemy ashore without interference from the Royal Navy. What is left of the Fleet in home waters sails to seek out and destroy the would-be invasion forces; but the enemy fleet very sensibly 'evaded the conflict at close quarters, and, sheering off, left behind them the fatal engines which sent our ships, one after the other, to the bottom'. The Government, it appears, had received warnings of the invention; but to the nation this stunning blow was utterly unexpected. These secret weapons—presumably mines or torpedoes—were the only weakness in the story. They caused Charles Yriarte, who translated the *Battle of Dorking* into French, to exclaim upon the 'affair of five lines' by which Chesney had so conveniently disposed of 'a force without rival in the world'.

But, once that improbability has been accepted, then the whole narrative moves forward with great vigour through vividly described incidents, which tell the sad story of a nation's failure to prepare for the evil day. The reader experiences the disaster in a succession of personal and national tragedies as they are related by Chesney. The Volunteer recounts the effect of the news on his family—father, mother, brother, sister; then comes the confusion at the office and the anxiety in the City; and then the difficulties of joining his unit and the hopeless incompetence of the attempt to destroy the invading force on the beaches. The story of the defence is a long tale of administrative chaos and inefficiency, made worse by the presence of large hordes of half-trained Volunteers, but relieved by attractive descriptions of familiar English scenery which make each disaster seem more terrible.

The commissariat fails to provide rations for the Volunteer's unit; and when they buy food in a village they discover that the regiment is without cooking equipment. But—far worse—when it takes up its position 'on the extremity of the ridge which runs from Guildford to Dorking', the regiment has no information whatsoever about the progress of the battle. The Volunteers deploy along their section of the line and wait for the enemy to arrive—without fear and without information. The least military-minded reader of *Blackwood's Magazine* could see that, in contrast to the German troops engaged in the war of 1870, the Volunteers were still prepared to fight in the manner of Waterloo. Chesney's description of a review by the commanding general suggests that the army is commanded by old-style generals ready for an old-style war:

At last the whole line stood to arms, the bands struck up and the general commanding our army corps came riding down with his staff. We had seen him several times before, as we had been frequently moving about the position during the morning; but he now made a sort of formal inspection. . . . He was a tall thin man, with long light hair, very well mounted, and as he sat his horse with an erect seat, and came prancing down the line, at a little distance he looked as if he might be five-and-twenty; but I believe he had served more than fifty years, and had been made a peer for services performed when quite an old man. I remember that he had more decorations than there was room for on the breast of his coat, and wore them suspended like a necklace round his neck. Like all the other generals, he was dressed in blue, with a cocked-hat and feathers—a bad plan, I thought, for it made them very conspicuous. The general halted before our battalion, and after looking at us a while, made a short address: We had a post of honour next her Majesty's Guards, and would show ourselves worthy of it and of the name of

Englishmen. It did not need, he said, to be a general to see the strength of our position; it was impregnable, if properly held.[6]

These fine last words to the troops are the prelude to Chesney's demonstration of heroic failure and monumental incompetence. In a quick succession of brilliantly observed incidents he shows that the Volunteers are brave fellows, but are not trained for a modern war. They leave their positions at the end of an engagement and a staff officer has to drive them back with a cry of 'Gentlemen, do, pray, join your regiments, or we shall be a regular mob'. Towards the end, as Chesney begins to hammer home the lesson, they realize where the fault lies: 'We felt, indeed, our need of discipline, and we saw plainly enough the slender chance of success coming out of troops so imperfectly trained as we were; but I think we were all determined to fight on as long as we could.'

There had never been anything to compare with this in English fiction before Chesney wrote the *Battle of Dorking*—neither in method nor in quality. For Chesney has the unusual distinction that his success helped to launch a new type of purposive fiction in which the whole aim was either to terrify the reader by a clear and merciless demonstration of the consequences to be expected from a country's shortcomings, or to prove the rightness of national policy by describing the course of a victorious war in the near future. The strong or weak points of a situation—moral, or political, or naval, or military—were presented in a triumphant or in a catastrophic manner according to the needs of the propaganda. This technique was well suited to a period of increasing nationalism and unending change in armaments. In consequence the *Battle of Dorking*, as handled by Chesney, gave rise to a European device. French, German, British, and a few Italian writers applied the Chesney formula of defeat and disaster to their own versions of an imaginary war of the future in which they sought to show that a national defeat was the result of a national failure to adopt the military, or naval, or political measures favoured by the authors. Before the *Battle of Dorking* there was little effective method in the few tales of imaginary warfare that had appeared. After Chesney there were few of these tales that did not apply the techniques that had alarmed a nation, annoyed a Prime Minister, and amazed a continent.

Gladstone had good grounds for feeling annoyed at the upheaval created by the *Battle of Dorking*. Hitherto it had always been the crisis that had been responsible for the flood of pamphlets on the state of the Fleet or of the national defences; but in 1871 it was the publication of the *Battle of Dorking* in the form of a pamphlet that had caused the commotion. To a politician like Gladstone, who had begrudged money for ships and fortresses, it must have seemed decidedly improper and unjust that a colonel of engineers should have caused a political sensation with a short story in a respectable middle-class monthly magazine. He paid unwilling tribute to Chesney's skill as a writer and to the effectiveness of his story when he felt it was necessary to warn the nation against the dangers of alarmism. In a speech at Whitby, on 2nd September 1871, he attacked the *Battle of Dorking* and all whom it had aroused. It was a heart-cry from the Treasury:

In *Blackwood's Magazine* there has lately been a famous article called 'The Battle of Dorking'. I should not mind this 'Battle of Dorking', if we could keep it to ourselves, if we could take care that nobody belonging to any other country should know that such follies could find currency or even favour with portions of the British public; but unfortunately these things go abroad, and they make us ridiculous in the eyes of the whole world. I do not say that the writers of them are not sincere—that is another matter—but I do say that the result of these things is practically the spending of more and more of your money. Be on your guard against alarmism. Depend upon it that there is not this astounding disposition on the part of all mankind to make us the objects of hatred.[7]

Gladstone could talk with some heat about the effects of Chesney's story, since it had set in motion a series of counter-attacks that lasted from May until September, when the success of the autumn manœuvres showed that an invading force had little hope of leaving its beach-head. During those five months the episode attracted international attention. Coming so soon after the German victories in 1870, and appearing in the midst of the greatest maritime power on earth, it was taken seriously outside the country. An indication of what the *Battle of Dorking* meant abroad can be seen in the editions immediately printed in Australia, Canada, New Zealand, and the United States, in the numerous translations, and in the thirty-six pages Charles Yriarte wrote for his preface to the French edition. If there was amazement abroad, at home the feeling ranged from satisfaction to alarm and indignation. Kinglake, the historian of the Crimean War, wrote to congratulate John Blackwood and hoped that the story would prove 'a really effective mode of conveying a much-needed warning'. From the Carlton it was reported that no one could take up

Blackwood's for five minutes without a waiter coming to ask if he had finished with it. By June the story had been reprinted as a sixpenny pamphlet and in a month over 80,000 copies had been sold, mostly to readers for whom it had never been intended. This fact impressed foreign observers. They regarded the appearance of the story in bookshops and on railway bookstalls as an indication that the whole nation was involved in the alarm, and not simply the readers of the select monthlies. In fact, the Press became a battlefield, as the counter-attacks and the anti-Chesney articles appeared in the papers and in the book-shops. Most of these began as short stories or articles in dailies like *The Times* and *St. James's Gazette*. All of them employed Chesney's methods against him in their attempts to prove there had never been a German victory at Dorking, or that after the initial disaster the Fleet had returned from overseas and had routed the enemy. The number of these pamphlets and tracts, and the fact that they attacked Chesney's theme, are a remarkable sign of the alarm and indignation the *Battle of Dorking* had caused. They appeared by the week and by the month with their stories of victory: *After the Battle of Dorking or What Became of the Invaders?*, *The Battle of Dorking: a Myth*, *The Battle of the Ironclads*, *The Cruise of the Anti-torpedo*, *The Second Armada*, *What Happened after the Battle of Dorking*, *The Other Side at the Battle of Dorking*, *Chapters from Future History*. For Chesney's tale of defeat they substitute victories; they show how the Volunteers, who had failed so signally in Chesney's story, prove to be as good as the best regulars. For example, in *What Happened after the Battle of Dorking* the anonymous author dwells on the good discipline and the excellent training of the Volunteer forces. On several occasions he goes out of his way to describe how regular officers marvelled at the efficiency of the Volunteers. When a battalion carries out a difficult flanking movement the regulars stand by: 'The old general and his staff had watched the admirable coolness with which this manoeuvre was executed. "Gad, colonel," he said to our commanding officer, "the smartest regiment of the Line couldn't have done that movement better." ' Not even the veterans of Sedan could hope to conquer troops like these.

These counter-attacks produced some extraordinary pamphlets. One army officer, Lieutenant-Colonel William Hunter, published an *Army Speech dedicated to those who have been frightened by the Battle of Dorking*. He wrote 'to revive the drooping courage, to calm the shattered nerves of those who have been too lightly alarmed by the predicted woeful results of the phantom *Battle of Dorking*'. He attacked 'the extraordinary invasion panics' and showed that the British people were well able to take care of themselves. Anything could have happened during this period when the excitement was still running high. One enterprising publisher produced a faked issue of the *London Gazette*, which set out 'The official despatches and correspondence relative to the Battle of Dorking, as moved for in the House of Commons. 21st July 1920.' But by the time Chesney's story had been set to music, it was clear that the panic had begun to subside, for the music halls were singing:

> England invaded, what a strange idea!
> She, the invincible, has nought to fear.
> John Bull in his sleep one day got talking,
> And dreamt about a battle fought at Dorking.

And then in September there was the first of what subsequently became the annual army manœuvres. They were a considerable novelty, for the German successes in the war of 1870 had been attributed in part to their practice of training troops in fire discipline and large-scale operations by means of annual manœuvres designed to test both staff and troops. In 1871 Cardwell, who had done so much for Britain as Secretary for War, introduced a Bill to make it permissible for troops to be assembled in large numbers for the purposes of manœuvres. The first of these began in September, and the innovation was closely watched by Press and public, since the aim of the exercise was to test the co-operation between regulars, militia, and volunteers. The scheme was for the home forces to engage and repel an invading enemy. The results were felt to be very encouraging. The Press gave signs of satisfaction and *Punch* celebrated the success of the manœuvres with a full-page drawing of Mr. Punch reviewing members of the Army, the Militia, and the Volunteers. The caption was *All's (Pretty) Well*! That summed up the feeling of a country recovering from the alarms of the *Battle of Dorking* episode. As the *Daily News* wrote: 'If the supposition on which these manœuvres were planned should ever become reality—if the fleet should be dispersed, the Channel crossed by an invading force, the armies along the coast defeated and scattered, and the enemy should have penetrated to the neighbourhood of the Hog's Back, on his way to London—some Sir Hope Grant of the time will render a very admirable account of himself.'[8] That was the end of the *Battle of Dorking* episode for 1871. The last state of the affair was that it became a stock joke to ask anyone with a trifling injury: 'Weren't you wounded at the Battle of Dorking?' The country had decided there was little danger of an invasion; and Chesney could now look forward to fame, reputation, and eventually a seat in the House of Commons. In the January of 1872 he was writing to Blackwood asking for a higher rate of pay; in the February he was asking Blackwood to use his good offices in his election to the Athenaeum; and in the April he sent Blackwood his grateful thanks for the sum of £279 8*s.* 10*d.* in final settlement for the *Battle of Dorking.*

The colonel of engineers had earned his money. Chesney had revealed the workings of a new literary device, which was admirably adapted to the mood and methods of the new epoch of belligerent nationalism. But he had not won a military victory, since there is no evidence that his story had any influence on the reorganization of the Army. Chesney had gained a great literary success, since his story established the pattern for a predictive epic on the victory or defeat of a nation-species in the international struggle to survive. It was a narrow and limited form of fiction; but it could be effective to the point of causing a national panic, if an earnest patriot could describe telling incidents in the Chesney manner, making actions speak with far greater force than lengthy arguments about the state of the nation's defences. It was for this reason that the form of the *Battle of Dorking* became dominant in its field throughout Europe and its influence lasted until the outbreak of the First World War. As late as the year 1900 that astute publisher, Grant Richards, calculated that the reputation of Chesney's story was still powerful enough to sell a book for him. His project was *The New Battle of Dorking*, an account of a successful French invasion, which he had commissioned from Colonel Maude 'in the hope that it might have the same kind of success that its predecessor had had three or four decades earlier'. Then, there was the American publisher, George Putnam, who paid a visit to England shortly before the outbreak of war in 1914. He went over the site of Chesney's battle with a copy of the story in his hand, and was amazed to find how closely Chesney had kept to the topography of the area. Finally, in 1940 the Nazis brought out a special edition under the menacing title of *Was England erwartet*!

There was the same interest in France. In the August of 1871 Charles Yriarte wrote his long preface to the translation, *Bataille de Dorking*, in which he made a detailed study of the reasons for the

Title-page of *Bataille de Dorking, Invasion des Prussiens en Angleterre*, with Preface by Charles Yriarte, 1871.

effectiveness of Chesney's story. He was so impressed by the vigour and ingenuity of the narrative that he wondered 'if such a book, published here in 1869, might not have had an influence on our future'. And, again in 1871, another Frenchman produced the first foreign imitation of Chesney when he recounted his comforting vision of a defeated Germany in *La Bataille de Berlin en 1875*, the first of many French fantasies of a war of national revenge for the humiliations of 1870. The author, Édouard Dangin, found considerable satisfaction in the hope that the burden of conscription and the indemnity paid by France would lead to the swift decline of Germany. His desire to make the Germans suffer for what they had done to France shapes the course of his imaginary war, which comes to a brisk finish with a proclamation designed for French readers rather than a conquered enemy: 'Germans! We do not come to conquer you. It is not you on whom we make war, but on your ruler who for four years has kept Europe in a state of war and troubled the peace of nations. Our sole desire is to break those iron fetters that oppress you and set you free.' The First World War, it would seem, had been desired and described long before it took place.

From 1871 onwards Chesney's story showed Europe how to manipulate the new literature of anxiety and belligerent nationalism. Between 1871 and 1914 it was unusual to find a single year without some tale of future warfare appearing in some European country; for, wherever certain conditions existed, there would also be these tales of coming war. The conditions were that a nation should be actively concerned in the international manœuvring of the time. Big power—or nearly big power—status alone qualified for entry into the new club. Spain and Serbia, for instance, are innocent of the new fiction; and Ireland only appears when Irish patriots from North or South are involved in the internal political struggles of their great power neighbour. The other conditions were that a nation should be troubled by naval or military problems; and that that nation should permit a free Press to operate. Thus, the United States (at the start) and Russia (for most of the time) are outside the conflict of the imaginary wars for different reasons. The United States lacked the strong and permanent sense of a foreign menace required to touch off tales of future wars, and Russia lacked the free Press and the free play of opinion that alone could produce private solutions for public perils.

Wherever these factors operated, then the name and the method of Chesney were remembered. Both Italy and Germany offer an excellent illustration of this connexion between the *Battle of Dorking* technique and the problems of a nation. About the end of the nineteenth century these two powers were both taken up with the question of their navies. On the Italian side it was a brief history of sharp decline, since the Italian fleet had failed to maintain its place at a time of rapid naval expansion. This was the characteristic Chesney situation; and in order to emphasize the danger to Italy the Lega Navale Italiana in 1899 published a story of future naval defeat, *La Guerra del 190–*. The story reveals the influence of the Chesney tradition. The author explains that he has taken for his model the *Racconto di un Guardiano di Spiaggia*, which was the *Battle of Dorking* translated and transposed to an Italian setting in 1872. The introduction indicates both the tradition and the intention behind the story: 'At a distance of thirty years the *Racconto di un Guardiano di Spiaggia* lives again in *La Guerra del 190–*. They are two signals of alarm, two cries of dismay, two invocations to the sea, to the nation, and to all who still believe in the Fatherland.' The author certainly carries out his promise of alarm and dismay, since he foretells how the French are able to destroy the Italian fleet, bombard La Spezia with impunity, and land in force at Viareggio.

There was a comparable propaganda situation in Germany at this time, when Tirpitz had called for a further expansion of the navy. The enabling bill was passed by the Reichstag in the June of 1900, after the Centre Party had forced the Government to cut the number of cruisers. Whilst the argument about the size of the fleet was in progress a German patriot, Gustav Erdmann, wrote his warning to the nation, *Wehrlos zur See*. The story was composed in the mood of the statement by von Bülow, the Foreign Minister, that 'in the coming century the German people must be either the hammer or the anvil'. For the purpose of his propaganda Erdmann chose to show that an inadequate navy accounted for the fact that 'Germany's sons rested with their ships at the bottom of the sea'. He describes a future war in which Russia, France, and Italy attack Germany, Austro-Hungary, and Turkey. Like Chesney before him, he relates in detail such moments of national humiliation as the destruction of the Baltic fleet, and a naval blockade that leads to starvation, typhus epidemics, and mass suicides. The responsibility for this disaster rests with the guilty party in the Reichstag:

'Through the fault of the Reichstag Germany has fallen in excusably behind other maritime nations in the expansion of her fleet.' And, again like Chesney, he ends the long tale of disaster by describing how Germany would be reduced to the level of a small power: 'British and American industry seized the German markets throughout the world for themselves; and once their rival had been overthrown, they were strong enough to keep him down. That German industry, which a few weeks earlier had a dominant position in the world, to which Germany owed its wealth, saw itself suddenly reduced to the level of a small-state economy.'

From all that has been said so far it will be evident that Chesney's ability as a writer was in part responsible for the continental success that made the *Battle of Dorking* a model to be copied by all who had something to say about the state of a nation. But this is a literary explanation that does not answer the far more important question: Why does the mass production of this type of fiction begin in 1871 and why does it become a standard device for many writers in Britain, France, and Germany? Part of the answer would seem to begin from the fact that the publication of the *Battle of Dorking* had coincided with the coming of a new mood throughout Europe. In one way this appeared as a general realization that the German victories in 1870 had altered the European power system and that in consequence, as Matthew Arnold wrote in the January of 1871, 'one may look anxiously to see what is in the future for the changed Europe that we shall have'. One result of the change was that in France after 1871, for example, a succession of tales about future wars began. They appeared almost every year, growing in detail and in length, until they reached a climax in the large-scale epic forecasts of French victories written by Capitaine Danrit during the eighteen-nineties. The authors generally described how the enemy of the day—Germany, or sometimes Britain—was soundly defeated by the superior abilities and resources of the French troops.

Another reason for the rapid growth of the new literature of imaginary future wars was the extraordinary development in every type of armament that took place during the last quarter of the nineteenth century. The frequent changes in military equipment and the often spectacular advances in the design of quite new naval craft posed questions about the conduct of the next war which at times could cause considerable anxiety. Further, with the coming of universal literacy and the emergence of the popular Press towards the end of the century, it became a general practice in the major European countries for writers to appeal directly to the mass of the people in order to win support for the military or naval measures they advocated.

The practice undoubtedly dates from the success won by the *Battle of Dorking*, since Chesney had by chance introduced a new device in the communications between a specialist group and a nation. As an engineer, he belonged to the then still small group of well-educated officers to be found in the British Army of the period: he could move from the direction of a large engineering college to a seat in the Commons, and he was as much at home with a staff paper as he was with writing an article for *Blackwood's*. He was in touch with the political and military thinking of his time; and when he suggested to John Blackwood that his idea for a tale about an imaginary invasion might be 'a useful way of bringing home to the country the necessity for a thorough reorganization', he was looking for a suitable medium through which he could communicate the convictions of a professional to an influential section of the community represented by readers of a monthly like *Blackwood's*.

Thereafter, once the tale of imaginary warfare had established itself as a natural propaganda device for the period before the First World War, it quickly became a favourite instrument with eminent persons, whether they could write effectively or not. Admirals, generals, and politicians turned naturally to telling the tale of the war-to-come, since it so conveniently allowed them to draw attention to whatever they thought was wrong with the armed forces. The rate of development in this field can be gauged from the fact that in 1871 an unknown colonel considered the middle-class *Blackwood's Magazine* to be a suitable channel for his ideas. By 1906 all the varied effects of the new mass dailies, universal literacy, the growth of armaments and the ending of British isolation came together in the episode of the *Invasion of 1910*. With the agreement and active encouragement of Lord Northcliffe, Field-Marshal Lord Roberts worked in close association with the popular journalist, William Le Queux, in preparing a story about a German invasion of Britain in 1910 for serialization in the *Daily Mail*. Lord Roberts saw it was an opportunity to spread his conviction that Britain must be better prepared for a modern war. As he wrote in his commendation of the *Invasion of 1910*: 'The catastrophe that may happen if we still remain in our present state of unpreparedness is vividly and forcibly illustrated in Mr. Le Queux's new book which I recommend to the perusal of every one who has the welfare of the British Empire at heart.'

The world learnt certain lessons of technique and method from Chesney and his successors. Wherever a patriot feared that France, or Germany, or the United States was falling behind in the cold war of armaments and military organization, the tale of warning followed the example set by Chesney. Thus, in 1874 an English writer followed in the master's footsteps with a story of German aggression. He arranged that 'England was to learn, though happily not at so terrible a price, the bitter lesson taught to the French in 1870, that no amount of enthusiasm, nor temporary self-sacrifice, will make up for pre-arrangement and steady discipline'. The story, *The Carving of Turkey*, started off from an account of the dangers to be anticipated if ever Germany went to war again. It was an object lesson for the British people on the need to be prepared for the swift warfare of great armies. When Germany quarrels with Austria, there is no breathing-space for the victim:

The conflict began. The German troops were mobilised with a speed and accuracy even greater than that displayed in 1870. Nor was this surprising. No day had passed since that eventful time which had not seen them more prepared for future war. There was not a country in Europe the invasion of which had not been worked out in detail by their generals. There was not a railway carriage unnumbered and undestined. There was not a man in the whole enormous army whose billet for each successive day had not been determined, assigned, and registered—a feat which would never have been possible but for the facilities of information afforded by the wide-spread employment of German waiters. It had become in fact the business of Germany to make war; and that Germans are excellent men of business is well known to all the world. Such was the finish of that exquisite engine of despotism that at the slightest touch each citizen became a soldier; and without noise, without confusion, almost without enthusiasm the entire nation revealed itself as a compact and disciplined army.[9]

The nationality of the writers does not in any way affect the medium of communication. Germans and French use the device of the imaginary war to advance the interests they have most at heart. Indeed, the similarity of the peril produces stories with so much in common that a simple change of names would make them useful propaganda for the country against which they were intended.

Contrast, for example, what was said about the Germans in the *Carving of Turkey* with what an American had to say about the British in 1890. Again, it is another anonymous author, and like the rest of them he applies *Battle of Dorking* methods to the situation in his own country. The anxieties of the author of *The Stricken Nation* were centred on the strength of the Royal Navy; they were part of a growing interest in the American Fleet that led to the United States becoming a first-class naval power by 1905. But in 1890 one American patriot thought the situation serious enough to write a fifteen-page pamphlet in order 'to arraign before the American people their representatives in Congress, who in their blindness and folly were responsible for the defenceless position of the great cities on this coast'. This is the characteristic Chesney theme in a transatlantic setting. It is interesting to know that in the eyes of one American propagandist the British are as villainous and as well prepared to do evil as the Germans were supposed to be in the *Carving of Turkey*. The British Fleet sails across the Atlantic and destroys most of the cities on the East Coast:

With nothing to fear in Europe, she could concentrate all her forces for an attack, which she well knew the United States was powerless to resist. For years her spies and agents had been at work in every Department of the American Government. She knew the weakest of our weak defences better than even our own engineers. She had on file plans of every port, charts of every harbor, tables of the valuation of every sea-port town, particulars of our torpedo arrangements; and she had her own soldiers specially detailed for the duty, in the guise of enlisted men in every branch of our service. There were British on our ships, British spies in our arsenals, and British influence had for years been powerful enough to defeat every attempt made to get appropriations for defence. This was accomplished by American representatives whose election to Congress to perform this very duty had been secured by a lavish outlay of British gold.[10]

This is the transatlantic version of perfidious Albion. It demonstrates the patriot's principle that controls so much of the feeling released in these tales of future warfare: all other nations are perfidious and the enemy nation of the moment is the most perfidious of them all.

Although this may show that the *Battle of Dorking* gave rise to an international practice in the composition of these imaginary wars, it fails to give a final answer to the question: Why does the device of the imaginary war spread throughout Europe from 1871 onwards? Although it is apparent that the starting-point for this new type of fiction is an urgent sense of anxiety over some problem of the day, it does not seem possible to account completely for the continental scale of Chesney's success by the simple technical explanation of a good story at the right time. Behind the European reception and imitation of the *Battle of Dorking* stand the varied and often concealed influences of the new sciences and the even newer technologies: first, in the facilities that the electric telegraph offered for the rapid dissemination of news; second, and more profoundly, in the general expectation of change engendered both by the fact of technological advance and by theories of progress and evolutionary development. Between the alarm caused by Louis Napoleon's *coup d'état* in 1851 and the flood of pamphlets following on the appearance of the *Battle of Dorking* in 1871 the new electric telegraph had brought all the cities of Europe, indeed almost all the great cities of the world, within a single communications system. The world had become a much smaller place since those days in 1839 when the Great Western Railway had installed the first telegraph line and the crowds had queued at Paddington to see 'this marvel of science which could transmit fifty signals a distance of 280,000 miles in a second'.[11] To meet the speed with which the news had begun to flash from one end of Europe to another there were quicker and more efficient type-casting and composing machines, which helped to reduce the cost and increase the size of publications. More people read more news sent more quickly than ever before. The incident of one evening could be read the next day in all the capitals of Europe. This fact was well understood by the Press. On the occasion of the finally successful laying of the Atlantic Telegraph Cable in 1865 the newspapers indulged in the favourite Victorian habit of imagining the shape of things to come. One of them declared that 'instantaneous communication between America and Europe means, of course, in its ultimate development, instantaneous communication all the world over. And so we shall have daily before our eyes a bird's-eye view of human affairs over the entire surface of the globe, and we shall be able to study all nations, as day by day they are making contemporaneous pages of history.' And so, when the *Battle of Dorking* affected nerves at home and curiosity abroad, it came to enjoy a notoriety that was not possible in the days before the rotary press and Wheatstone's automatic printing telegraph.

Technology was behind the whole process of advance as it was seen and felt by the Victorians. Technology provided the power and the equipment for incessant change; it was a major source from which the nineteenth century derived evidence for the gospel of progress; and it had a decisive influence on the establishment of the new futuristic fiction that began to spread throughout Western literature after 1800. All the great advances from the steam engine and the railway to the laying of the Atlantic Cable, the opening of the Suez Canal, and the ending of cholera epidemics—all these had helped to convert the evident fact of change into the dogma of unending progress. The realization of constant change carried over into the imagination to produce an entirely new literature of forecasts, inquiries about the future condition of mankind, as well as satires, ideal states, and romances placed in the centuries ahead. Within a generation of the first balloon ascents and the first steam engines a new literature of futuristic fiction had begun to emerge in Europe: steam balloons, steam ploughs, passenger kites, and electrical road vehicles were to be expected, so writers imagined, in the very different world of time-to-come. Change, progress, and improvement were the new catchwords. As Jane Webb explained in a Gothic romance of 1827, *The Mummy: a tale of the twenty-second century*, the future would be a time when 'education became universal and the technical terms of the abstruse sciences familiar to the lowest mechanics'. Similarly, on the evening of 1st February 1827, Goethe told Eckermann that he was confident of continued change, because 'through my whole life down to the present hour one great discovery has followed on another'. For this reason he felt like 'one who walks towards the dawn and, when the sun rises, is astonished at its brilliancy'. Ecstasies of this kind were common to the emergent industrial societies of the West. Poets agreed with engineers that technological development undoubtedly meant social—and often moral—improvement. By the eighteen-forties it had become accepted social doctrine that science had led mankind to a new and desirable order of existence. With this went the characteristically modern attitude to time as a process of development, and to the present as a necessary but preliminary stage on the way to a better and more advanced future. This Goethean delight in the dawn of a new order of human existence is admirably expressed in the rhapsodic verse of Tennyson's *Locksley Hall*. Tennyson was deeply moved by his contemplation of the 'wondrous Mother-Age'. It was heaven to be alive at a time when technology was leading men to final beatitude in a realizable future:

Saw the heavens fill with commerce, argosies of magic sails,
Pilots of the purple twilight, dropping down with costly bales;

Heard the heavens fill with shouting, and there rain'd a ghastly dew
From the nations' airy navies grappling in the central blue;

Far along the world-wide whisper of the south-wind rushing warm,
With the standards of the peoples plunging thro' the thunder-storm;

Till the war-drum throbb'd no longer, and the battle-flags were furl'd
In the Parliament of man, the Federation of the world.

Since the rate of change and the scale of innovation were so different from all that had previously occurred in human history, comparisons have to be made in terms of geological time. The marvels of that first industrial morning, when science was revealing its powers in an explosion of inventions across the world, can compare with 'the abominable mystery' of the Cretaceous Period, as Darwin called it, when the flowering plants suddenly appeared upon the earth and changed the course of life as it was then developing on this planet. The two events are related in size and in consequences. Indeed, the Tennysonian phrase about the 'Triumphs over time and space' comes straight from the new awareness of unprecedented changes and from the general realization that there was a real future—distinct and discernible—before the human race. The Prince Consort had said it was 'a period of most wonderful transition'; and an American had told de Tocqueville in 1832: 'There is a feeling among us about everything which prevents us aiming at permanence; there reigns in America a popular and universal belief in the progress of the human spirit. We are always expecting an improvement to be found in everything.'

The epoch of extrapolation had commenced. Men knew that the modifications of one day would the day after give rise to the improved model. And this knowledge was in its turn responsible for the vast literature about the future that ranges from a serious analysis of the prospects before democracy in America, as in de Tocqueville, to tales of future warfare and Wellsian visions of better worlds to come. In keeping with the methodology of science a new race of investigators began to examine the present so that they might discern the forces that would shape the future. Thus, in 1831 the French administrator and aristocrat, de Tocqueville, obtained leave of absence from his post of *Juge auditeur* and set off to study the new world of the United States. He began from the central fact of the political situation which he wished to examine: 'It is evident to all alike that a great democratic revolution is going on among us.' In the manner of the social scientist he considered it would be necessary to study the United States, because it was the model of the system to which all things were tending in Europe: 'I confess that in America, I saw more than America; I sought the image of democracy itself, with its inclinations, its character, its prejudices, and its passions, in order to learn what we have to fear or to hope from its progress.'[12] The answers he expected to find in his journey across the United States would throw light on the likely course of development in Europe: 'I have undertaken not to see differently, but to look further than parties, and while they are busied for the morrow I have turned my thoughts to the Future.'

This conviction of a completely different future meant that in politics the advocate of a new measure had to present his case in terms of the better state of affairs to be expected from the changes he wished to see introduced. And conversely it meant that a forecast of coming disasters might be an even more forceful device for pushing through a desirable reform. From this came the new fiction that aimed to persuade the reader to support present changes so that something better might emerge in the future. It was a popular form of enterprise and effort that grew rapidly until in the last quarter of the nineteenth century it became one of the most favoured modes of commenting on the state of society. It had a place for men as different as Lamartine, the French poet turned politician, and that colonel of engineers who wrote the *Battle of Dorking*. Both employed the tale of the future as a means of driving home to their contemporaries the points they had to make. With Lamartine it was an affair of idealistic politics. The earnest poet had become a liberal under the Orléanist monarchy, and in 1843 he described a future state of Europe in which all the best possible reforms had been realized. His intention was to enhearten and encourage good republicans by showing them his vision of an improved Europe in the year 1943. The majestic design calls for an 'Ibergallitalian Federation' comprising France, Italy, Spain, Portugal, and the Netherlands. The poet's vision is curiously familiar, since his plan for a United Europe is as much aimed against Britain as it is meant for the advancement of the nations forming the Federal Congress. He exhorts his readers in 1843 to note that it was the treaty of alliance 'between the Germanic nation and the Ibergallitalian confederation, a political and commercial treaty to which Sweden and Denmark were admitted, which preserves Europe from the two greatest dangers that impend over it, the military despotism of Russia, and the commercial monopoly of England'.[13]

Lamartine describes the benefits and blessings that attend upon universal suffrage, a wise federal system of government, and free schooling for all children. There are still armies, but these are composed of contingents from all the member states, so that even military service is an advantage, because 'the moving about of all these contingents favours the study of the idioms, and changes the conditions of life in which each soldier has been brought up. On returning to his native hearth he carries back with him agricultural, industrial improvements, of which he has seen the advantages.' In this way the picture of the future unrolls in attaction after attraction. The intention is to pile benefit upon benefit in order to demonstrate the advantages of a republican federation. As Lamartine remarked: 'The progress of human nature is the fundamental basis of our political religion.'

The circumstances that prompted Lamartine to describe an ideal state of the future in 1843 anticipate the comparable circumstances that caused Chesney to offer his story to John Blackwood in 1871. The two stories show how the desire to teach combined with the characteristic nineteenth-century sense of the future to produce the new literature of prediction. Chesney's story grew out of a preoccupation with the state of Britain's defences, just as Lamartine's picture of the ideal republican federation of 1943 derived from a radical's dissatisfaction with the corrupt France of his time. Both writers projected whatever pleased or displeased them into a future that could tell its own tale of consequences in the admirable results of republican theory or in the disaster awaiting a nation not prepared to fight the new war of great armies and rapid movement. But the difference between the two writers was that in the period between 1843, when Lamartine had composed his ideal state, and the publication of the *Battle of Dorking* in 1871 a collection of progressive and evolutionary ideas had come together under the label of Darwinism. This was the final mechanism required for the smooth functioning of the tale of the future, since it brought the apparent certainty of scientific law to the general conviction of progress. And so the interest that followed on the publication of the *Origin of Species* in November 1859 had the effect of providing a biological explanation for the constant technological progress and social struggle that all knew to be going on around them. By 1868 the *Saturday Review* noted that the influence of the *Origin of Species* had been rapid and far-reaching: 'So rapid has been the hold that it has taken on the public mind that the language incident to the explanation of the "struggle for life", and the gradual evolution of new forms consequent thereon, has passed into the phraseology of everyday conversation.'[14]

Evidence for this can be seen in the sudden flowering about this time of the new fiction of the future, which owed as much to Darwinian ideas of change and development as it did to the more general notion of progress. The first main phase opened in France in 1863 with the publication of *Five Weeks in a Balloon* by Jules Verne; and from that date until his death in 1905 there was only one year in which Verne failed to delight his readers throughout the world with his tales of high adventure beneath the sea, in the air, and under the earth. By 1870 he had already turned out seven books, when the second phase in the development of futuristic fiction opened with the appearance of *The Coming Race* by Bulwer Lytton in 1871 and *Erewhon* by Samuel Butler in 1872. Unlike Verne, the two Englishmen did not aim at wonder for the sake of wonder. Their use of science was entirely subsidiary to the primary purpose of satire. Both writers obtained much of the material for their attacks on Victorian society from Darwinism. With Butler the idea of evolution is central to the thought and method of his satire: the inhabitants of his imaginary land had long ago forbidden the use of machines, because they discovered that 'the machines were ultimately destined to supplant the race of man, and to become instinct with a vitality as different from, and superior to, that of animals, as animal to vegetable life'. This suggestion of a conflict avoided, of a struggle for survival between two groups, is developed more fully in Bulwer Lytton's story of the highly advanced Vril-ya. Like Butler, he deals with the future relative rather than with the future absolute; his subterranean race exists contemporaneously with the Victorian world of 1871, but it has gained a degree of scientific knowledge and a control over nature far in advance of anything the Victorians had achieved. It is Verne's world of technological marvels—from robots and flying machines to the mysterious fluid, Vril, which gave them control of 'the natural energic agencies'. But there all similarities with Verne finish, since the aim of Lytton's story is to apply Darwinian ideas to his theme of social evolution. He explains the superiority of the Vril-ya by 'the intensity of their earlier struggles against obstacles in nature amidst the localities in which they had first settled'. And he ends on a note of menace, as he looks forward to the day when the human race may have to wage a great war for survival against the more advanced species from below the earth. Lytton's parting shot comes straight from the *Origin of Species*: 'If they ever emerged from these nether recesses into the light of day, they would, according to their own traditional persuasions of their ultimate destiny, destroy and replace our existent varieties of man.'

The sudden emergence of tales about the future,* which were based on Darwinism and on the idea of progress, followed on the war of 1870; and in that war two great nations had demonstrated the fact of technological progress in a savage struggle to survive. In 1815 the infantry had used a smooth-bore musket which had a moderately effective range of fifty yards; in 1870 they had rifles which were accurate up to twelve hundred yards. The slow and clumsy muzzle-loading cannon had given place to the Prussian field batteries equipped with the new breech-loaders from Krupps, which gave such a devastating performance at the Battle of Froeschwiller. This was frightening evidence of progress. It makes it easy to see how Chesney's *Battle of Dorking* could have shocked a nation and at the same time have established a new literature of imaginary warfare; for the Franco-German War had taken place at the time when ideas of natural conflict and the struggle to survive were merging with the earlier dogma of unending progress. It was widely assumed that human society was an integral part of nature and that it would therefore be controlled by the universal mechanism of the struggle for life. Nature's first law for mankind seemed to be an extension of De Candolle's principle that 'all the plants of a given country are at war with one another'. Ideas about the universal process of war came as naturally out of the Darwinian discourse about man and society as they did from the

* Some of the first to appear at this time were:
J. F. Maguire, *The Next Generation*, 1871.
Octogenarian (pseud.), *The British Federal Empire*, 1872.
E. Maitland, *By and By*, 1873.
Anon. (A. Blair), *Annals of the twenty-ninth century*, 1874.
Anon., *In the Future*, 1875.

popular kings-and-heroes history of the period. Had not the Normans conquered the English and had not the warlike Arab race swept out of the desert to overrun an effete Byzantine civilization? In India and Africa the advanced and better peoples of Europe were subduing the lesser races by a natural right to conquer. When one looked at the war between the French and Germans, it seemed to bear out Darwin's conclusion at the end of the *Origin of Species* that 'from the war of nature, from famine and death, the most exalted object which we are capable of conceiving, namely, the production of the higher animals, directly follows'.

Ideas of this kind were in full circulation at a time when, after decades of argument and anxiety about the nation's ability to prevent invasion in an epoch of steamships and ironclads, the sudden destruction of what had been considered the greatest military power in Europe gave rise to grave doubts about the future. Chesney worked on these anxieties and gave a military twist to Darwinian ideas by showing that in the new warfare of conscript armies and high-speed artillery only the fittest nation could hope to survive. And fitness meant military preparedness. His story was presented in terms of progress, the need to be ready for a new form of warfare, and the fact of a natural conflict between groups. He began with a picture of the days when 'London was growing bigger and bigger'; he goes on to the clamour that 'the army ought to be reorganized, and our defences strengthened against the enormous power for sudden attacks which it was seen other nations were able to put forth'. He finished by showing how the great conflict, which ended Britain's day as a dominant power, turned ultimately on the internal struggle that led to the nation's decline and fall: 'Power was then passing away from the class which had been used to rule, and to face political dangers, and which had brought the nation with honour unsullied through former struggles, into the hands of lower classes, uneducated, untrained to the use of political rights, and swayed by demagogues.' This was a soldier's application of Walter Bagehot's principle, put forward in 1868, that 'those nations which are the strongest tend to prevail, and in certain marked peculiarities the strongest are the best'.

The period of 1870–1 represents a grand climacteric in international affairs and in the complex of the popular notions about progress and evolution that are behind the emergence of the tale of the future as a major literary device. The war of 1870 had altered the power system in Europe and in a more general way it was considered to have revealed the working of the Darwinian mechanism for the rise and decline of species. In fact, on the Continent the war had an immediate influence on the development of Social Darwinism, since the struggle between the French and Germans had the apparent characteristics of a struggle for survival two rival species. In Britain, according to Lord Wolseley, the lesson of 1870 was that the country would have to change the army system or cease to be a great power:

> Before the Franco-German War we had rather modelled ourselves upon the French army. In the Crimea we had found our military system in all its methods and phases to be hopelessly out of tune with modern ideas, and were astonished when we realized that it was obsolete when compared with that of the army which the Emperor Louis Napoleon had sent into the field. . . . But yet, though all thoughtful men who had served before Sebastopol realized how much our whole Army System needed reform, none of any real importance was effected. The Franco-German struggle at last opened the eyes of our people to the real state of our out-of-date Army, and to our absolute military inefficiency.[15]

The German victory was considered a triumph for the ideal of the nation-in-arms and a demonstration of the fact that in modern warfare only those best adapted to the new conditions could hope to survive. It was thought that the Germans had won because they were better. Soldiers like Wolseley argued that their organization was better and that the training of their officers—especially of the general staff—gave them a decided superiority over the French. The consequences of this were profound and far-reaching. They ranged from the establishment of great conscript armies in most European countries to the general adoption of the new literature of imaginary warfare, which was dedicated to the task of preparing nations for the new type of war. That was the central point in the *Battle of Dorking*. Chesney took his facts from the German campaign, added the device of secret weapons, and showed what would happen to Britain if it did not secure 'the defences of the nation by the enforced arming of its manhood'.

Already in 1871 the First World War was being prepared in fact and in fiction. The terrible slaughter of the Somme and Verdun was the direct consequence of the lessons taught by the German victory; for the nations took note that if they were to survive they would have to have the biggest armies and the most murderous weapons possible. From 1871 onwards the major European powers prepared for the great war that Bismarck had said would come one day. And for close on half a century, while the general staffs and the ministries argued about weapons, estimates, and tactics, the tale of the war-to-come was a dominant device in the field of purposive fiction. For the most part, certainly from 1871 to the appearance of the mass Press in the eighteen-nineties, the writers were naval and army officers who had something they thought it important to say at a time of rapidly changing armaments. Like Chesney, they confined themselves to the areas of influence and effective opinion represented by the middle-class journals and the more important daily newspapers. They turned out short stories designed for publication in *The Times, St. James's Gazette, Le Journal des Débats, Blackwood's Magazine, Le Monde Illustré*. Everywhere the method was the same: the authors composed a piece based on a few statistics in manpower, armaments, or organization. Usually they kept very close to Chesney's method of relating the disaster through the experiences of a survivor who picks out the causes—bad training, the construction of a Channel Tunnel, the lack of capable engineer officers in the Royal Navy—that brought on the catastrophe. It was a British export to Europe that became an international commodity, since the fears of one country were frequently translated to provide pleasant reading in another. In the December of 1884, for example, an anonymous English author brought out *The Siege of London*, in which he attacked Gladstone's policies by showing that 'those who for years had been frittering away England's power' were responsible for a successful French invasion. Such a view had considerable appeal to a French audience, and six months later there duly appeared a translation, *La Bataille de Londres en 188–*. In the preface there is a very interesting analysis of the purpose and workings of the new tale of future war: 'Like the *Battle of Dorking*, which was first attributed to Disraeli and then to a general in the British army, and like the *Battle of Port Said*, the author of which is reported to be a senior officer in the Royal Navy, *The Siege of London* belongs to a type of publication in which the English seem to excel, especially since the War of 1870. It can be classed under the heading of *Batailles imaginaires*. The purpose of these stories is either to criticize the actions of the party in power, or to exert enough influence on public opinion to oblige the government to take precautions against possible troubles or probable conflagrations, and by these means secure the increase and improvement of the means of defending the country.'

The range of these stories goes from the strictly tactical examination of possible fleet actions or army movements to nationalistic fantasies in which French—and later German—writers describe the last days of perfidious Albion. Many of these tales went the rounds of the European publishing houses, often in the route followed by an account of a naval war between France and Britain which was written by Spiridion Gopčević, an officer in the Austro-Hungarian Navy. This began as a story which appeared between the July and September of 1886 in the *Internationale Revue über die Gesamten Armeen und Flotten*. The story was *Der grosse Seekrieg im Jahre 1888*, a flat and painfully detailed account of an imaginary engagement between British and French naval forces in the Channel. It was very much a staff officer's piece, for it had more to do with lectures on strategy in a naval training establishment than with the art of fiction. After its appearance in the *Internationale Revue* the story was published as a pamphlet and it was then translated by a commander of the Royal Navy and published by a Portsmouth firm in 1887. After that it waited until 1891, when French naval policy in the Mediterranean was affecting relations between Britain and France, and the French then brought out a translation, *Comment la France conquit l'Angleterre en 1888*.

On other occasions the to-and-fro process of publication and translation started in France. This can be seen at work in the publishing history of a French tale of stupendous revenge. It began in 1887 with the anonymous *Plus d'Angleterre* which ran through six editions in the first year of publication. The following year it was translated into English as *Down with England* and in the same year of 1888 it provoked a counter-attack, *Plus encore d'Angleterre*. The original was an apocalyptic vision of triumph and revenge in which the British suffered a swift and humiliating defeat. As in all these tales, the plot of *Plus d'Angleterre* started from a recognized fact in contemporary history. On this occasion the point of origin was the ill feeling between the French and British over the occupation of Egypt in 1882. 'Is it not clear enough,' the author wrote, 'especially since 1882, that the English oligarchy has resumed its old struggle to the death with France?' The rest of the story was composed according to a formula of vengeance and victory, an early specimen of the nationalistic fiction of future warfare that was to be very popular in France, Germany, and Britain between

1890 and 1914. The tone of these stories can be gathered from the opening pages of *Plus d'Angleterre:*

We admit that there is something great, even something enormous, about England; and that is her audacity. This island kingdom, as they call it, which exploits the whole world and works night and day to embroil the European powers, has only its talent for intrigue with which to defend its approaches. The three great European powers comprise 180 million people and have 3 million soldiers under arms. The mistress of 310 million subjects, the ruler of the empire on which the sun never sets, has not even 200,000 regular troops that could be deployed for action, and of these half are in India and the colonies. Any one of the great powers with a quarter of its effective forces could finish off the schemer in her den, because the famous silver streak is no longer a defence and at the decisive moment her scattered fleet would be inferior to that of France.[16]

At this distance from the passions and indignation of a French patriot writing in 1887 it is possible to see the comic side of an international dispute that caused an anonymous Frenchman to find in Britain both the form and the occasion for his attack. He based his style on that 'ingenious fiction called the *Battle of Dorking*'; and he planned his book as a condemnation of a 'certain boorish Chauvinism' that prevailed on the other side of the Channel. Forgetful of what was then being said in France about Britain, he protested with good reason against the arrogance of the British people: 'It was an axiom that one English soldier was as good as three of any other nationality, and that every foreigner was an inferior and contemptible creature. It was taught in their schools that Britain had beaten the Russians in the Crimea without the French Army.' But there is a justice in the tale of the future that arranges the destinies of nations according to an international system of rewards and punishments. The proud and fickle British are condemned to perpetual seclusion in what remains of their island kingdom and suffer the loss of all their overseas possessions. The French—virtuous and deserving much—are given Dover, the Channel Islands, Gibraltar, Malta, West Africa, the West Indies, Tasmania, New Zealand, and most of the British islands in the Pacific. There is a clause in the peace treaty that reflects French cultural interests: 'The Egyptian antiquities taken from France after the Battle of Aboukir, and at this moment in the British Museum, will be returned to France together with the Elgin

Marbles.' And finally, after this best of all possible wars has made the Germans see the wisdom of returning Alsace and Lorraine to France, the epic closes on a chauvinist's vision of the world reorganized to suit French interests through an arrangement by which 'France and Germany agreed on the terms of a reciprocal disarmament. The active army of either nation was not to exceed 200,000 men, and each was to be allowed full liberty to choose her form of military organization.'

But there were not many like this before the eighteen-nineties. Most of these stories—British and foreign—were short and practical pieces. They confined themselves to a pamphlet of thirty or forty pages in which the authors dealt with a single matter. For the most part they were all 'little Europeans' until the 'nineties. No doubt this was a result of thinking in one-topic terms of the Channel Tunnel, the state of the nation's morals, the dangers of Irish self-government, and the indifference, mismanagement, and parsimony so many naval writers complained about for so long and so bitterly. The greater themes of world-wide warfare only became general with the full-length stories that writers like Capitaine Danrit in France and Louis Tracy in Britain produced for the new literate masses. But even before the 'nineties there were occasional stories that had caught the theme of the great globe, world communications, and the need to arrange the human race to suit the convenience of a dominant group. One of these pictures of the future anticipates the later visions of H. G. Wells: *Three Hundred Years Hence*, first published in 1881 by William Delisle Hay. The story sums up many of the great aspirations of the period: a world state, the Sahara irrigated and under cultivation, the seas farmed by 'algoculturists', flying machines, television, and all the desirable goods of applied science. It is an epic tale on the great Victorian theme of unending progress; and yet there are elements drawn from Darwin and the whole complex of evolutionary ideas that help a citizen of the post-Hiroshima world to understand how ordinary men could contemplate without a blink the tales of death and destruction that poured from the presses of Europe between 1871 and 1914.

The author has a whole chapter on what he calls 'The Fate of the Inferior Races'. After describing the development of a form of world Socialism, he comes to the conflict between the white and the non-white races. His ideas look forward to the Nuremberg rallies:

The old idea of universal fraternity had worn itself out; or rather it had become modified when elevated into the practical law of life. Throughout the Century of Peace, gradually, but steadily and surely, men's minds had become opened to the truth, had become sensible of the diversity of species, had become conscious of Nature's law of development. The incompatibility of certain races of men with others, that prevented their admixture with the general mass, and that held them aloof from the advantages of civilisation, was slowly recognised. The stern logic of facts proclaimed the Negro and the Chinaman below the level of the Caucasian, and incapacitated from advance towards his intellectual standard. To the development of the White Man, the Black Man and the Yellow must ever remain inferior, and as the former raised himself higher and yet higher, so did those latter seem to sink out of Humanity and appear nearer and nearer to the brutes. The Social impulse had blindly proclaimed the equality of these races with the highest, theology had declared them the equals of the Teuton and the Sclav, but Nature decreed these doctrines to be impossible, and showed the Inferior Races but a step above the beasts, a wide degree below intellectual man. It was now incontrovertible that the faculty of Reason was not possessed by them in the same degree as the White Man, nor could it be developed in them beyond a very low point. This was the essential difference that proved the worthlessness of the Inferior Races as contrasted with ourselves, and that therefore placed them outside the pale of Humanity and its brotherhood.[17]

This truly Hitlerian act of semantic cheating and self-deception was native to the time; it had fed on the pseudo-science of so many ideas about the survival of the fittest. When grafted on to the sense of mission in an imperial people and the natural vanity that came from belonging to a dominant power, these ideas issued into fantasies of a world made safe for the White Man. It was the most brutal self-interest masquerading under the convenient notion that 'the duty of a rising race is either to absorb or to crush out of existence those with which it comes in contact, in order that the fittest and best may eventually survive'. The solution is still the Stone Age remedy of slaughtering the enemy; and the author gives an account of the wars and air battles that butcher all who stand in the way of the White Man. The air armadas fly across China and Japan, sending down beneath them 'a rain of death to every breathing thing, a rain that exterminates the hopeless race, whose long presumption it had been that it existed in passive prejudice to the advance of United Man'. *Dulce bellum inexpertis.*

Chapter Three

Science and the Shape of Wars-to-Come, 1880–1914

BEFORE the beginning of the eighteen-nineties the first phase in the growth of the tale of imaginary warfare had come to an end. Although the methods revealed by Chesney were not forgotten, the second and major phase of this literature began with a change in the direction and with a rapid expansion of the new fiction. An early sign of the new influences at work was the appearance in 1884 of the popular and aggressive French story, *Les Malheurs de John Bull*; and this was followed in 1888 by Arnold-Forster's attempt to describe the likely course of a future naval engagement in his short story, *In a Conning Tower*. What had hitherto been a middle-class exchange between the service writers and the readers of the monthly reviews and *The Times* quickly became an open market in which distinguished admirals competed and sometimes co-operated with enterprising journalists for the attention of the general reader. Behind this change, and shaping the stories of the period throughout Europe, were the increasingly powerful forces of mass journalism, mass literacy, and the mass emotions of extreme nationalism. The new tales of future warfare had the marks of a raw and frequently brutal epoch. At times they were violent and vindictive both in matter and in manner; they were often nationalistic to the point of hysteria; and they displayed an eagerness for novelty and sensation at the level of entertainment provided by the new journalism in publications like *Answers* and the *Daily Mail*. The cool tone, the objective approach to contemporary problems, the controlled emotion of Chesney now gave way on many occasions to excited language, crude emotionalism, and an often foolish idealization of the nation as the sole source of justice and the supreme arbiter in human affairs.

At the same time there was a corresponding change in the form of these stories. During the Chesney period the account of the imaginary war had usually appeared as a short story, designed to be one item amongst many for one issue of a newspaper or of a monthly periodical. By the eighteen-nineties, following on the great expansion of the daily and weekly Press, the new stories very often began as serials and, if successful, were immediately reprinted as full-length books. In this way it was often possible to combine the interest of matters of immediate political importance with the demand for excitement and adventure. This fact was noted by a new race of popular journalists like Louis Tracy, George Griffith, and William Le Queux. They had a standard formula for dealing with every situation: a major anxiety of the moment plus a racy and exciting narrative plus the introduction of eminent contemporary figures who would talk to the reader in the intimate manner favoured by the columnists of the *Daily Mail*. These were the distinctive features of much of the new fiction; and in essence it was the Chesney technique adapted to include romantic interludes and the treatment of personalities as practised by the popular Press.

Another change appeared in the way the new tales covered a wide field of national interests. The writers looked into every aspect of future warfare from the effects of new and as yet untried weapons to wild fantasies of anarchist uprisings throughout the world. Thus, Hugh Arnold-Forster, later to be Secretary of State for War, set out in 1888 without any political intentions to give the readers of *Murray's Magazine* 'a faithful idea of the possible course of an action between two modern ironclads availing themselves of all the weapons of offence and defence which an armoured ship at the present day possesses'. His story, *In a Conning Tower*, was a simple exercise of the imagination; and it proved to be so congenial to the interests of the period that it went into eight editions and was translated into five languages. In complete contrast there was the case of William Le Queux, the tireless exploiter of any scare or anxiety that would 'make a story'. Most of the war fiction he produced was extraordinarily successful, partly because he chose to write on matters of great national concern and partly because his handling of his themes never rose above the level set by the new mass newspapers. A notable example is to be found in the history of his first really profitable venture, *The Great War in England in 1897*, which first appeared as a serial in *Answers* during the war scare of 1893. Then, having helped to increase the circulation of *Answers*, it came out as a book in 1894 with a preface by Lord Roberts. It sold five editions in the first four weeks of publication; and it drew letters of commendation from the Duke of Connaught, Lord Wolseley, and other eminent personages. By 1899 it had gone through sixteen editions and had been accorded leading articles in the Paris *Figaro*, the Rome *Opinione*, and the *Secolo* of Milan.

The variety and number of the new publications reflect many forms of opinion and interest. In fact, they differ so much in quality and subject-matter, from sober military forecasts to tales of demon scientists eager to destroy humanity, that it is impossible to contain them all within a single explanation beyond noting that they all display a far greater interest in the details of armed conflict than had ever appeared before. War in all its fascination and terror was one theme that found its way into even the most purposive and political tales of future warfare. At every level in the nation the subject of 'the next great war' attracted constant discussion and description. The boys' magazines were filled with serial after serial[1] describing invasions by every possible enemy—French, German, Russian, even Chinese. In this the boys were only following the interests and preoccupations of their elders, for the new journalism represented by *Answers* and the *Daily Mail* saw that the public got what the editors thought their readers wanted. Much of this took the form of detailed accounts of war. It was a Harmsworth principle that 'war not only created a supply of news but a demand for it. So deep-rooted is the fascination in war and all things appertaining to it that . . . a paper has only to be able to put on its placard "A Great Battle" for its sales to mount up.'[2] This principle can be seen at work in the very respectable middle-class and imperialist illustrated weekly *Black and White*, which had started publication in 1891, one of the many new illustrated magazines then beginning to appear. The editor was an experienced journalist who tried out many devices during the early months of the magazine in order to increase his sales. His most spectacular and successful enterprise appeared within twelve months of the first number. It was *The Great War of 1892*, the first lavishly illustrated account of an imaginary war to appear in English. The editor revealed his intentions in the editorial he wrote to introduce the serial in January 1892. It is evident that he expected an increase in circulation figures from a story that combined imperialist ambitions with the novelty and excitement of the next war:

The air is full of rumours of War. The European nations stand fully armed and prepared for instant mobilisation. Authorities are agreed that a GREAT WAR must break out in the immediate future, and that this War will be fought under novel and surprising conditions. All facts seem to indicate that the coming conflict will be the bloodiest in history, and must involve the most momentous consequences to the whole world. At any time the incident may occur which will precipitate the disaster.

The Editor of *Black and White*, considering that a forecast of the probable course of such a gigantic struggle will be of the highest interest, has sought the aid of the chief living authorities in international politics, in strategy, and in war; and in the present number appears the first instalment of a suppositious record of this future War. In the construction of this imaginary but possible history, Admiral Sir Philip Colomb, Mr. Charles Lowe, Mr. D. Christie Murray, Mr. F. Scudamore, and other experts in military campaigns have taken part. From week to week the course of events will be narrated as though an actual war were in progress, and the Proprietors have obtained the assistance of Mr. F. Villiers, their own War Artist, Mr. C. W. Wyllie, Mr. J. Finniemore, Mr. W. F. Calderon and other artists, for the purpose of illustrating the scenes and episodes incident to the War. The various campaigns and political crises involved in the scheme, will be treated by writers and artists who have a particular knowledge of their subject, and the whole narrative will, it is hoped, present a full, vivid and interesting picture of the GREAT WAR of the Future—as it may be.

Although the war of 1892 could not in any sense be described as 'the bloodiest in history', certainly not by modern standards, the editor's hopes were fully realized. As the story came out week after week, supported by vivid illustrations, it aroused considerable interest and discussion. It quickly appeared in book form and was then translated into several European languages. By 1894 the German version, *Der grosse Krieg von 189–*, had reached its fifth edition. In an introduction to the German text General von Below attributed the great interest shown in the forecast both to what was said and also to the eminence of those who said it, especially Admiral Colomb. The German general considered that the *Great War of 1892* was an important work; and his reasons suggest an explanation for the general popularity enjoyed by these stories in Europe: 'So far there has been no shortage of stories about future battles in the German press. These stories have all aimed at describing the course of future battles and engagements from a military point of view . . . but this work has a higher aim. It concerns itself with the subject of international politics in Europe.'

The widespread European success enjoyed by stories as different as the straightforward forecast of the *Great War of 1892* and the simple imaginative projection of *In a Conning Tower* shows clearly that Britain, France, and Germany were united in spite of themselves by an interest in tales of future wars that described how these nations fought and defeated one another. But behind this common interest there were far more varied and unusual reasons than the simple anxieties that explained the excitement following on the *Battle of Dorking*. New drives and new forces began to reveal themselves in the eighteen-eighties, and these gathered strength until they exerted a decisive influence on the form and direction of many of the new-style stories produced in the 'nineties. A taste for the exotic, a delight in the marvels of military technology, a desire for adventure, an aggressive spirit of nationalism, the constant appeals from demagogues in Press and politics—these were some of the discernible influences that began to play with increasing effect upon the pattern of the imaginary war. The result was a flood of new stories that ranged from the innocent curiosity of *In a Conning Tower* to the completely romantic attractions of a world at last subject to the British Empire as described in *The Final War* by Louis Tracy. His preface revealed the purpose behind the numerous romantic tales of future wars that came out during the 'nineties: 'I have taken the whole world as my theme and its chief citizens are my characters. I can only hope that I have given no offence . . . I have tried to write a story of adventure.'

Although the contemporary interest in adventure provided the motive for many of these stories, there were quite different reasons behind the other types of the imaginary war as they developed in this period. Many of the stories fall into distinctive categories. They were deliberately shaped by their authors to present a military or a naval forecast, to teach a political lesson, or to give a demonstration of scientific marvels still to come. And they were all so taken up with the shape of 'the next great war', as it was so often called, that they had no space to display any interest in peace, except by way of conquest and the domination of other peoples. This is the one great ironic fact that must strike every reader who comes to these stories with a knowledge of what has happened during the last fifty years. The period from the eighteen-eighties to the long-expected outbreak of the next war in 1914 saw the emergence of the greatest number of these tales of coming conflicts ever to appear in European fiction. Save for rare exceptions, they are distinguished by a complete failure to foresee the form a modern war would take. The slaughter of the trenches, the use of poison gas, the immense damage caused by submarines, the very scale of a world-wide industrialized war were mercifully hidden from the admirals, generals, politicians, and popular novelists who joined in the great enterprise of predicting what was going to happen.

This was inevitable. It was the result of the now familiar time-lag between the rapid development of technology and the belated abandonment of ideas, mental habits, and social attitudes that the new machines and the new industries had rendered out of date. When men thought of war they did not foresee the struggles of great armies and anonymous masses of conscripts that finally came to pass. Instead, drawing on an imagination still burdened by a long tradition, which presented war as an affair of brief battles and heroic deeds by individuals, they underestimated the scale of actual warfare. Further, some were influenced by the widespread expectation that the new science would reduce and perhaps even end the danger of wars, others by the equally widespread doctrine that war was a profitable undertaking, or by evolutionary notions about the naturalness of war, and most of all by the characteristic Victorian interest in the novelty and romance to be found in new weapons and new forms of warfare.

As will be seen, a major paradox of the period was the way in which the Victorian sense of human achievement tended to make men regard science as an unmixed blessing. In consequence, the Victorians were as much interested in new weapons as they were in new engineering undertakings. As Macaulay saw science, there were no disadvantages at all:

> It has lengthened life; it has mitigated pain; it has extinguished diseases; it has increased the fertility of the soil; it has given new securities to the mariner; it has furnished new arms to the warrior; it has spanned great rivers and estuaries with bridges of form unknown to our fathers; it has guided the thunderbolt innocuously from the heaven to earth; it has lighted up the night with the splendour of the day; it has extended the range of human vision; it has multiplied the power of human muscles; it has accelerated motion; it has annihilated distance; it has facilitated intercourse, correspondence, all friendly offices, all dispatch of business; it has enabled man to descend the depths of the sea, to soar into the air, to penetrate securely into the noxious recesses of the earth, to traverse the land in cars which whirl along without horses, to cross the ocean in ships which run ten knots an hour against the wind. These are but a part of its fruits, and of its first-fruits; for it is a philosophy which never rests, which has never attained, which is never perfect. Its law is progress.[3]

The same gratitude for the wonders of science and the same sense of immense accomplishment ran through the *Lives of the Engineers* as described by Samuel Smiles. He saw them as demigods who had conquered nature for the benefit of mankind. 'Our engineers,' Smiles wrote, 'may be regarded in some measure as the makers of modern civilization'; and he declared that his intention in his *Lives of the Engineers* was 'to give an account of some of the principal men by whom this nation has been made so great and prosperous as it is—the men by whose skill and industry large tracts of fertile land have been won back from the sea, the bog, and the fen, and made available for human habitation and sustenance; who, by their industry, skill, and genius, have made England the busiest of workshops'.[4] Such ideas affected the mood of the nineteenth century; and in spite of occasional moments of anxiety and alarm this unqualified optimism ran its course until 1914. What Macaulay and Samuel Smiles said in their histories was echoed in the fiction and poetry of the period. Walt Whitman summed up the greatness of nineteenth-century man in phrases that are closely related to the epic fantasies of the new science described by Jules Verne:

> His daring foot is on land and sea everywhere,
> he colonizes the Pacific, the archipelagos,
> With the steamship, the electric telegraph,
> the newspaper, the wholesale engines of war,
> With these and the world-spreading factories
> he interlinks all geography, all lands.

Whitman's verse is a programme for the series of books that Jules Verne poured out between 1863 and his death in 1905. This pious Catholic, who won the commendation of Leo XIII for the purity of his writings, had so perfectly sensed the spirit of his time that he became the first writer to make a fortune by using science as material for fiction. In his stories the machine becomes the object of fiction and the technologist is the Promethean genius who uses science to make the Victorian dream come true by the conquest of the oceans and of the air. His heroes are from the same stock that produced the engineers celebrated by Samuel Smiles; but where Smiles relates the glories of great achievements in the past, Verne looks to even more glorious achievements still to come. The heroes of the past, as Smiles wrote, were men who were 'strong-minded, resolute, and ingenious, and were impelled to their special pursuits by the force of their constructive instincts'. The heroes of the future are men who have outdistanced the greatest triumphs of the Victorians. Their adventures reveal the prospect of conquests still to come; Captain Nemo has achieved the age-old dream of penetrating the depths of ocean and Robur has anticipated the inventors with his aeronef. 'And now who is this Robur?' wrote Verne. 'Robur is the science of the future. Perhaps the science of tomorrow. Certainly the science that will come.' This was something quite new in fiction. Before Verne the marvels of science had on occasions been incidental to stories of romance; but Verne gained a world-wide success by his ability to make technological achievements a subject for fiction. His heroes are scarcely real in any sense of the word. At best they are manifestations of tremendous energy —men who have learned how to control the great powers of nature. Their adventures are simply occasions for demonstrating man's new-found capacity to shape things to his will.

This delight in the limitless capacities of science was intimately associated with much of the literature of imaginary warfare that appeared after the eighteen-eighties. In fact, it seems that only a matter of temperament prevented Jules Verne from following in the steps of predecessors and contemporaries to develop some of the military possibilities implicit in his stories. There is, for instance, an indication of the havoc that could have been caused by the *Nautilus* in Captain Nemo's death-bed story of how he sank one of the hated British frigates. The suggestion that his machines could be used in war becomes explicit in a remarkable episode from the adventures of Robur in the *Clipper of the Clouds*. Verne demonstrates the beneficent result of the white man's inventions by describing how Robur saved the intended victims from the annual sacrifice in Dahomey. The aeronef cruises over the place of sacrifice and at the right moment 'the little gun shot forth its shrapnel which really did marvels'. It was enough to convince Robur's unwilling passengers of the advantages of his machine, and 'in this way did Uncle Prudent and Phil Evans recognize the power of the aeronef and the services it could render humanity'. But even clearer than this is the hint of what scientific warfare might achieve as described in *The Begum's Fortune*—the nearest Verne's imagination ever came to contemplating the type of war made possible by specially devised weapons. It is a strange story, a lesson on good and evil, France and Germany, the peaceful and warlike uses of science. Two scientists, one French and the other

German, use the wealth they have inherited to build two cities in the United States. Professor Schultz of Jena builds Stahlstadt, a crude anticipation of *Nineteen Eighty-Four*, in which rigid discipline and totalitarian methods contrast effectively with the happy conditions in the ideal city of Franceville. In these circumstances the German scientist plots to destroy the French city. His secret weapon—the first of many successors—is an enormous cannon with a range of thirty miles; its purpose is to fire a single vast shell that holds enough carbonic acid gas to wipe out the 250,000 inhabitants of Franceville in an instant.

Verne is important both because his work represents the high tide of European delight in the marvels and possibilities of science, and because he stands half-way between the earlier occasional and incidental treatment of future warfare in fiction and the full development of that theme in the last fifteen years of the nineteenth century. It is a telling indication of the speed with which the potential of science had begun to affect the imagination that there is only a century between the sensation caused by the balloon ascents of 1783 and the first large-scale vision of technological warfare in *La Guerre au vingtième siècle*, published in 1883 by the French draughtsman and satirist, Albert Robida. His sketches of air bombardments, armoured fighting vehicles, submarine attacks, and gas warfare marked a major stage in the interaction that had been taking place between science and the Western imagination. Since the appearance of Robida's forecast the gap between what was imagined and what finally came to pass has continued to narrow until in our own day science has at last caught up with fiction. Now, for the first time in the course of these imaginary wars, the general staffs and the politicians agree with the story-tellers that the next war is likely to be over before it can be reported and that the only task left for fiction is to describe the post-warfare state of the world.

This is the present stage in the sequence of scientific discoveries that began with the Renaissance dream of the conquest of nature and the supremacy of man. The scientific fantasies of Wells, Verne, and Kurd Lasswitz were the sophisticated nineteenth-century products of a process of development that went back to a man like Leonardo da Vinci. They described to millions of interested readers the shape of many things that had not yet appeared, whereas Leonardo set down his ideas in his notebooks. He bent his restless imagination to designing giant ballista, a steam gun, bombs, armoured chariots, multi-barrelled guns, and an underwater craft, of which he wrote in his notebook: '. . . this I do not publish or divulge on account of the evil nature of men who would practise assassinations at the bottom of the sea by breaking the ships in their lower parts and sinking them together with the crews who are in them.' Similarly, the magnificent ideal states of the nineteenth century—Bellamy's *Looking Backward* and Mantegazza's *L'Anno 3000*, for example—belonged to the tradition inaugurated by Bacon's *New Atlantis*. They prescribed a mixture of science and centralization as the certain cure for all the problems of their time; they planned for the whole world the type of highly organized society Bacon had imagined for the island community of the *New Atlantis*. The technological utopia of the nineteenth century had been designed on the Baconian principle that 'the end of our foundation is the knowledge of causes, and secret motions of things; and the enlarging of the bounds of human empire, to the effecting of all things possible'.[5]

The favourite Victorian dialogue between today and tomorrow, the advance from the evidence of things accomplished to the vision of the even greater things still to be done, could only begin from the developments of modern science. Verne and Wells followed in a tradition that went back to the eighteenth century, for it has already been shown that an immediate result of the success of the first Montgolfière and Charlière balloons was a flood of prints that attempted to depict how the invention could be used in warfare. Indeed, the year of 1783 had not run its course before a twenty-two-page tract had been published in Amsterdam and Paris. It discussed the possibilities of the new 'flying globes' and described how they might be used to capture Gibraltar. Again, in 1784 Benjamin Franklin asked: 'And where is the Prince who can afford so to cover his Country with Troops for its defense, as that ten thousand men descending from the clouds might not in many places do an infinite deal of mischief before a force could be brought together to repel them?' In this way, and from this time onwards, fact and prediction began to advance in parallel with fiction and prophecy. The last decades of the eighteenth century saw the start of a strangely innocent delight in trying to imagine warlike applications for peaceful inventions. In 1791 the aspiring natural philosopher Erasmus Darwin celebrated the great success of the new steam engine in abominable verses that looked forward with complete equanimity to its use both in peace and war:

Soon shall thy arm, UNCONQUER'D STEAM! afar
Drag the slow barge, or drive the rapid car;
Or on wide-waving wings expanded bear
The flying-chariot through the field of air.
Fair crews triumphant, leaning from above,
Shall wave their fluttering kerchiefs as they move;
Or warrior-bands alarm the gaping crowd,
And armies shrink beneath the shadowy cloud.

The possible application of these discoveries to war seems to have had a peculiar fascination for the early nineteenth century. In 1800 the German writer A. K. Ruh produced a romance of the twentieth century, *Guirlanden um die Urnen der Zukunft*, in which he set a commonplace and sentimental tale against a background of imaginary future changes. This new direction in fiction owed as much to the sense of change born of the great scientific discoveries as it did to the considerable European popularity enjoyed by Sebastian Mercier's account of an ideal state of the future, *L'An 2440*, which had played a great part—especially in Germany—in causing writers to present their hopes in the form of a tale of the future. Most of these early stories were either simple romances or not too serious attempts to foresee the pattern of civilized life in time to come.* The story by A. K. Ruh, for instance, related a long series of adventures that befall the hero whilst in the service of the Emperor of Germanien. The impression of a different future was established by such devices as an air postal service and a sail-driven balloon squadron used for air reconnaissance. The same theme of balloons in the service of the military appeared more fully in *Ini*, a story of the twenty-first century published in 1810 by Julius von Voss, a former lieutenant of the Prussian Army. His picture of the new age is striking evidence of the way in which the possibilities of technology had begun to fascinate the imagination long before Tennyson wrote of 'the nations' airy navies grappling in the central blue'. The story looks forward to a single European state, ruled by an Emperor in Rome. His writ runs from Sicily to Moscow—a reflection of the time when Napoleon was at the

* Some of the first tales of future times to appear were:
Jean-Baptiste de Grainville, *Le Dernier Homme*, 1805.
Mary Shelley, *The Last Man*, 1826.
Jane Webb, *The Mummy*, 1827.
Lord Moresby (pseud.?), *A Hundred Years Hence*, 1828.
R. F. Williams, *Eureka: a Prophecy of the Future*, 1837.

height of his power and it was impossible to go from Rome to Hamburg without passing through French-controlled territory. Wars are now fought against the barbarian peoples of Asia; and artillery has become so powerful that cities have deep underground shelters (with all the amenities of shops and churches) to protect their inhabitants in time of war. Once again, the popular fantasy of dirigible balloons appears in the description of the aerial reconnaissance groups: 'These had the task of observing the enemy from afar and reporting on the number and disposition of his troops. Since they had ascended high enough, the enlarged field of vision was a considerable help in observation; but the height also meant that they could be seen for twenty miles. But the enemy, eager to conceal his intentions, did not hesitate to send up his own light craft in order to drive back the enemy balloons; and so in the heavens above skirmishes developed between advanced patrols as had once taken place between Hussars and Cossacks centuries before.'[6]

Here, then, in the initial exuberance and general innocence with which men welcomed the first scientific advances one can discern the beginnings of the later European habit of forecasting the course of future wars. The habit was a consequence of regarding war as an affair of small armies, of the exhilaration of living in a period of unprecedented development, and of the assumption that there was no foreseeable calamity in the production of increasingly lethal weapons. Throughout the century there was a widespread belief that, although wars may have been unpleasant and might become horrible, war remained a possible and profitable activity for nations. For instance, the inventor Robert Fulton tried to persuade Congress in 1810 to adopt his torpedoes on the grounds that they would sweep British ships from the seas: 'In all my reflections on this kind of war, I see no chance for their escape other than by retreat; and the moment the English ships of war retreat before torpedo boats, that moment the power of the British marine is for ever lost, and with it the political influence of the nation.'[7] Few thought of—few were able to think of—the cumulative effects of the constant growth in the size and destructiveness of new instruments of war. Even the brilliant and humane pioneer of the aeroplane, Sir George Cayley, answered Lord Stanhope's fear that men might abuse the power of flight by arguing in 1817 that the discovery of the ship had brought good as well as evil. It was ordained that the aeroplane would or would not succeed: 'A new and extended power—commensurate with the still further state of civilisation contemplated for our race—now, in my view of the case, presents itself; some evils may possibly be in its train, but let us rest assured either that the subject is *impracticable* and therefore not designed for our use, or *practicable* in which case as a most *powerful* engine it must have been designed for our use. Our business seems to be to put the practicability to the test, and never to hesitate as to the result. Your Lordship seems to think that the means of conveyance will be increased whilst the means of defence remains the same: surely the defendant may use the same instrument as the assailant. I conceive we are looking too far in attempting to unravel all the workings of a power like this. Society may improve commensurably with the improvement of this power and we cannot estimate the moral influence of such improvement.'[8]

Since civilized life had demonstrably improved, it was widely felt that war might also moderate its terrors to the point when the possibility of war would have disappeared entirely. Looking at the changes going on about him in 1829, Robert Southey expected that in the matter of warfare 'the chemist and the mechanist will succeed where moralists and divines have failed'. Southey's argument was repeated frequently throughout the rest of the century. He thought that 'the novel powers which, beyond all doubt, will be directed to the purposes of destruction, are so tremendous, and likely to be so efficient, that in their consequences they may reasonably be expected to do more toward the prevention of war than any or all other causes.'[9] On 8th December 1834, when the distinguished French physicist, Dominique Arago, delivered the *Éloge* in honour of James Watt to the Académie des Sciences, he looked forward to a future full of hope and abundance. He forecast that 'a time will come, when the science of destruction shall bend before the arts of peace'. By the eighteen-seventies this view was becoming almost traditional teaching; for one of the more curious results of the Franco-German War was to encourage the belief that, since war had become swifter than ever, it had thereby become more humane than ever before. This was the moment when the nineteenth century had begun to turn in upon itself and contemplate the great progress that had been made since the beginning of the century. It was the time when histories of science began to replace the lives of the engineers, when books about the romance of science were beginning to find an ever-growing demand. These books generally included a chapter on fire-arms and armaments, which were introduced with enthusiastic remarks on the way the spirit of progress had affected the battlefield. As one writer began: 'Some idea of the marvellous achievements of the inventor on the battle-field—or, rather, in preparing for the battle-field—may be formed by a brief reference to recent statistics on the subject. There are said to be at the present time about 37,000 pieces of cannon in existence in the world.'[10] Another writer proclaimed that 'the man who invents the most rapid and the most effectual means of destruction, as regards war, is the greatest friend to the interests of humanity'. In an exultant chapter on the marvels of 'Gun-powder and Gun-cotton' he told his young readers: 'We are quite sure, however, that if any man could invent a means of destruction, by which two nations going to war with each other would see large armies destroyed, and immense treasure wasted on both sides, in a single campaign, they would both hesitate at entering upon another. We repeat, therefore, that in this sense the greatest destroyer is the greatest philanthropist.'[11]

The historians and the scientists joined with the generals and the novelists in claiming that war had become too terrible to continue, or that it had become so rapid in its results that the modern battle was now far more humane than the dreadful engagements of the bad old days. Behind this confused attitude to war there was a mass of assumption that derived as much from old-fashioned notions as from a general and no doubt unavoidable failure to foresee what might happen when the major industrialized nations went to war. In effect, war was regarded as an international process that resulted in convenient changes for the victor and no markedly unfortunate results for the loser. War had brought nations to power in Europe; it was extending the territories of European countries across the face of the earth; and as Ferdinand Foch told his students at the end of the century, when he was professor of military history at the École Supérieure de Guerre, 'if war is still national today, it is for the sake of securing economic benefits and profitable trade agreements'.

The argument for war had all the answers in its favour: it could no longer happen; or, if it did happen, then the consequences would not be disastrous. In this way it came to be accepted that there would be another war, because there had always been wars, and there could always be more wars. The imagination tolerated the idea, since it lacked the capacity to foresee the devastation, the immense casualty lists, the chaos and destruction that lay ahead. In 1883, Baron Colmar von der Goltz, the German military writer and later Governor of Belgium, put the case in favour of technological warfare in his book, *The Nation in Arms*. He recognized the force of the complaint that 'all advances made by modern science and technical art are immediately applied to the abominable art of annihilating mankind'. His answer was to demonstrate that the conduct of war had improved almost out of recognition: 'The fact that each new invention and each mechanical improvement seems somehow, in these days, to find its way into military service need not, therefore, alarm us, much less be regarded as a step backward in humanity and civilisation. By these means, on the contrary, the battle is only the more rapidly decided and the war brought to an end sooner than in the days of old.' This defence of war was common doctrine throughout Europe; it was not confined to recruiting speeches by German generals. The English version can be found in a plain history of science, *Discoveries and Inventions of the Nineteenth Century*, which put the militarist case at the beginning of a chapter on fire-arms:

We often hear people regretting that so much attention and ingenuity as are shown by the weapons of the present day should have been expended upon implements of destruction. It would not perhaps be difficult to show that if we must have wars, the more effective the implements of destruction, the shorter and more decisive will be the struggles, and the less the total loss of life, though occurring in a shorter time. Then, again, the exasperated and savage feelings evoked by the hand-to-hand fighting under the old system have less opportunity for their exercise in modern warfare, which more resembles a game of skill. But the wise and the good have in all ages looked forward to a time when sword and spear shall be everywhere finally superseded by the ploughshare and the reaping-hook, and the whole human race shall dwell together in amity. Until that happy times arrives . . . we may consider that the more costly and ingenious and complicated the implements of war become, the more certain will be the extension and the permanence of civilization. The great cost of such appliances as those we are about to describe, the ingenuity needed for their contrivance, the elaborate machinery required for their production, and the skill implied in their use, are such that these weapons can never be the arms of other than wealthy and intelligent nations. We know that in ancient times opulent and civilized communities could hardly defend themselves against poor and barbarous races. . . . In our day it is the poor and barbarous tribes who are everywhere at the mercy of the wealthy and cultivated nations. The present age has been so remarkably fertile in warlike inventions, that it may truthfully be said that the progress made in fire-arms and war-ships within the last few years surpasses that of the three previous centuries. Englishmen have good reason to be proud of the position taken by their country, and may feel assured that her armaments will enable her to hold her own among the most advanced nations of the world.[12]

This compound of complacency, ignorance, and innocence was the primary condition for the great growth of war fiction during the last quarter of the nineteenth century; and the new genre became so well known that writers and reviewers commented on the latest stories as specimens of *les guerres imaginaires, der Zukunftskrieg*, or the tale of 'the next great war'. There was so little to hold back the imagination from trying to foresee the shape of a future war. In fact, almost everything was a direct encouragement. The singularity of new weapons, the exciting possibilities in the development of the aeroplane and the submarine, the sense of immense achievements past and still to come, the traditional and heroic ideas of warfare—all these factors coincided with the start of the naval arms race and with the growing spirit of nationalism. The result was an entire new fiction of warfare that opened with the strictly political appeal introduced by Chesney and ranged through long stories in aid of new weapons or new ships to tales of 'what it will be like' in destroyers.

The abundance is embarrassing, but not overwhelming; for most of these writers were single-minded enough to turn out stories that kept strictly within their chosen fields of the political, the marvellous, or the romantic. One of the earliest examples of the more serious attempts to examine the pattern of future warfare was a naval application of Chesney's method. It appeared in the *Battle of Port Said*, an anonymous story reputed to be by an admiral which was first printed in *Engineering*. After causing a considerable stir at home and abroad, it was republished as a pamphlet in 1883 and then translated into French. The technique was still pure Chesney—the argument from defects to disaster. The intention in the *Battle of Port Said*, the author wrote, was 'to expose certain weaknesses in the construction and management of our war ships'. The proof is the outbreak of a war in which Britain and Germany side with Egypt against France, Russia, and Turkey. The result is a resounding defeat for the Royal Navy in which all the weaknesses of machinery and unskilled engineers are made clear.

The reasons behind the story were the many changes then going through at bewildering speed in naval construction. The arms race had begun, and much of the naval expansion that dates from about 1880 was a race between rival nations to keep pace with bigger guns, thicker armour, more effective projectiles, and faster ships. What this meant can be seen from the unending competition between guns and armour. When Britannia's wooden walls had become ironclad warships, the struggle of gun against plate had started. As guns increased in accuracy and effectiveness, the armour had to grow steadily thicker. Thus, the first wrought-iron plates had a thickness of between four and five inches. This increased to twenty-four inches; and then came the new compound armour of iron faced with steel; and finally there was steel alone. It was the same with naval guns: the *Dreadnought* had been launched in 1875 with 12.5-inch muzzle-loaders which could penetrate eighteen inches of iron; by 1902 the latest 12-inch breech-loaders fired a projectile that could get through a thickness of forty-six inches. Such a swift sea-saw development makes it clear why so many writers sought to describe the shape of wars-to-come. In fact, no one could say with certainty what a war at sea would be like, since the rate of naval development had been so hectic, and had been based on so many theories of offensive and defensive tactics that even the admirals—to judge from what some of them wrote—were not sure how things would turn out at sea. This is one reason for the sudden burst of predictions in which writers fought out the battle of gun against armour, ram against gun-fire, torpedo against battleship, and speed against defence. And, as had happened with the earlier pamphlets on the dangers of invasion, many of these stories went the rounds of international translations, since the anxieties and fears of one maritime power were of considerable interest to the others. The process can be seen at work with the *Battle of Port Said*. It had appeared at a time when, in the opinion of a distinguished naval officer like Lord Charles Beresford, the French naval vessels had better guns, better armour, and were generally more efficient than the British. So, when the *Battle of Port Said* had done its best for the Royal Navy, it was next discussed in French service journals and published in book form with a special introduction for French readers. The editor commented on the general interest aroused by the story and noted that the author's intention was 'to make known to his fellow citizens the defects that he finds in the construction of the British ships and in the training of their officers and men'.

Any defect, any reason, any fear provided the starting-point for these completely purposive stories of the disaster that could only be avoided by better ships, better guns, or better treatment for engineers. One long story published in 1896, *The Naval Engineer and the Command of the Sea* by F. G. Burton, began as a serial in *The Practical Engineer* with the sole intention of showing that 'the growing importance to the Navy of highly trained engineer officers and skilled mechanics has not yet been sufficiently recognised by the Authorities and the result has been a deep feeling of discontent throughout all branches of the engine-room staff. It is in order to direct public attention to this discontent, which threatens serious disaster to us in the event of war, that the following pages have been written.'

If the swift advance from wooden walls to steam turbines caused some to look anxiously to the future, there were many others who found it interesting, even exhilarating. There was a large audience throughout the nation for the factual and exciting account of the way in which future wars, especially future naval battles, would be fought. That was the discovery of Arnold-Forster, who pioneered a development of the imaginary war with his account of a ramming action between two warships. His motives explain the intentions of his many successors: 'an attempt has been made to throw into a popular form the teaching of various trials and experiments which have from time to time been made, and to introduce into the story of an actual engagement the results of a long course of careful observations of modern naval progress'. What he wrote, however, was little more than an English adaptation of a famous incident in the Battle of Lissa which had had a considerable influence on the theory of naval warfare in Europe. On 20th July 1866 Admiral Tegetthoff led the Austrian fleet out of Pola in order to engage the Italians. In the action that followed Tegetthoff steered his own ship, *Erzherzog Ferdinand Maximilian*, straight for the Italian *Re d'Italia*, rammed and sank her. 'Far underneath the water-line', so ran the account by the narrator in Arnold-Forster's story, 'the protruding ram had struck a blow from which no human power could save the victim. For a moment all was still, save for the sound of the stretching and rending of the iron; then suddenly, with a steady

The illustrator of *Trafalgar Refought* by Sir W. L. Clowes and A. H. Burgoyne, 1905, shows Nelson with the gun's crew of a twentieth-century warship.

but certain heave, the great ship seemed to bow down towards us. I watched her for a moment; long enough to see the surface of the deck as it showed up with the heel of the ship, and then I knew no more.'

The style of these new accounts of imaginary battles gives the impression that George Henty had collaborated with Samuel Smiles in describing the conduct of future naval engagements. The most striking qualities of a story like *In a Conning Tower* are a delight in the marvels of the new technology and an eager interest in the seemingly epic nature of a future battle. Arnold-Forster describes the conning tower of a warship of the eighteen-eighties in this way:

Here in this spot is concentrated the whole power of the tremendous machine which we call an ironclad ship. Such power was never since the world began concentrated under the direction of man, and all that power, the judgement to direct it, the will to apply it, the knowledge to utilise it, is placed in the hands of one man, and one only. What is this power? Talk of Jove with his thunderbolts, of Nasmyth with his hammer; the fables of mythology and the facts of latter-day science! where has there ever been anything to compare to it? Here in the Conning Tower stands the captain of the ship, and beneath his feet lie hidden powers which the mind can hardly grasp, but which one and all are made subservient to his will, and his will alone. Picture him as he stands at his post before the battle begins; all is quiet enough, there is scarcely a sound save the lapping of the water against the smooth white sides of the ironclad, and no outward sign of force save the ripple of parted waters falling off on either side of the ram as it sheers through the water.[13]

The same enthusiasm directed the work of the French officer who wrote under the *nom de plume* of Capitaine Danrit (see p. 117). Between 1889 and 1893 he had started on his career as a patriotic writer by turning out a series of books on the common theme of the next war against Germany. They were all published under the general title of *La Guerre de Demain*. Each book was a large two-volume account devoted to one aspect of future warfare as Danrit thought it would develop: *La Guerre en forteresse, La Guerre en rase campagne,* and *La Guerre en ballon*. Although Danrit's stories were far more political in aim than Arnold-Forster's *In a Conning Tower,* they gave considerable space to descriptions of new weapons and new machines of war. All the stories in the trilogy of *La Guerre de demain* dealt with the same war between France and Germany; and all were written in the spirit of Danrit's preface to the first of the series:

On every side the nations are arming and preparing for war. By writing this book in the form of an imaginary story I have tried to inspire my French readers with confidence in the outcome of the struggle. With this in mind I reveal to them the resources of our country, and I demonstrate the weapons that will be used in the coming battles: Melinite, the Lebel rifle, and the dirigible balloon.

In describing his imaginary war of the future Danrit kept his promise to give the reader confidence, to reveal the resources of the country, and to show the new weapons in action. In each book he described the probable conduct of infantry engagements, of fortress troops in the defence of strategic areas, and of the new airmen in their observation balloons and dirigibles. In many ways Danrit's stories were the French military equivalent of the British naval tales about the handling of destroyers and battleships in a future war. But, as will be seen later, his intentions were far more serious. His constant aim in everything he wrote was to prove that French troops and French equipment were always and in all places better than anything on the German or the British side. He continually breaks off the narrative in order to describe how a photographic section operating from a dirigible is able to obtain invaluable information about the size of a German column on the march; or to show how the French rifle is far more efficient than the German model; or to relate how the complicated business of mobilization goes forward rapidly and faultlessly in accordance with long-prepared plans.

Whilst Danrit was busy giving the French his picture of the conduct of the next war, in Britain a complete school of fiction had followed on the success of Arnold-Forster's *In a Conning Tower*. The new writers kept their narratives strictly to accounts of naval battles in which the Whitehead torpedo, the destroyer, and the battleship fought it out according to the theories of the day. They wrote tales like *The Captain of the 'Mary Rose'* by William Laird Clowes in 1892, *The Great War of 1892* by Admiral Colomb and his associates in 1892, the Earl of Mayo's *War Cruise of the 'Aries'* in 1894, F. T. Jane's *Blake of the 'Rattlesnake'* in 1895, and J. Eastwick's *The New Centurion* in 1895. Their simple treatment of future warfare continued until in 1905 it reached its most curious development, when the naval writers William Laird Clowes and

Alan Burgoyne joined forces to write *Trafalgar Refought*. The authors combined the taste for novelty with the potent appeal of tradition to produce, as they said, 'a vivid picture of likely happenings at sea had Nelson lived in this present year of grace'.

It was a crowded field in which the authors never hesitated to explain their intentions to their readers. William Laird Clowes set out in *The Captain of the 'Mary Rose'* 'to give a readable tentative answer to the question: 'What will the sea-fighting of tomorrow be like?" ' Although he cast his story in the form of a war between France and Britain, he was quick to point out that he had 'been animated by no unfriendly and by no unfair feelings towards France'. For James Eastwick the story of *The New Centurion* was meant to answer 'the not unnatural query what fighting with automatic weapons would be like'; and with a sour reference to his competitors he warned the reader that he would have to limit the account, 'otherwise it would be sure to end in describing one of those mythical contests between an unheard-of ironclad and an equally unheard-of enemy, of which we have too many already, and from which nothing ever has been learnt or ever will be'. There was the same declaration of intention and the same desire to apologize in the introduction to F. T. Jane's *Blake of the 'Rattlesnake'*. His aim was 'to work into story-form some of the romance that clings thick around the torpedo service'. And he included a note for the opposition: 'I would say one final word to those who object to these "future war yarns" on the grounds that they are likely to set other nations, at present friendly to us, by the ears. Foreign nations are frequently turning out similar stories, describing the utter destruction of the British Navy by their own; yet I have never heard of any of us bearing them ill-will for it. May our Warfare of the Future long be confined to the pages of books; as, indeed, it will be, so long as foreign nations know that we are ready to tackle the lot of them if need be.'

This was the idea of progress applied to the future of warfare. It was the product of a European preoccupation with technology and change that could never let the imagination rest. It was part of a general speculation that covered such diverse interests as the strictly professional fiction from members of the armed forces and the more daring conjectures of writers like H. G. Wells and Conan Doyle. Whilst the naval and military writers confined themselves to the immediate and the practicable, others like Albert Robida and H. G. Wells played with the possible and tried to imagine what might happen if the aeroplane, the submarine, even dynamite and Röntgen rays were developed for use in warfare. The new interest was only the most recent phase in the constant attempt to understand the new circumstances of the epoch, to foresee coming changes, to adjust to a rate of change that had been accelerating steadily ever since technology had begun to transform war as well as peace. In 1660 Robert Boyle had observed that 'the invention of gunpowder hath quite altered the condition of martial affairs over the world, both by sea and land'. In fact, the invention of fire-arms had meant the end of war as an occupation for warriors; it was beginning to be a profession for soldiers. By the end of the seventeenth century the cannon and the musket had brought about changes in tactics and strategy that in their turn demanded a new military discipline. And then, as weapons went on increasing in number and complexity, the soldier had to turn himself into a professional, dedicated to the service of an arm like the artillery or the engineers. Uniform, drill, regulations, general staffs, conscript armies, balloon observer companies, railway transport battalions, and machine-gun regiments were a consequence of the industrial revolution and of the advice given by Lazare Carnot to the Committee of Public Safety in August 1793—that the nation should organize a *levée en masse*. The idea of the nation-state coincided with the opportunities of science; and science being universal and neutral, knowing neither good nor evil, offered its gifts for men to use them as they wished. But once technology had been committed to the conflict between nations, it was inevitable that one day war would become fully automatic. In the half-century after the Franco-German War the general staffs toiled away to perfect techniques for launching great armies like so many offensive missiles. The logic of this union between war and technology—the military physics of speed and mass—has brought us to the point of completely mechanical warfare. The rows of buttons, the winking lights, the brisk ritual of the count-down—everything now waits for the electronic command that will trigger off the first fully automated war.

Today the tale of future warfare has little attraction for the imagination, since fiction cannot say more than is already known about the terror of the hydrogen bomb. But in the half-century before 1914 there was still enough curiosity about the future and men had enough sense of wonder about technological possibilities to attempt forecasts of the next war. For the service writers this was often a matter of communication, a desire to tell the civilian what the armed forces were planning; and this has persisted down to our own time in occasional stories like *War—1974* by the American tank officer Lieutenant-Colonel Robert B. Rigg. The difference is, however, that no military writer before 1914 ever began his story with the warning given to the reader in *War—1974* that, if war is to be prevented, 'people must know, beforehand, the shapes and forms that future conflict could assume. Unless people and governments know and understand the likely proportions of any conflict to come they are ill-equipped to prevent the occurrence of such an event.'

The old world before 1914 was still lost in the dream of constant progress. Warfare too often took on 'the romance that clings thick around the torpedo service' for men to question Treitschke's assertion that 'the mere fact of the existence of many states involves the necessity of war'. So, writers applied themselves to the business of describing what they thought would happen when the British and French Fleets met in battle, or when the French armies crossed over into Germany to win the great war of revenge. In attempting this they were trying to strike some sort of balance between war as it had been and what they thought it might become as a result of the many changes in artillery, projectiles, and tactics. In 1887 Prince Kraft zu Hohenlohe, who had commanded the Guard Artillery in 1870, showed the way he thought things might go in the lessons he drew from the Franco-German War: 'The manner in which the campaign was opened on the part of the Germans will, therefore, remain a standard pattern so long as new inventions do not create new strategical means such as aeronautics might do.'[14] Again, in the preface to the 1890 edition of his *Nation in Arms* Baron von der Goltz wrote that 'military science is at present undergoing revolutionary changes, which may influence the details of the military art, though in essentials it will probably remain unaffected while national armies of huge masses remain in existence'. Who could foresee the battles of the future, when in the 'nineties the French were complaining that they had changed the model of their rifle three times since 1870? An even more spectacular development was the discovery in the 'eighties of a smokeless powder, the famous *Poudre B* of the French chemical industry, which was so named out of compliment to the Minister of War, General Boulanger. By ending the usual fog of war, the new powder had totally transformed the conditions of the battlefield. Up to the appearance of *Poudre B* it had been standing practice for the artillery to engage the infantry over open sights. In 1870 the war correspondents had often reported the dense smoke created by bursting shells and the striking scene when the red trousers of the French infantry suddenly showed through the smoke as battalions advanced at the double in close column of troops towards the German positions. The simple chemistry of gun-cotton and the nitration process had in the course of a few brief years done away with the sense of spectacle that had always surrounded the great set battles; and it had presented a host of problems for the commanders to solve. Here, for example, is the old-style engagement described by Prince Kraft zu Hohenlohe in his *Letters on Cavalry*, written just before the introduction of smokeless powder. Discussing the problem of when to commit the cavalry, he states that 'at a distance of two miles it is exceedingly hard to judge as to the condition of the enemy, and as to the favourable moment for taking part in the action. Thick clouds of smoke overspread the locality of the combat, lines are seen swaying backwards and forwards, hurrahs mingled with the clatter of the infantry fire and with the thunder of the guns create such a hubbub that the whole seems one long roll of sound, and it is impossible to judge at all as to the condition of the engagement.'[15]

The stories thrown up by these incessant changes in the conditions of warfare began with military and naval writers—British, French, and German. Most of these stories were at first presented as a fictional version of a staff exercise; and it was not until the emergence of the mass Press in the 'nineties that service writers like Admiral Colomb and the French officer Émile Driant began to produce full-length stories for serialization in the new dailies and weekly magazines. Whilst *Black and White* was serializing Admiral Colomb's *Great War of 1892*, Capitaine Driant was turning out his trilogy, *La Guerre de forteresse, La Guerre en rase campagne, La Guerre en ballon*. In all this fiction there is a correlation between national attitudes and the type of stories these writers produced. The French were usually concerned with the coming war of reconquest to be waged against Germany; and except for the period of dispute with Britain in the 'eighties and 'nineties, when some of these stories turned into a French conquest of Albion, their writers continued to describe the multifarious forms they imagined for the great task of *la revanche*. The Germans were markedly different. They produced very little in the field of imaginary warfare until after 1895, when the expansion of the fleet set them on a collision course with Britain. In fact, until the appearance of the propaganda for a bigger fleet in *Wehrlos zur See* in 1900, German writers were far more interested in translating predictions made in other countries, or in turning out very plain pamphlets that were little more than military appreciations for the general public. The publications of the military historian Karl Bleibtreu are characteristic of this aspect of the tale of imaginary warfare in Germany. In the late 'eighties he produced a series of three battle pieces under the general title of *Die Entscheidungsschlachten des Europäischen Krieges, 18 . . .* They are exceptionally tiresome and long-winded. Indeed, the only element of interest is his contempt for foreign publications of the same kind and his conviction that a future war would be a fast-moving affair in the manner of 1870. In his account of a war fought by Russia against Germany and Austro-Hungary he relates in great detail the advance of the cavalry divisions, followed by the engagement of infantry patrols. Then the main forces begin their manœuvring, and the campaign is swiftly decided by a single major battle. The enemy, it is shown, have been defeated by the superior capacities of the German staff and the greater abilities of the troops. Even the German attempts to describe the next war, Bleibtreu asserted, were better than anything written in other lands. In the introduction to his third story, *Die Schlacht bei Châlons*, Bleibtreu destroyed the reputation of all foreign competitors with his claim that 'the foreign pamphlets about the next war are simply the chatter of the ignorant; the German accounts, both in strategy and in tactics, are workmanlike studies. Moreover, the attempt to describe a future war in such minute detail is completely new.' But Bleibtreu's view, too, was simply the chatter of the ignorant.

The great paradox running through the whole of this production of imaginary wars between 1871 and 1914 was the total failure of army and navy writers to guess what would happen when the major industrial nations decided to fight it out. Even when one takes account of the fact that many of these writers were presenting a special case for changes in equipment or organization by projecting success or disaster into the future, it still remains true that the intense conservatism of the armed forces and years of studying pre-technological battles from Cannae to Waterloo had induced a habit of expecting that wars would continue to be more or less as

La Guerre au vingtième siècle by Albert Robida (Paris, 1887—the edition in book form of Robida's work which first appeared in his periodical *La Caricature* beginning in 1883).

they had always been. In consequence, the naval and military prophets generally saw war as an affair of adaptation and improvisation. They rarely thought of what their new equipment might do. None of them ever seems to have imagined that technology might be able to create new instruments of war. That was left to the civilian; for in the fifty years before the First World War the only writers who came anywhere near to seeing how science and industry might change the traditional pattern of warfare were Albert Robida, H. G. Wells, and Conan Doyle. One reason is that the imaginative writer, free from the specialist preoccupations of the professional, could allow his mind to move freely over the whole area of the possible. This comes out clearly in the first major vision of technological warfare ever presented, *La Guerre au vingtième siècle* by Albert Robida, which appeared during 1883 in the French periodical *La Caricature*. The visions of this remarkable engraver, lithographer, caricaturist, architect, and writer represent a distinct phase in the growth of the idea of the future. Robida comes midway in the development that begins with the total optimism of Jules Verne in the eighteen-sixties and ends with the first prediction of the universal horror of atomic warfare in *The World Set Free* by H. G. Wells in 1914. The two writers, Robida and Wells, had an unusual awareness of the destructive potential of technology when used for military purposes. As Wells put the matter in 1914, when he described the atomic bombs used in the world war of 1959, science had begun to confront the human race with a choice between total war and total peace:

Certainly it seems now that nothing could have been more obvious to the people of the earlier twentieth century than the rapidity with which war was becoming impossible. And as certainly they did not see it. They did not see it until the atomic bombs burst in their fumbling hands. Yet the broad facts must have glared upon any intelligent mind. All through the nineteenth and twentieth centuries the amount of energy that men were able to command was continually increasing. There was no increase whatever in the ability to escape. Every sort of passive defence, armour, fortifications and so forth was being outmastered by this tremendous increase on the destructive side.[16]

The first stage of this realization appears in the text and drawings of Robida's *La Guerre au vingtième siècle.* They present a picture of future warfare that was very different from what all the admirals and generals had been saying. Unlike Wells, however, Robida is not entirely serious in his forecast of war in the twentieth century. He looks into the possibilities of scientific warfare with all the ironical detachment of a satirist who has no illusions about the readiness with which men would use the most frightful weapons in order to conquer; but the difference between the realities of 1883 and what might happen in the future war of 1945 was still big enough to provoke amusement rather than terror and despair. Robida's position is closer to Verne than to the Wells of *The World Set Free*; he is hardly attacking warfare, but rather the folly of human beings who might one day, if they were so foolish, really develop all the weapons he drew with such admirable ability. He foresaw most of what appeared later on: submarines, underwater troops, mines, torpedoes, smoke-screens, automatic small-arms fire, air bombardments of cities, a chemical corps complete with poisonous shells, a bacteriological warfare company to spray the enemy with microbes, and the *blockhaus roulants*, the forerunners of Wells's land ironclads. If many of the weapons belonged to the future, the world picture of 1945 was still a derisive projection of the anxieties of 1883: 'The first half of the

Two drawings by Albert Robida: a tender ferries crew-members to an aerial cruiser and (below) a successful attack by a one-man submarine. From Robida's *La Guerre au vingtième siècle* (Paris, 1887)

year 1945 had been particularly peaceful. Except for the usual goings-on, that is to say a little civil war of three months in the Danubian Empire, an American expedition against our coasts which was driven off by our submarine fleet, and a Chinese expedition smashed to pieces off Corsica—except for these—Europe had enjoyed complete peace.'

And then war breaks out. The hero joins the 6th Squadron, 18th Territorial Aeronautics, and is forthwith committed to the swift war of electrically powered aircraft, tanks, and cyclist troops. Outside one town an enemy chemical battalion takes up its position. Four bombs describe a brief parabola through the air: '. . . a sentry who had seen suspicious shadows was about to raise the alarm, when the first projectile exploded in a greenish cloud. A loud cry, a puff of smoke . . . Three more shells followed. And then there was a great silence. The camp fires were extinguished and everything went dead, even the miserable inhabitants remaining in the town who had been suddenly asphyxiated in their homes. But these are the accidents of war to which we have all grown accustomed as a result of the recent advances of science.' However, it is only on rare occasions that so serious a note sounds through the text. For the most part the story proceeds at breakneck speed as the hero moves from one unit to another, in turn air gunner, infantryman, second-lieutenant of a machine-gun company, torpedo engineer in the submarine fleet, and finally commander of the *Voltigeur aérien No. 39* in which he accomplishes great deeds against the enemy air fleets.

As a writer, however, Robida is a light-weight in comparison with his contemporary, H. G. Wells; and any final judgement has to recognize that only the exceptional imagination shown in the drawings makes it possible to contrast *La Guerre au vingtième siècle* with the several Wellsian visions of the wars to come. Nevertheless the two men had a number of things in common: they were fascinated by the immense potential of science; they both had an intuitive awareness of the ways in which the conduct of war might be changed; and they both had an interest in violence and destruction that was characteristic of so much European writing during the last two decades of the nineteenth century. All these qualities, however, appeared more strongly in Wells and were all given much freer rein in his fiction before 1914. In fact, a sense of groups divided and in conflict seems to have been central to Wells's imagination from the start. He began in *The Time Machine* in 1895 by looking into the far-off future world of 802701, and there he found that humanity had degenerated into two different species, the effete Eloi and the obscene subterranean Morlocks, who were engaged in a fearful Darwinian struggle to survive. This idea of a war to the finish between races had appeared earlier in Bulwer Lytton's *Coming Race* and more spectacularly in W. D. Hay's account of the all-victorious white race in *Three Hundred Years Hence*. But Wells's handling of the theme was very different; it was far more pessimistic. The Time Traveller discovered there was no glorious future ahead for the human race. He grieved 'to think how brief the dream of the human intellect had been' after he made the terrible discovery that 'these Eloi were mere fatted cattle, which the ant-like Morlocks preserved and preyed upon—probably saw to the breeding of'. The law of unending progress had clashed with the greater law of nature—'that intellectual versatility is the compensation for change, danger, and trouble'. In consequence, the human race had split into the divergent species of the Eloi and the Morlocks; and out of that split came the great war of nature.

Three years later the war of nature assumed cosmic proportions. Wells returned to the theme of conflict and in the best of all his scientific romances, *The War of the Worlds*, he took the Darwinian struggle for survival, combined it with contemporary ideas of a war between peoples, and projected the results upon a planetary scale. This most forceful tale of the Martian invasion of earth is still better than any of the tales of interplanetary warfare that have derived from the great success of the prototype. In fact, the *War of the Worlds* is the perfect nineteenth-century myth of the imaginary war; it says many things about war in many different ways. At first sight the *War of the Worlds* is all that it claims to be: the invasion of earth by a warrior force from the more highly advanced civilization on Mars. At this level the story keeps close to the original idea, which was suggested to Wells by his brother Frank during a walk in the peaceful Surrey countryside. ' "Suppose some beings from another planet were to drop out of the sky suddenly," said Frank, "and begin laying about them here!" Perhaps we had been talking of the discovery of Tasmania by the Europeans—a very frightful disaster for the native Tasmanians! I forget. But that was the point of departure.'[17] From that the story grew into a true fantasy of the subconscious. In addition to handling the central theme of adventure and horror, Wells's imagination sought to work out three principal ideas: the violence of colonial warfare, the Darwinian idea of a struggle between competing groups, and the devastating potentialities of an advanced military technology. That is to say, his ideas derived from: warfare as the Europeans—especially the British—had experienced it during the great imperial expansion in the last twenty years of the century; warfare as the biologists declared it to be experienced in the universal world of nature; and warfare as it might be experienced if science were turned to the task of producing the most efficient possible weapons.

The first of these themes, although the least important, decided the shape of the story. In fact, it was present from the very beginning in the thought of what had happened to the Tasmanians when the superior technology of the West had 'opened up' their lands. Wells stood colonial expansion on its head, presented Britain as a backward area, and gave the Martians a degree of technological achievement that made the miserable defenders of imperial Britain look rather like the unhappy Tasmanians. The theme of an interplanetary war was an ironical inversion of nineteenth-century imperialism. It was a retort on behalf of the Tasmanians to the lament of Cecil Rhodes: 'The world is nearly all parcelled out, and what there is left of it is being divided up, conquered and colonised. To think of these stars that you see overhead at night, these vast worlds which we cannot reach. I would annex the planets if I could; I often think of that. It makes me sad to see them so clear and yet so far.'[18] This imperialist point of view, when raised to an interplanetary level and combined with the principle of the universal struggle to survive, explains the purpose of the Martian descent on our planet:

And we men, the creatures who inhabit this earth, must be to them at least as alien and lowly as are the monkeys and lemurs to us. The intellectual side of man already admits that life is an incessant struggle for existence, and it would seem that this too is the belief of the minds upon Mars. Their world is far gone in its cooling, and this world is still crowded with life, but crowded only with what they regard as inferior animals. To carry warfare sunward is indeed their only escape from the destruction that generation after generation creeps upon them. And before we judge of them too harshly, we must remember what ruthless and utter destruction our own species has wrought, not only upon animals, such as the vanished bison and dodo, but upon its own inferior races. The Tasmanians, in spite of their human likeness, were entirely swept out of existence in a war of extermination waged by European immigrants, in the space of fifty years.[19]

The twin themes of colonial and evolutionary warfare run right through the story. It explains the devastating success of the Martian invaders in the language of interplanetary imperialism:

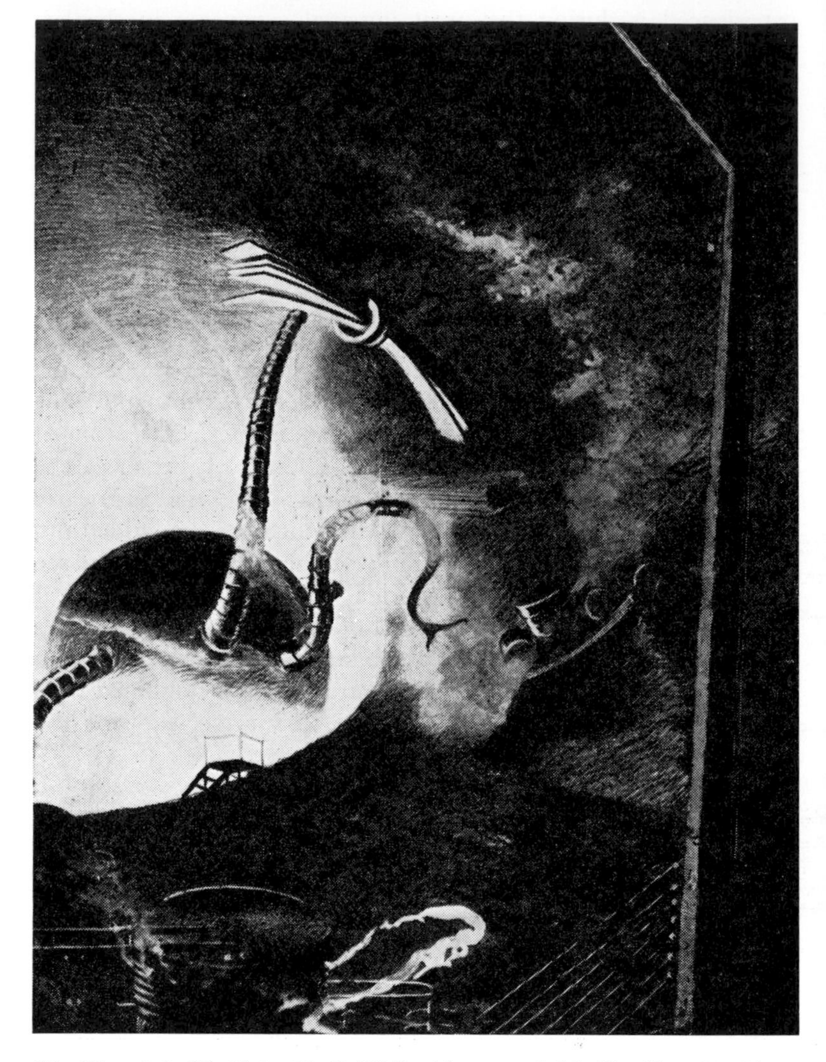

The War of the Worlds by H. G. Wells: 'the remarkable Handling Machines, and the tall war vehicles in which the Martians stalked over southern

'We men, with our bicycles and road-skates, our Lilienthal soaring-machines, our guns and sticks, and so forth, are just in the beginning of the evolution that the Martians have worked out.' And at the very end it explains the irony of earth's salvation. It was a victory won for mankind by 'the putrefactive and disease bac-

England . . .' Illustrations by a Belgian artist, Alvim-Correa, from the Belgian edition of Wells's book, published by Van Damme, Brussels, 1906.

teria'. The microbes had conquered in the name of Darwin: 'These germs of disease have taken toll of humanity since the beginning of things—taken toll of our pre-human ancestors since life began here. But by virtue of this natural selection of our kind we have developed resisting-power . . . But there are no bacteria in Mars, and directly those invaders arrived, directly they drank and fed, our microscopic allies began to work their overthrow.'

It was a famous victory for the allies and something more than a highly convenient ending to a story; it was a profound humiliation for man. Men had not conquered. In fact, under the conditions imagined by Wells they could not conquer. The warriors may have come from Mars for the purpose of the fiction; but their terrible weapons and the immense destruction they caused might one day emerge from Western industrialism, if science were to create the most lethal possible armoury. The marvels of the poisonous Black Smoke, the Heat Ray, the remarkable Handling Machines, and the tall war vehicles in which the Martians stalked over southern England, calling *ulla, ulla, ulla* to one another—all came from the immensely fertile imagination of Wells as he thought with a fear (half recognized for what it was) of the destruction that would follow on a full-scale industrialized war. This fear appears from time to time in a rudimentary form in the *War of the Worlds*. 'Never before in the history of warfare,' he wrote, 'had destruction been so indiscriminate and so universal.' And again, when all southern England is at the mercy of the invaders, he writes that 'had the Martians aimed only at destruction, they might on Monday have annihilated the entire population of London, as it spread itself slowly through the home counties.' The greatest industrial nation upon the planet Earth was defenceless before the power of science. As the Commander-in-Chief announced in a calamitous dispatch, flight was the only way out:

> The Martians are able to discharge enormous clouds of black and poisonous vapour by means of rockets. They have smothered our batteries, destroyed Richmond, Kingston, and Wimbledon, and are advancing slowly towards London, destroying everything on the way. It is impossible to stop them. There is no safety from the Black Smoke but in instant flight.

At this point the *War of the Worlds* parts company with the mass of imaginary war fiction as it had developed since the time of the *Battle of Dorking*; for Wells's story transcends all the limitations of national politics, international disputes, and contemporary armaments that had engaged the attention of most practitioners in this field. A scientific education, a logical mind, an exceptionally rich and original imagination had acted on his intense realization of incessant change to create this prevision of the possible. Behind it there was a two-stage logic, which began with Wells giving the invaders everything any army could hope for in terms of protection, speed, and fire-power. For Britain the consequences were total defeat, roads crowded with terrified refugees, and the abandoned city of London. For these reasons and because of the high quality of the narrative the *War of the Worlds* is still the most remarkable fantasy of imaginary warfare that has so far appeared in the history of the genre. The theme was scientific warfare taken to the limit. It was the prelude to a sequence of similar stories, *War in the Air, The World Set Free, The Shape of Things to Come*, in which Wells went on to deal with the conflict between outdated but still-with-us institutions and the urgent need to adjust everything (techniques, education, attitudes of mind, social practices) to the new world that science had called into existence. The struggle between the old and new tormented Wells. In one way he saw it as the struggle between traditional practices in education and the new approaches required to prepare the citizens for life in a technological epoch. Another form was the contrast he saw between the old-style close combat battles of the Victorian school primers and the swift world-wide wars of the future. The one reflected the other. As he saw the situation when he produced *Anticipations* in 1902, two of the principal factors working to change the course of human life in the twentieth century were 'the steady development of a new and quite unprecedented educated class as a necessary aspect of the expansion of science and mechanism' and 'the absolute revolution in the art of war that science and mechanism are bringing about'. War and science, therefore, demanded a better and more widespread form of education, or else a nation would go under in the new international struggle to survive. Wells's thesis was very simple: we must educate or perish. 'The law that dominates the future', he wrote, 'is glaringly plain. A people must develop and consolidate its educated class or be beaten in war.' The reasons were obvious to him: 'The nation that produces in the near future the largest proportional development of educated and intelligent engineers and agriculturists, of doctors, schoolmasters, professional soldiers and intellectually active people of all sorts . . . will certainly be the nation that will be the most powerful in warfare as in peace, will certainly be the ascendant or dominant nation before the year 2000.'[20] It took the British people fifty years of slow change, two world wars, and half a dozen reports on educational reform, before they began to catch up with the Wellsian proposition.

Wells was one of the few writers of his time who had the requisite imagination and technical competence to understand the social changes then taking place as well as the ability to foresee the ways in which science would continue to affect the conduct of human life. Contrast, for example, Wells's ideas about future warfare with these concluding lines from a *History of Our Time*, written by the historian G. P. Gooch in 1911. His verdict was peace in our time: 'We can now look forward with something like confidence to the time when war between civilised nations will be considered as antiquated as the duel, and when the peacemakers shall be called the children of God.' The scientist turned writer was much nearer the mark than the professional historian. In the chapter on 'War' in *Anticipations*, Wells wrote:

All this elaboration of warfare lengthens the scale between theoretical efficiency and absolute unpreparedness. There was a time when any tribe that had men and spears was ready for war, and any tribe that had some cunning or emotion at command might hope to discount any little disparity in numbers between itself and its neighbour. Luck and stubbornness and the incalculable counted for much; it was half the battle not to know you were beaten, and it is so still. Even today, a great nation, it seems, may still make its army the plaything of its gentlefolk, abandon important military appointments to feminine intrigue, and trust cheerfully to the home-sickness and essential modesty of its influential people, and the simpler patriotism of its colonial dependencies when it comes at last to the bloody and wearisome business of 'muddling through'. But these days of the happy-go-lucky optimist are near their end. War is being drawn into the field of the exact sciences. Every additional weapon, every new complication of the art of war, intensifies the need of deliberate preparation, and darkens the outlook of a nation of amateurs. Warfare in the future, on sea or land alike, will be much more one-sided than it has ever been in the past, much more of a foregone conclusion.[21]

Wells was not always so far-sighted. Although he expected that the military would have to create some form of armoured fighting vehicle, a land ironclad as he described it in a famous short story, he could not foresee 'any sort of submarine doing anything but suffocate its crew and founder at sea', and in 1902 he did not expect a successful aeroplane to have flown much before 1950. But by 1907, when he set out to write the *War in the Air*, at a time when the Zeppelin was still an experiment and Blériot had not yet flown the Channel, Wells returned to the prophetic style of his earlier fantasies. His new thesis was 'that with the flying machine war alters its character; it ceases to be an affair of "fronts" and becomes an affair of "areas"; neither side, victor or loser, remains immune from the gravest injuries, and while there is a vast increase in the destructiveness of war, there is also an increased indecisiveness'.

He describes the great air battles that follow on the sudden raid made by the German Air Fleet on New York; he relates the destruction of the American Fleet in the Atlantic, the North Sea battle that ended German hopes of naval glory, the epidemics, diseases, the destruction of great cities, the spread of war to every corner of the globe, the collapse of trade and commerce. He explains why it all happened in a paragraph that is even more relevant to the period since 1918:

The accidental balance on the side of Progress was far slighter and infinitely more delicate and complex in its adjustments than the people of that time suspected; but that did not alter the fact that it was an effective balance. They did not realise that this age of relative good fortune was an age of immense but temporary opportunity for their kind. They complacently assumed a necessary progress towards which they had no moral responsibility. They did not realise that this security of progress was a thing still to be won or lost, and that the time to win it was a time that passed. They went about their affairs energetically enough, and yet with a curious idleness towards those threatening things. No one troubled over the real dangers of mankind. They saw their armies and navies grow larger and more portentous; some of their ironclads at the last cost as much as their whole annual expenditure upon advanced education; they accumulated explosives and the machinery of destruction; they allowed their national traditions and jealousies to accumulate; they contemplated a steady enhancement of race hostility as the races drew closer without concern or understanding.[22]

Wells came back six years later to this favourite thesis of science and the coming world conflict in the *World Set Free*, which was written during 1913 and published early in 1914. In many ways it is his most striking forecast, although by no means one of his best stories of the future. Two things make it stand out: his argument that 'because of the development of scientific knowledge, separate sovereign states and separate sovereign empires are no longer possible in the world'; and—even more remarkable—his prediction that scientists would have discovered how to use atomic energy by 1953 and that in consequence a world-wide atomic war would break out. The account of the lecture by the professor of physics at the beginning of the story is one of those rare occasions when fiction becomes truly prophetic. The subject is radioactivity. Holding a phial of uranium oxide before the audience, the professor foretells what would happen when men tapped 'a source of power so potent that a man might carry in his hand the energy to light a city for a year, fight a fleet of battleships or drive one of our giant liners across the Atlantic . . . Every scrap of solid matter in the world would become an available reservoir of concentrated force.' Long before the mushroom cloud over Hiroshima one man had guessed what might result from the work of Einstein and Rutherford. A quarter of a century before Einstein wrote his letter to warn President Roosevelt that the discoveries of the nuclear physicists had made possible the development of 'extremely powerful bombs of a new type', Wells had already given the term 'atomic bomb' to the English language.

Unfortunately the story in the *World Set Free* is much more prosaic than the extraordinary leap of the imagination that described the discovery of atomic energy and the manufacture of atomic bombs. The tendency to preach, so characteristic a feature of much of Wells's writing after the early scientific romances, undoubtedly weakens the story. The nearer he comes to the facts of science and society, the more pedestrian he is. But when one contrasts what he thought might happen to the conduct of war in the *World Set Free* with the old-style engagements described in so many contemporary tales of imaginary warfare, Wells is still the major prophet. Here, for instance, is the description of the first atomic war as he imagined it in 1913:

For the whole world was flaring then into a monstrous phase of destruction. Power after power about the armed globe sought to anticipate attack by aggression. They went to war in a delirium of panic, in order to use their bombs first. China and Japan had assailed Russia and destroyed Moscow, the United States had attacked Japan, India was in anarchistic revolt with Delhi a pit of fire spouting death and flame: the redoubtable King of the Balkans was mobilising. It must have been plain at last to every one in those days that the world was slipping headlong to anarchy. By the spring of 1959 from nearly two hundred centres, and every week added to their number, roared the unquenchable crimson conflagrations of the atomic bombs; the flimsy fabric of the world's credit had vanished, industry was completely disorganised and every city, every thickly populated area, was starving or trembled on the edge of starvation. Most of the capital cities of the world were burning; millions of people had already perished, and over great areas government was at an end.[23]

But the Wellsian forecast of unheard-of weapons seemed too far-fetched, too far away in the barely discernible future, to attract the attention of the general reader in 1914. A prophecy much more to the point in those days was Sir Arthur Conan Doyle's notorious short story of unrestricted submarine warfare, *Danger*, which won the interest of all Europe and the scorn of most naval experts. The story, which first appeared in the July number of the *Strand Magazine* in 1914, was written about eighteen months before the outbreak of the First World War. Doyle was quite as deliberate as Wells had been. He wrote, he said, in order 'to direct public attention to the great danger which threatened this country'. He went to the nation with a story of the way in which the submarine fleet of one of the smallest powers in Europe defeated the entire might of the British Empire by sinking all vessels approaching United Kingdom ports.

The story was propaganda in aid of the Channel Tunnel project; and the form was the familiar Chesney method of showing what ought to be done by demonstrating the consequences of failing to do it. Conan Doyle opens with an arrogant ultimatum from the British Government to a small and imaginary European country. Captain John Sirius, commander of submarines, urges his government to oppose the British demands and he proposes that his submarines should take up stations off the major British ports. When the ultimatum expires, and the British Government is left with an easy war to win, unidentified submarines begin to sink merchant vessels all around the British Isles. The submarine blockade is complete. Food supplies begin to run out and the Government has to sue for peace terms from the despised but victorious small power.

Conan Doyle's forecast appeared two months before Kapitänleutnant Otto Weddigen showed what the U-boats could do when he sent the *Aboukir, Hogue*, and *Cressy* to the bottom, and seven months before Vize-Admiral von Pohl, Chief of the German Admiralty Staff, proved the accuracy of *Danger* by proclaiming a submarine blockade of the British Isles. All waters around Great Britain and Ireland were declared to be a military area in which Allied shipping would be destroyed and neutral vessels would be in danger of a like fate. Three months later the Cunard liner *Lusitania* was torpedoed off the south coast of Ireland with a loss of 1,198 lives. Conan Doyle was right and the admirals were wrong. In part, British naval thinking had expected that the

"THE SHIP LAY WITHIN TWO HUNDRED YARDS OF US, AND IT WAS EASY TO SEE THAT SHE HAD HER DEATHBLOW."

(See page 1.)

DANGER!

Being the Log of Captain John Sirius

By A CONAN DOYLE

Illustrated by E. S. Hodgson

The Opinions of Naval Experts on this striking story, appear on page 20.

It is an amazing thing that the English, who have the reputation of being a practical nation, never saw the danger to which they were exposed. For many years they had been spending nearly a hundred millions a year upon their army and their fleet. Squadrons of Dreadnoughts costing two millions each had been launched. They had spent enormous sums upon cruisers, and both their torpedo and their submarine squadrons were exceptionally strong. They were also by no means weak in their aerial power, especially in the matter of hydroplanes. Besides all this, their army was very efficient

Danger! by A. Conan Doyle: opening of the story as it appeared in the *Strand Magazine* for July 1914. By permission of the proprietors of the *Strand Magazine*.

submarine would only affect Fleet actions. In part, the admirals were not so cynical as the civilian; they did not expect that submarines would attack unarmed vessels. As Admiral Penrose Fitzgerald said of *Danger*: 'I do not myself think that any civilised nation will torpedo unarmed and defenceless merchant ships.' For Admiral Sir Algernon de Horsey the story was 'a very interesting but, as most would say, fantastic account of an imaginary war'. Another admiral, Sir Compton Domvile, had the same opinion: 'I am compelled to say that I think it most improbable, and more like one of Jules Verne's stories than any other author I know.' And Admiral William Hannam Henderson, although agreeing that the submarine had modified aspects of naval warfare, rejected the opinion 'that territorial waters will be violated, or neutral vessels sunk. Such will be absolutely prohibited, and will only recoil on the heads of the perpetrators. No nation would permit it, and the officer who did it would be shot.'[24]

Three weeks after these views had appeared in the *Strand Magazine* the fateful ultimatum had been sent to Serbia. And out of that came the first world-wide conflict which most of the authors of these imaginary wars had failed to foresee. On 4th August 1914 the long European peace ended. The Germans set the Schlieffen Plan in operation and along the whole line of the French frontier seven German armies moved forward. One and a half million men were up on their start lines or in support positions. Opposite them some seventy French divisions were engaged in the task of defeating the enemy according to the scheme laid down in Plan XVII. What followed is a matter of history, of military strategy, and national legend. By 23rd August the situation on the French left had become most critical as two German armies sought to roll up the Fifth Army. At the same time in the Mons area German troops had made contact for the first time with the British Expeditionary Force. A full-scale engagement developed. It opened with a bombardment by six hundred guns, the prelude to a frontal attack by German infantry who advanced in mass formation. The British troops, all highly trained marksmen, used their rifles to such effect that their fire halted the frontal attacks. From this incident came the first great legend of the war; for it is a curious commentary on the mentality of the British people at that time that their favourite myth was the story of the Angels at Mons. It began in a commonplace manner as *The Bowmen*, a short story written by Arthur Machen which appeared in the *Evening News* of 29th September

1914. Thereafter, the myth grew in size and detail; the bowmen became angels and the clouds shone with the glory of the great host of heavenly warriors who fought on the side of the British soldiers. And with this story, which became a popular legend, half a century of imaginary wars came to an end. Never again would so many writers describe the shape of wars to come with so much eagerness and ignorance. After all the predictions the final paradox is that the last tale of imaginary warfare to be published in 1914 was Machen's account of the visionary English archers. The ultimate irony is that in their moment of greatest anxiety, and at the start of the first great technological war in history, the people of a highly industrialized world power should find comfort and hope in a legend of angels who fought upon the clouds. So, the whole sequence of these stories—from Chesney to Wells and Conan Doyle—ends with the cry of *Adsit Anglis Sanctus Georgius* and the strange appearance of the bowmen. According to the narrator in Machen's story, 'the roar of the battle died down in his ears to a gentle murmur; instead of it, he says, he heard a great voice and a shout louder than a thunder-peal crying, "Array, array, array!" His heart grew hot as a burning coal, it grew cold as ice within him, as it seemed to him that a tumult of voices answered to his summons. He heard, or seemed to hear, thousands shouting:

"St. George! St. George!"
"Ha! messire; ha! sweet Saint, grant us good deliverance!"
"St. George for merry England!"
"Harow! Harow! Monseigneur St. George succour us."
"Ha! St. George! Ha! St. George! a long bow and a strong bow."
"Heaven's Knight, aid us."

And as the soldier heard these voices he saw before him, beyond the trench, a long line of shapes, with a shining about them. They were like men who drew the bow, and with another shout, their cloud of arrows flew singing and tingling through the air towards the German hosts.'[25]

Chapter Four

Politics and the Pattern of the Next Great War, 1880–1914

MODERN readers seem to find the imaginary wars described by Wells and Robida far more interesting than the many tales of destroyers in action and the even more numerous forecasts of the invasion of Britain that appeared in the thirty years before the outbreak of the First World War. For every person who has read Arnold-Forster's best-seller, *In a Conning Tower*, there must be thousands today who have read Wells's *War of the Worlds*. There are obvious differences of quality here, since Wells was a far better writer; and there is the added fact that we are still able to feel surprised at the singularity of an accurate forecast like Conan Doyle's description of unrestricted submarine warfare in *Danger*. Even half a century after the publication of the *World Set Free* a reader is impressed by the way Wells could take abstruse scientific ideas from a paper by Frederick Soddy in 1909 and work them into a forecast about the development of atomic energy in 1933—the very year when Frédéric and Irène Joliot-Curie were concluding important investigations that showed how to achieve artificial nuclear radiation. High narrative qualities and the Leonardo-like capacity of some authors to surprise by describing what could happen are reasons that explain the continued popularity of a few stories like the *War of the Worlds* and the *Riddle of the Sands*, whereas the mass of these imaginary war tales leave the reader with strong feelings of the quaint, the almost archaic, and the often unreadable. But when these books were appearing for the first time, the interests of the reading public were very different. To judge by the number of editions and the large sales made by some of them it is clear that, although readers were then interested enough in the Wellsian type of future war story, the themes capable of arousing the greatest excitement were matters affecting the military or naval security of a nation and the dangers to be anticipated from a foreign power or a combination of foreign powers. In the major European countries the golden tribute of the large editions came from stories like Capitaine Danrit's *La Guerre fatale*, August Niemann's *Der Weltkrieg*, and Le Queux's *Invasion of 1910*. All of these dealt in a very factual way with the conduct of a war in the immediate future between France and Britain, or between Germany and Britain.

It is remarkable how much these rival tales had in common. Behind the various slogans of the competing nations it is difficult to find any great difference in the anxiety or the arrogance that had provoked so many visions of British, French, or German victories. From 1880 to 1914 the progress of the tale of future warfare presents a perfect mirror image of the international situation at the time of writing. The changes that take place in the pattern of European power relationships are indicated by sudden outpourings of these stories. Each moment of international crisis—the French alliance with Russia in 1894, the Fashoda incident in 1898, the Tangier landing in 1905—at once sets off an outburst of propaganda stories and warning visions of the future. These continued for a year or two and then they died down until the next crisis began the process once again. What all this meant in the shape of national attitudes and in the scale of book production can be seen from a comparison of publications for the years from 1882 to 1888 and for the closing years of the period in 1913 and 1914.

The initial phase coincided with a time of increasing tension between Britain and France which began when Wolseley secured Egypt after the battle of Tel-el-Kebir in 1882. From that date the Anglo-French understanding started to deteriorate, especially after 1887, when the French opposed the British efforts to reach a settlement with the Turks over Egypt; and in 1888 opinion in the United Kingdom was further excited by a naval panic touched off by rumours of the mobilization of the French fleet. The temperature was ideal for a spontaneous patriotic explosion. On both sides of the Channel the propagandists began to open fire in the first great imaginary war to be fought between France and Britain since the fantasies of a French invasion that were turned out during the period of the Great Terror when Napoleon was planning to invade Britain. The first shot in the new war was fired in France, a ranging round from Camille Debans, who wrote in 1884 a violently chauvinistic tale of the total destruction of British power, *Les Malheurs de John Bull*. The appearance of Debans' story marks the beginning in France of a new development in the literature of imaginary warfare. The language and the sentiments of Camille Debans reflect the mob oratory of men like Paul Déroulède, who founded the Ligue des Patriotes in 1882, one of the many movements that led to the great outburst of patriotism and the nationalistic ideas of Boulangism in the 'eighties. The same chauvinism and the same violent language appear in the anonymous *Plus d'Angleterre*. The author opens his story with an incident that must have seemed quite likely to Frenchmen in 1887, for the trouble between Britain and France begins in Egypt when British soldiers attack the French consulate in Cairo. As the narrative unrolls with victory after victory for the French and humiliation upon humiliation for the British, it is evident that the style of *Plus d'Angleterre*, like that of *Les Malheurs de John Bull*, is far more popular and nationalistic than anything that had appeared since the *Battle of Dorking*. These stories, like the fiction of Le Queux in the 'nineties, appealed directly to chauvinistic prejudice by presenting an idealized picture of a dedicated nation triumphing at last over the despicable enemy of the moment. Already present in *Plus d'Angleterre* are those elements of violence, hatred of the enemy, and the desire for absolute victory that distinguish so many of these stories right up to the outbreak of the First World War. In general the authors are so angry and so nationalistic that they lack the humour to see how foolish they are at times. The anonymous author of *Plus d'Angleterre*, like later German and British writers, can only see the wickedness of the enemy; and he writes a book full of French nationalism to attack the evils of British nationalism.

On the British side feelings had not yet reached this degree of animosity. That was to come after the Franco-Russian agreement of 1894, when the British imaginary wars came to rival the invective of the French ten years earlier. Only after 1894 did stories begin to appear like the *Sack of London in the Great French War of 1901*, which replied in kind by explaining French ill will as a matter of pure envy—'envy of England's great Empire, envy at her freedom, envy of the stability of her Government, of her settled monarchy, and of her beloved Queen'. Before this, however, most of the imaginary wars published in the United Kingdom were concerned with the performance of ships and armaments in a future war, or with political demonstrations in favour of measures to improve the safety of the nation in time of war. Certainly these were the usual types of war fiction that appeared between 1882 and 1894.

The first political differences with France in 1882 coincided with a national debate on the scheme for a Channel Tunnel, which Sir Edward Watkin had put before Parliament in the form of a Private Member's Bill. The uproar that followed provides an interesting lesson on differences in national attitudes. On the part of the French there were no tales of imaginary invasions by British troops who came suddenly and treacherously into France by way of the Channel Tunnel. The French Press looked on the extraordinary commotion then taking place in the United Kingdom as one more example of the eccentric goings-on of a very odd neighbour. One observer, Georges Valbert, remarked with great shrewdness that the panics and protests were not military but psychological in origin. On the day the Channel Tunnel was completed, he wrote, Britain would be no longer an island: 'It will be a prodigious event in the life of an insular people, when they find that they are islanders no more. Nothing is more likely to excite and alarm them, or to affect and upset their preconceived ideas.'[1] How right he was can be seen in the alarm about French intentions shown in the debate on the Channel Tunnel and in the sudden crop of invasion stories during 1882 and 1883.

The typical British reaction to the proposals of the Channel Tunnel Company and the Submarine Continental Railway Company was like that of Palmerston twenty-five years earlier. The Prince Consort had spoken to him with all his usual enthusiasm for great technological enterprises in an attempt to gain his support for Thomé de Gamond's scheme to construct a tunnel. The reports of that famous interview relate that—'without losing the perfectly courteous tone which was habitual with him'—the Prime Minister told the Prince Consort: 'You would think very differently if you had been born in this island.' These sturdy British sentiments explain the reaction against a tunnel, from the thundering of *The Times* and the spate of imaginary invasions by way of the Channel Tunnel to the action of the angry Londoners who smashed the windows in the Westminster offices of the Channel Tunnel Company. The substance of the argument for the opposition was that to build a tunnel would be an act of folly, since it would leave the country open to sudden invasion. The case against the Channel Tunnel was put by a popular ditty sung in 1882:

> By the Great Ruler of the Earth and Heaven
> This Island from a Continent was riven;
> Where mountains could not shield from spoil and slaughter
> He—for a national Bulwark—gave THE WATER!

Opposition to the proposed Channel Tunnel was a popular and national movement that affected every level in society. One of the most striking demonstrations came from that reputable periodical the *Nineteenth Century* during the height of the upheaval in April and May 1882. The editor, James Knowles, took the unusual step of organizing a mass petition against the tunnel—a device considered to be a very great novelty in the magazines and reviews at that time. The petition was signed by many distinguished figures of the day: Browning, Tennyson, Huxley, Cardinal Newman, Spencer, the Archbishop of Canterbury, The Mackintosh of Mackintosh, the editors of the *Spectator, Morning Post, St. James's Gazette, Lloyd's Weekly News*, five dukes, ten earls, twenty-six Members of Parliament, seventeen admirals, fifty-nine generals, about two hundred clergymen, and some six hundred other eminent persons. All put their signatures to this protest: 'The undersigned, having had their attention called to certain proposals made by commercial companies for joining England to the Continent of Europe by a Railroad under the Channel, and feeling convinced that (notwithstanding any precautions against risk suggested by the projectors) such a Railroad would involve this country in military dangers and liabilities from which, as an island, it has hitherto been happily free—hereby record their emphatic protest against the sanction or execution of any such work.'[2]

It was the *Battle of Dorking* panic in another form. Tracts, pamphlets, military forecasts of the consequences of building a tunnel, and tales of imaginary invasions by the French poured off the presses during 1882 and 1883. Letters to newspapers, special articles, and editorials showed that the country was not yet mentally prepared to accept the brutal engineering that would terminate for ever the convenient isolation of 'this fortress built by Nature for herself'. The emotional inheritance, loaded with the magnificent literary tradition inaugurated by Shakespeare's well-remembered lines about 'this scepter'd isle', was far too strong for the less romantic facts of commercial and technological advantage. And yet, when one asks why so many eminent gentlemen should have subscribed to the protest against the Channel Tunnel organized by the *Nineteenth Century* the only answer can be that they feared the country would be ruined. In this they had the support and example of military and naval opinion. The considered view of the Duke of Cambridge, writing from the Horse Guards in his capacity as the Field-Marshal Commanding-in-Chief, was set down in a memorandum of 23 June 1882. He argued against a tunnel on the grounds that, since the Fenians only a few years before had attacked Chester Castle, it might be possible to take Dover Castle by surprise; that no device could be certain to prevent others using a tunnel, because during the war of 1870 the French had left the splendid Vosges tunnels intact for the Germans to use; that British military forces could not hope to oppose any great Continental power after it had seized the Channel Tunnel; and that if a tunnel were ever built, then 'we might, despite all our precautions, very possibly some day find an enemy in actual possession of both of its ends, and able at pleasure to pour an army through unopposed'.

The same suggestion of sudden menace and of strange forces moving on Dover at the dead of night came out in another memorandum of June 1882, written by Lord Wolseley in his office as Adjutant-General. One of his arguments against a tunnel gives good cause to claim him as the originator of the fifth-column story that became very popular with writers of imaginary invasion tales. He seems to have fathered the tales of French waiters with rifles packed in their baggage from which grew the stories of German waiters training secretly in London that were a stock feature of the imaginary invasion fiction published before 1914. For the Adjutant-General argued in all seriousness that 'a couple of thousand armed men might easily come through the tunnel in a train at night, avoiding all suspicion by being dressed as ordinary passengers, or passing at express speed through the tunnel with the blinds down, in their uniform and fully armed'. He warned the country that it would be possible for a force of five thousand men to attempt to seize the tunnel installations. Nay, 'half that number, ably led by a daring, dashing young commander, might, I feel, some dark night easily make themselves masters of the works at our end of the tunnel—and then England would be at the mercy of the invader'.

Whilst the chairman of the South-Eastern Railway, Sir Edward Watkin, was arguing the case for his tunnel against the doubters in the scientific committee of inquiry, the railway bookstalls were covered with stories of imaginary invasions written in the great cause of the nation versus the tunnel. The titles carried their message of warning: *The Seizure of the Channel Tunnel, The Channel Tunnel; or, England in Danger, The Story of the Channel Tunnel, Battle of the Channel Tunnel, How John Bull Lost London, Surprise of the*

Channel Tunnel, The Battle of Boulogne. None of them was able to improve in any way on the warnings given by the Duke of Cambridge and Lord Wolseley. They told a tale of sudden attack by French tourists, or by picked groups of Zouaves, or by soldiers disguised as waiters. As the author of the *Surprise of the Channel Tunnel* explained, 'the great increase in size and prosperity that the Tunnel brought to Dover caused a large number of French restauranteurs, waiters, bootmakers, milliners, pastrycooks etc. to settle in that town'. Any patriot could have guessed the results. Those seeming civilians were all trained soldiers, even the milliners; and according to plan they seized their rifles on N-night, rushed from their lodgings, occupied the tunnel installations, and sent the signal that brought the entire French Army pouring into the sleeping land of Britain. In another story, *How John Bull Lost London*, which caused a minor sensation in Britain and provided an occasion for derisive comment in France, a party of French tourists suddenly leaped from their excursion train and opened the way for the invasion forces. According to the author of *The Channel Tunnel*, the invaders would spread terror wherever they went:

> The sudden seizure of the tunnel by the French would produce such a panic in England that law and order would probably become impossible, fear and fury would be dominant, and those who had property, or the honour of wives and daughters to save from the French soldiery, would be busy taking speedy measures to escape from London with their valuables.

Propaganda of this kind was completely single-minded in its attempt to influence public opinion against the Channel Tunnel. It is clear from the popular appeal of some of these stories that the authors were in many ways anticipating the methods developed in the mass fiction of the eighteen-nineties, since several of them were clearly no longer writing for an exclusively middle-class public, as Chesney had done with the *Battle of Dorking*. These stories show that, in step with the increase in literacy and with the growing importance of the new electors following on the Education Act of 1870 and the various Reform Acts, the conduct of war was ceasing to be a private matter for the higher levels of the nation. It was rapidly becoming a matter for everyone, as the new daily newspapers would demonstrate in the last decade of the century.

An obvious relationship exists between this type of fiction and the political situation at the time of writing; for these stories occupied the attention of the public for a year or two whilst the anxiety behind them ran its course from panic to prostration, and then they disappeared for ever. This principle is evident in the burst of imaginary invasions caused by the Channel Tunnel controversy in 1882 and 1883. It can be seen at work again in 1887 and 1888, when anxiety at the state of the Royal Navy and anger at the French attitude to British attempts to solve the Egyptian problem produced another crop of imaginary wars between Britain and France: *The Great Naval War of 1887, The Battle off Worthing, An Omitted Incident in the 'Great Naval War of 1887', The Capture of London, The Taking of Dover, Plus encore d'Angleterre*; *or, the Repulse of the French.*

In their different ways these stories all reflect a general anxiety at the condition of the Royal Navy, which had begun in September 1884 when the astute and influential journalist, W. T. Stead, published a series of articles in the *Pall Mall Gazette* designed to tell 'The Truth about the Navy'. In the view of Lord Charles Beresford, Stead's articles 'did more than any other Press representations before or since to awaken public opinion to the true condition of our defences'. The articles were certainly effective, since Stead's demands for a more efficient Fleet and for more cruisers and improved coaling stations were at once repeated throughout the national Press. The First Lord of the Admiralty, Lord Northbrook, was the subject of much criticism; and in 1885 he had the misfortune to inspire a violent attack on himself from the Poet Laureate:*

> You—you—*if* you have fail'd to understand
> The Fleet of England is her all in all—
> On you will come the curse of all the land,
> If that Old England fall,
> Which Nelson left so great—
>
> You—you—who had the ordering of her Fleet,
> *If* you have only compass'd her disgrace,
> When all men starve, the wild mob's million feet
> Will kick you from your place—
> But then—too late, too late.

* The poem provided a title for the story of an imaginary war: C. Gleig, *When all Men Starve*, 1897.

The passion of Tennyson's verse was symptomatic of the public's anger and alarm on discovering that the Navy had fallen behind in the race for technological development and that its direction was often inefficient and inadequate. In 1885, when Britain and Russia were in dispute over Afghanistan, it had taken two months to complete the naval preparations. Again, it was only in 1886, on a suggestion from Lord Charles Beresford, that a Naval Intelligence Department was established to deal with the many problems of the new-style war at sea. The Royal Navy was preparing to meet the challenge of the ironclad and the torpedo. From this point in the eighteen-eighties public interest in the past and future achievements of the Navy grew rapidly; and this was matched by a rapid growth of imaginary war stories in which the ships of the Fleet sailed out to glorious triumphs or humiliating defeats according to the intention of the author. At times these were simple yarns about the way in which a future naval engagement might develop, like Arnold-Forster's *In a Conning Tower*. The first of the more purposive stories of naval warfare appeared in 1887, when William Laird Clowes and A. H. Burgoyne wrote a serial for the *St. James's Gazette*, a special piece called *The Great Naval War of 1887*, which was intended to show the consequences of an inefficient scheme of mobilization. War breaks out between Britain and France. Mobilization follows, but in the manner of Chesney the authors rub in the bitter lesson that 'the machinery of the Admiralty and War Office collapsed under the strain that was so suddenly thrown upon it, and incredible confusion resulted'. For the rest it is the Chesney formula of brave men and incompetent leadership and the brutal fact that it was all 'the natural result of years of indifference, mismanagement, and parsimony'. The answer soon became a standard item in these naval stories: more funds for the Fleet.

In the eyes of writers like William Laird Clowes the greatest of all the sins against the Royal Navy was parsimony. As the nation discovered when the Naval Defence Act of 1889 was introduced into Parliament, there had to be more funds. The proposals to build eight first-class battleships and thirty-eight cruisers were essential if the British hoped to maintain their traditional policy of isolation. Until the naval scares of the eighteen-eighties policy had depended on the supremacy of the Navy and on the fact that continental countries could be expected to be so occupied with their own quarrels that they would not think of combining against

Britain. But both these cardinal principles were in doubt after 1884. A bigger and better Fleet was the immediate answer to one of the problems; but when the French allied themselves with the Russians in 1894, and so threatened British naval supremacy in the Mediterranean, the only answer to a European combination was to look for allies abroad. In the history of imaginary warfare these political facts took the shape of future wars fought by the British against the French and their allies until in 1903 the great popularity enjoyed by the *Riddle of the Sands* signalled the beginning of a sudden shift to stories of the coming German invasion of the United Kingdom.

Before the beginning of the Anglo-French Entente in 1904 the *guerres imaginaires* had been almost as much concerned with wars against Britain as against Germany. The one difference was that before the disagreement over Egypt the French stories dealt exclusively with the future war of reconquest to be waged against the Germans: *La Guerre future* in 1875, *La France et l'Allemagne au printemps prochain* in 1876, *La Guerre franco-allemande de 1878* in 1877, *La Guerre prochaine entre la France et l'Allemagne* in 1881. Plans for the sacred task of *la revanche* continued year by year until 1914; but in parallel with this stream of anti-German tales a series of triumphant imaginary wars against the British began to appear after the publication of *Les Malheurs de John Bull* in 1884, and these continued down to 1904. They were generally less methodical in their plans of campaign, less concerned with military detail and much more impassioned in their language than the anti-German stories of this period. The difference between these two forms of imaginary warfare in France turned on a matter of attitudes. Whenever French writers set about describing the next great war against Britain or Germany, they apparently acted on the principle that, even if the Germans were enemies, the British were undoubtedly their most hated enemies. Anger, resentment, and the desire to destroy utterly were the dominant emotions in most of the tales about the humiliation of proud Albion. This condition was a natural product of the Napoleonic tradition which seems to have infected most of these writers whenever they turned their attention to a war against the British; and in the political climate of the time it reflected the steady deterioration in the relations between the two countries which reached their lowest level at the time of the Fashoda incident in 1898. To understand the difference between the two styles of imaginary warfare, contrast the plain and matter-of-fact titles given to the anti-German stories with the inflammatory and vindictive style of *Plus d'Angleterre* in 1887, *La Prise de Londres au XXe siècle* in 1891, *Mort aux Anglais* in 1892, and *L'Agonie d'Albion* in 1901. In the last analysis, however, the differences in the two kinds of story reflect a division of interest between the civilians and writers in the armed forces. Most of the narratives about a future war against Germany were produced by army officers. They wrote matter-of-fact accounts in the manner of *La Bataille de Damvillers; récit anticipé de la prochaine campagne*. They repeated the ideas and plans talked over in the mess and the military academy. The description of the war against Britain was usually left to the civilian writers, no doubt because only those ignorant of naval matters would be rash enough to attempt an account of a successful invasion of the British Isles. There can be no better illustration of this dual attitude than in the numerous publications of Capitaine Émile Danrit, or as he really was—Capitaine Driant:

DRIANT, Émile Auguste Cyprien. Son of Joseph Driant and Adélaide-Virginie de Fäy. Born 11 September, 1855. Educated at the Lycée de Reims; entered St. Cyr in 1875; and in 1877 commissioned as second-lieutenant in the 54th Infantry Regiment. Promoted lieutenant in 1882; in 1886 transferred to the 4th Regiment of Zouaves. In 1888 appointed adjutant to General Boulanger at the Ministry of War. On 29 October, 1888, married Marcelle, younger daughter of General Boulanger. From 1892 to 1896 served as instructor at St. Cyr. Recalled to regimental service and in 1898 appointed to command the 1st Battalion Chasseurs à Pied. In 1906 resigned his commission and took part in the elections of that year but without success. In 1910 was elected a deputy for Nancy. In 1914 recalled to command a battalion. Protested against failure to make adequate preparations for the defence of Verdun. Killed in action at the Bois des Caures whilst directing heroic defence against mass of the German XVIII Corps.

As might be expected from a man who was adjutant to General Boulanger at the time of his greatest triumphs and had married the general's daughter, everything Driant wrote was filled with the glories of military service and with a spirit of intense nationalism. His many stories about future wars against the Germans or the British belong to the great body of *revanchiste* literature that sprang up rapidly in the eighteen-eighties. What he wrote was only a demonstration of the ideals and intentions to be found in such popular songs of the day as *Réveil de la France, La Marseillaise de la*

Revanche, À la frontière, Notre Général bien-aimé, as well as in the poetry of Paul Déroulède. One of the closing stanzas of Déroulède's poem, 'Vive la France', reveals the spirit of reconquest that shaped the French literature of imaginary warfare:

> Et la revanche doit venir, lente peut-être,
> Mais en tout cas fatale, et terrible à coup sûr;
> La haine est déja née, et la force va naître:
> C'est au faucheur à voir si le champ n'est pas mûr.

An English variant of these sentiments can be found in the aggressive imperialism of W. E. Henley, who wrote frequently of the 'iron beneficence' of war. In 1892, for instance, he published in the *National Observer* a poem by one of his young writers. It began:

> Give us, O Lord,
> For England's sake,
> War righteous and true,
> Our hearts to shake.

'On every side', Capitaine Danrit wrote in the preface to *La Guerre de demain*, 'the nations are arming and preparing for war.' Danrit was at once the William Le Queux and the Admiral Colomb of France. His books are filled with the arrogant nationalism of stories like *England's Peril* and they make the same use of expert military knowledge that can be seen in the *Great War of 1892*. Running through his stories and through many similar stories by other writers there is a sense of anger at past defeat, of military honour cast down in 1870. To compensate for past humiliation the army had to be the symbol of the nation's pride and the guarantee of future revenge. At a time when respect for the military uniform, for the officer, and for the tricolour was greater than in any previous period, it was to be expected that Danrit's stories should turn out to be one sustained glorification of France, the Army, and the great business of *la revanche*. This, no doubt, was the reason why the French Academy crowned *La Guerre de demain* and gave Danrit the Prix Montyon.

The political background of Danrit's three stories of the campaign against Germany was the international situation of the period about 1890. Like Admiral Colomb in the *Great War of 1892*, he thought in terms of a war between France and Germany in which the Russians would come in on the side of the French. The style of the writing recalls the demonstrations before the

An illustration from *La Guerre en rase campagne* by Captain Émile Danrit (pseudonym of Émile Driant). German troops shoot an aged French civilian.

veiled statue of Strasburg in the Place de la Concorde which in those days was still covered up with the prophetic slogan, *Qui vive? La France. 1870–18—*, and with the initials of the Ligue des Patriotes. For a soldier and a patriot the picture of the future was a vision of French troops driving the enemy out of occupied France. With this in mind Danrit dedicated *La Guerre en rase campagne* to the men of his own 4e Régiment de Zouaves: 'It has been my hope to have gone off with you to the Great War which we are all expecting and which is still delayed. But, if there is a god of battles and if he hears me, I still hope to take part in the war under your banner. To pass the time whilst waiting, I have dreamed of this Holy War in which we will conquer, and this book is my dream.' The same sentiments, enlarged to national proportions, inspire the proclamation of war and the appeal to the French as Danrit describes the moment when the Germans make their sudden and undeclared onslaught on France:

Francais!

In violation of the law of nations our country has been invaded without a declaration of war. German troops are advancing towards the Meuse. The hour of our revenge has struck. The holy war has begun. Frenchmen, young and old, conscripts, soldiers, territorials—to arms!

To arms in the supreme struggle that will restore to us our lost provinces and our place in Europe! To arms for the defence of our homes! Let all the powers of France rise up to punish the barbarians who want to remove our name from contemporary history and our country from the map of the world. The French Army will not be surprised. Every day it has been expecting to do battle, ready to defend or to attack. Our troops will march against the enemy as their fore-fathers did in the heroic past. They will carry on their banners the old words—Victory or Death!

Behind them and by their side stand all those of you who love your country but for reasons of age have not been called to the colours—children, old men, even the infirm. Start now on this war to the death! Answer this treacherous invasion by a war of extermination. Burn your villages before the Germans enter them. With your own hands destroy anything that could help the enemy. Let the East of France become the tomb of our ancient enemy.

Be of good heart! This German empire, a thing of bits and pieces, will collapse at the first reverse! Be of good heart! A powerful ally is about to join forces with us! Frenchmen, have confidence! From today all quarrels among ourselves have disappeared—buried beneath an ardent love for France![3]

The actions Danrit relates have for their tonic and dominant the ideal of national supremacy and the desire for total victory over the ancient enemy. A certain utopian element appears in the selection and projection of all that he considers is best and most admirable in French life. Indeed, his stories, like so many of the contemporary imaginary wars in English and later in German, are perfect para-utopias for an epoch of exaggerated nationalism. Politics and self-persuasion work together to create a vision of the nation imposing its will upon the enemy of the moment. Any comparison of these stories in English, French, or German will show how the nationalistic emotions of the period found their natural outlet in a new mythology of imaginary wars which were no more than a picture of the world rearranged to suit a nation's desires. So, Danrit concludes *La Guerre de demain* on the comforting thought that 'France united with Russia is today the arbiter of Europe and the world'. The same demand that the world should be a reification of national ambitions can be seen in *The Final War* by Louis Tracy. His theme is a variant on the French nationalism of Danrit: 'The Saxon race will absorb all and embrace all, reanimating old civilizations and giving new vigour to exhausted nations.'

On the surface Danrit's stories, like the stories of George Griffith, Louis Tracy, and August Niemann, were all concerned with a likely political situation in the near future; but in reality Danrit and his contemporaries were creating wish-fulfilment fantasies of a noble people, united in true brotherhood, engaged on the great task of winning for the nation its rightful place in the world. In Danrit's dream—and he called it a dream—all sections of society are joined in the work of *la revanche*. Simple peasants fight as partisans, officers die with conspicuous heroism at the head of their troops, and even the village curé (*le vieux bon homme*) is ready to leave his flock and take up a rifle against the enemies of the sacred soil of France. It is no different in Tracy's account of the Franco-German attack on Britain in *The Final War*. Everything is quite perfect: 'The splendid calm of the House of Commons, amid all the varying fortunes of the war, and its phlegmatic pride, its stern attitude of quiet resolution, formed a striking example of the indomitable character of the English people.' Overnight all political quarrels are forgotten, as in Danrit's stories, and the rich help the poor with the result that within a few weeks from the outbreak of war 'there was more practical Socialism to be seen in the internal economy of London and other important centres of population than had been dreamed of or spoken of by philosophical reformers in as many centuries'.

At this stage the narratives begin to move away from the realities of the contemporary political situation. The element of fantasy increases and the stories turn into a species of nationalistic utopia in which the superior virtues, intelligence, and vigour of the fatherland defeat an enemy without honour, without honesty, and without intelligence. The central principle in all of them is that the whole world conspires against the enemy. In Tracy's tale of *The Final War* the American Navy intervenes on the British side, Russian revolutionaries capture the Tsar, the Indian Army storms across Persia to attack Russia, and the new Thomson Electric Rifle gives the British troops a devastating secret weapon. Similarly, in Danrit's account of the Franco-German war, the threat of an Italian invasion from the south is conveniently removed by the action of the Pope, who puts the Italian Government under an interdict and then leaves for Spain. A two-day revolution follows in Rome; the Italian Government falls, and the war with France ends almost before it had really begun. It is an understatement to call such extravagance a wish-fulfilment fantasy. Danrit and his contemporaries were projecting an idealized image of the nation in arms. Their stories have all the force and the directness of popular and purposive fiction. The events and the characters are seen in black and white; everything is presented in the form of the polar opposites of the unspeakable enemy and the glorious nation. Since the nation is an object of worship in these stories, the enemy must equally be an object of detestation. This is the other side to the utopian tale of national triumph: complete virtue faces total wickedness. In fact, it would seem that war guilt had been apportioned long before 1914, since some of the British reactions to the Germans in the First World War appear to be stereotyped behaviour patterns carried over from the literature of the imaginary wars. This is especially true of the enemy agent. In all these tales the spy is the supreme symbol of enemy evil, the antithesis of the nationalist thesis of unity, courage, and victory.

One of the major ironies in the literature of future wars is that all European countries expect the worst of the enemy. Espionage represents the depths of villainy on the other side, for the spy always appears where he can do a country the greatest harm. In the *Great Naval War of 1887* the authors relate that 'it was well known that the whole south of England was full of French spies'. The enemy could always be expected to take the meanest advantage of a hospitable nation, even to the point of employing renegades and traitors against their own country. The plot in Max Pemberton's very popular *Pro Patria* of 1901 turns on the treachery of Robert Jeffery, a one-time candidate for entry to Woolwich, who directs the French plan to invade Britain by a tunnel secretly constructed under the Channel. What happened and how it all ended can be seen in the last paragraphs, which show how these stories flourished on the ill-feeling between countries:

That France attempted to build a tunnel under the Channel to England is no longer denied. That her engineers had been engaged upon the

'All that I could see . . . betrayed a vast activity': illustration in Max Pemberton's *Pro Patria*, 1901, concerning the French military operation of secretly constructing a Channel Tunnel.

work for many years is equally well known. Her prospects of success, should such an attempt be repeated, are variously esteemed. We have seen that the more daring capitalists and fanatics of Paris, having compelled the French government to thrust out a tunnel from Calais, sought to open that tunnel here by taking a farmhouse in an Englishman's name. . . . The vigilance of one man defeated this great scheme; he shut the gate, as he says, in the face of France. But the tube of steel still lies below the sea. No living man, outside the purlieus of the secret, can say how far that tunnel is carried, or where the last tube of it is riveted. It may come even to Dover's cliffs; it may lie many miles from them.

During this period it was a convention with writers of imaginary wars to describe in detail the despicable behaviour of enemy spies. Even the Italians, whose tales of future wars were the rarest and mildest of them all, did not fail to dwell on the ill doings of the enemy. In a tale of 1899, *La Guerra del 190–*, the narrative describes how a patrol of Alpini arrested two French officers 'who were caught red-handed in the act of spying, complete with plans and sketches in their baggage'. This attitude to espionage is one of the bigger hypocrisies of the literature before 1914. Civilization, truth, and justice are for the purpose of the story identified with Britain, France, Germany, or Italy; and in this situation the spy has a special role to play, since he can be used to point a moral and reinforce the sense of national virtuousness in the reader. In support of this attitude there was the unquestioned fact that espionage had been increasing since the war of 1870, and could be expected to go on increasing as long as new weapons were devised, fortifications built, and strategic plans prepared for the defence of frontiers. If espionage was a condition of the new epoch of industrialized warfare, it was also a fact in the new popular mythology of the imaginary wars. Most of Danrit's stories, for example, make great play with the activities of the spy who, unlike the dignified and humane French officers, is decidedly unchivalrous. He is even devious and conveniently stupid into the bargain. The first rule for the use of enemy agents is that they are always found out in time. The second is that our own agents are always successful. Both rules can be seen in operation in William Le Queux's notorious tale of 1899, *England's Peril*. The French Embassy in London is a nest of spies: 'Attached to the Embassy were many spies, for of recent years the French Secret Service had grown almost as formidable in its proportions as that of Russia, and their constant reports from political and official centres in London would have surprised the Admiralty and War Office. Officially they were unrecognized, being controlled by one man, a renegade Englishman.' There is, however, no real cause for alarm, since our own agents know what is going on: 'The British Secret Service, although never so prominently before the public as those unscrupulous *agents provocateurs* of France and Russia, is nevertheless equally active. It works in silence and secrecy, yet many are its successful counterplots against the machinations of England's enemies.'

Change the names and Danrit could have written those lines, for he was as certain as Le Queux that enemy agents were at work in many places. And he was right in so far as, unknown to him, Colonel Schwartzkoppen had started to operate from the German Embassy in 1891 and was beginning to collect French military documents, the famous *bordereau* that led to the Dreyfus Affair in 1894. In his *Guerre de forteresse* Danrit maintained that 'out of the 25,000 officers who appear in the German Army List 15,000 volunteered of their own free will for espionage duties. They honour that sort of work with the name of secret mission.' And as the *Guerre de demain* unrolls, the spies and *saboteurs* appear in a variety of cunning disguises. Two Alsatian refugees turn out to be enemy agents and are caught only minutes before they would have passed on vital information to the enemy. An amiable young priest, who claims to be the curé of Bazoilles, is proved to be no priest at all but a member of the German intelligence network. And there is the ridiculous Englishman, Sir John Byde, a pantomime spy with long teeth, side-whiskers, an impossible French accent and immense arrogance, who operates in the German interest with a comical lack of success.

This black-and-white characterization is part of the implicit contract between the writer and his readers that they will be able to join in the greatest actions of which a nation is capable—war and the reconstruction of the world. The subject-matter of these stories is not the behaviour of recognizable individuals, as it is in the novel; it is the nation, the enemies of the nation, the new instruments of war, and the future greatness of the fatherland. What characters exist in the narrative are there to play chorus and interlude to epic dramas in which the principals are some or all of the great powers. The process of idealization begins with the way writers describe their wars in the language of gallantry and glory, and not in terms of the courage and endurance needed in real warfare. They are, of course, describing war as they would like it to be right down to the last victorious battle and the future that will be for ever British, or French, or German. This can be seen in the many stories turned out by journalists like George Griffith, Robert Cromie, and Louis Tracy. In 1899 Griffith produced the *Great Pirate Syndicate*, a prodigious tale of imperialistic politics and of secret weapons that give instant victory to the Anglo-Saxon powers. By the end of the story the whole world has been subdued and the happy victors find that 'foreign sea-borne trade had practically disappeared, for no competition with the enormously wealthy firms of Anglo-Saxondom was possible'. An Anglo-Saxon peace in our time completes the happiness of all: '. . . as no other nation could hope to cope with the colossal forces at the disposal of the Anglo-Saxon Federation, there was every reason to believe that the world was entering upon an era of profound peace as well as unexampled prosperity.' The French version of this optimistic nationalism can be seen in Danrit's account of the invasion and conquest of the British Isles, *La Guerre fatale: France-Angleterre*, which was first published in 1901. Like so many of these stories written at the beginning of the twentieth century, Danrit's fantasy goes to the limit in describing the swift and merciless destruction of the enemy. The Russians sweep through Afghanistan and conquer India. The new submarines of the French Fleet convoy an invasion force across the Channel in full view of an impotent Royal Navy. And the British troops prove to be as second-rate and incompetent as any enemy general could hope. The French storm up the beaches to pealing trumpets and shouts of victory, for 'the British Army had little importance in the eyes of our soldiers since it had been shown to be so weak in South Africa'. The fortunate invaders find that 'the worst faults of Lord Methuen and Sir Redwers Bulwer [*sic*] in the Transvaal' have been repeated on their home ground.

In this way the story of the nation's next great war changes into a vulgar utopian vision of total triumph written according to the political specifications of the international situation. For the first time in the course of history the epic tale of great national achievements had ceased to be told only in retrospect. During the last two decades of the nineteenth century the epic had moved out of the legendary past; it became a popular and prospective myth projected into the near and seemingly realizable future. In the hands of writers like Louis Tracy, Capitaine Danrit, and August Niemann the tale of future warfare developed into an attractive and spectacular demonstration of how a nation could satisfy its every desire. Victory is, therefore, always absolute, even to the detailed and exultant description of the entry into the enemy capital and the final symbolic act of surrender before the massed battalions of the invader. Danrit closes *La Guerre fatale* with the reading of the peace terms in the shattered ruins of the House of Commons. Similarly, in Niemann's story published in 1904, *Der Weltkrieg*, the Germans land at Leith and rapidly overrun the United Kingdom. The German author ends on the happy thought that 'His Majesty the Emperor will enter London at the head of the allied armies. Peace is assured. God grant that it may be the last war which we shall have to wage for the future happiness of the German nation.'

In their own strange way these writers were trying to create a Beowulf myth for an industrial civilization of ironclads and high-speed turbines, a new and violent *chanson de geste* for an age of imperialism, told in the inflammatory language of the mass Press. They were popular epics for a period of universal literacy, the counterpart of the many tales about the deeds that won the Empire, all written to the glory of the nation-state; for in the closing years of the nineteenth century the aggressive nation-states of Europe had everything on their side except common sense. They were supported by a steady growth in the power of central governments, and especially by the immensely powerful associations of the national flag, anthems, magnificent uniforms, and traditional ceremonies. Most of all in the nineteenth century the nation-state meant the glories of war. From the moment when Kellermann called for cheers for the nation as he rode along the line of raw recruits at the Battle of Valmy, war had become the maker of nations. That was the moment when, in the words of Foch, 'a new era had begun, the era of national wars that are fought under no restraint whatever.' And since the cardinal virtues of the nation-state were love and hate—ourselves against the rest—it followed that any prospective vision of the nation triumphing in war would be set in terms of life and death, of total victory and total defeat. So, the tale of imaginary warfare could start from some incident or possibility in international politics; it could then grow into a species of nationalistic rhetoric by means of which a writer was able to demonstrate national values and objectives at one and the same time. This is one reason why in so many of these stories, although the weapons were the very latest instruments of destruction, the language and the attitudes recall the epic moments of Austerlitz and Waterloo.

And here it is necessary to point out that a difference runs through this literature. Although writers may all be agreed on the immediate end, the defeat of the enemy, it must be emphasized that their motives and purposes vary considerably. Guy du Maurier's play, *An Englishman's Home*, displays an effulgent patriotism. Very different is the unquestioned opportunism shown by Harmsworth when he commissioned an invasion story as part of his scheme for the general election of 1895. In that year Harmsworth stood as one of the two Conservative candidates for Portsmouth. To further his campaign he bought the *Portsmouth Mail* and obtained the services of William Laird Clowes, who collaborated with one of Harmsworth's young men, Beccles Wilson, in concocting a shocking tale of what might happen if the Navy could not prevent an enemy fleet from approaching the coast. The story, *The Siege of Portsmouth*, began on 17th June and continued every day for three weeks. The nasty compound of commercialism and electioneering that caused the story to be written is admirably illustrated from the announcement advertising the first issue. The following text appeared under a drawing of the tower of Portsmouth Town Hall collapsing beneath a rain of shells:

On Monday next the 'Mail' will commence a startling new 'forecast' of the Great War of 189–. Day by day we shall print a stirring narrative, written by distinguished naval and military authorities, dealing with the story of the Siege of Portsmouth, and how our country was invaded by the French and Russians. The names of prominent townsmen will be introduced in this remarkable work, and all those who do not wish to be left behind in the rush for the 'Mail' should go to their newsagents today and give an order for the paper to be delivered at their house regularly.

On Monday next the guaranteed issue of the 'Mail' will exceed 40,000 copies, and advertisers who wish for publicity in the paper should bring their advertisements to the office at once.

One of the incidents of the Siege, the blowing up of the Town Hall, is depicted in the above illustration, which will also be found on a larger scale on most of the hoardings in the neighbourhood.

The story was well calculated to play upon current anxieties in the Conservative interest. It started from the then obvious fact of

British isolation in 1895, when 'the enhanced hereditary hatred between France and ourselves was unfortunately coincident with a growing coolness between ourselves and Germany'. Here it is possible to detect the hand of William Laird Clowes himself in the account of the war that follows on the visit to Brest by the Russian Baltic Fleet. The episode was a clear reference to the naval scare that blew up over the visit of a Russian squadron to Toulon in 1893. Clowes was largely responsible for the scare, since he went to Toulon as *The Times* special correspondent and sent back a highly alarming report in which he declared that the days of British naval supremacy in the Mediterranean were ended. In his *Siege of Portsmouth* he repeats this technique of exaggerated and alarmist prophecy; he adds fact to fantasy in a deliberate attempt to excite and startle the reader. The story is presented in the usual contrasting terms of the noble and unsuspecting nation surprised by brutal and treacherous enemies. On the British side there is Rudyard Kipling, Poet Laureate by this time, who composes a song to Old England's glory which was sung by seventy thousand men on Hampstead Heath. On the enemy side the French display all the meanness and treachery that Capitaine Danrit attributed to the British. Our ambassador leaves Paris and then the mob do their worst:

> The mob which remained behind at the Embassy were not slow to take advantage of the opportunity, and before nightfall a blackened heap of ruins represented what had been for many decades the proud official residence of Her Majesty's Plenipotentiary at the French capital.
>
> The Embassy had been stormed at and execrated during many crucial epochs; but the French government had always afforded it protection until then . . . Anglophobia was at its height. The journalists of the Boulevards heaped scorn and contumely upon the English. The French spat upon our countrymen in the streets. The gallant defence made by a party of belated tourists at Rouen gave the signal for a cowardly massacre, the details of which caused a thrill of horror throughout England when it became known.

The enemy employ the meanest and most despicable ruses, because they have to be as vile as election propaganda would have them. The French land at Eastbourne—'whose streets ran blood and whose walls echoed the shrieks of the dying and defenceless'. The miserable citizens endure the agony of seeing 'their sons, their wives, and their daughters at the mercy of a foe who, reared on carnage, hate, and oppression, knew no mercy'.

Portsmouth, however, manages to hold out against incessant attacks; the Channel Fleet steams back from the Azores, and the Franco-Russian squadrons are decisively defeated in a tremendous naval engagement off Spithead. But why had it happened? The reason was to be found in the Conservative case against the Liberals in the election of 1895: not enough money had been spent on the Royal Navy and no one had learnt the lesson of the 1894 naval manœuvres which revealed that the Fleet was seriously undermanned.[4] As Clowes asked:

> And why had Portsmouth been thus pressed, and England thus imperilled? Because men had not sufficiently remembered that 'England's Navy is her All in All'. Because, while creating a big fleet, they had been remiss in the equally important matters of manning and organisation. Because they had allowed the Fleet Reserve to be nominal rather than real. Because they had been so blind as to accept the annual partial mobilisations, at dates known long beforehand, as evidence that the Navy was fit at any and every moment to do all that might be required of it. Because, in one word, they were NOT READY.

The events in the *Siege of Portsmouth* provide a most instructive case-study of the tale of imaginary warfare in all its varieties and applications. It illustrates every device and attitude to be found in this form of fiction: the projection of contemporary anxieties into a specially contrived future, hatred of the enemy, the horror figure of the spy, brutal and violent incidents, fierce nationalistic sentiments, appeals to tradition and to prejudice, the dread picture of the nation alone in adversity and on the edge of defeat, the final swift and facile destruction of the enemy fleet. But more important than these was the attitude of mind to be seen in the unquestioning acceptance of war as a customary exercise between nations, and in the applied art of a story that had been designed to play on mood and sentiment for political and commercial ends. War, as Harmsworth knew, was good for business; but the war described by Clowes and so many others, in spite of the apparent modernity of fleet actions, was still presented in terms of the old-world pattern of Trafalgar and the Crimea. The Western attitude to war was still determined by what might be called the Othello Syndrome:

> . . . the neighing steed and the shrill trump,
> The spirit-stirring drum, the ear-piercing fife,
> The royal banner, and all quality,
> Pride, pomp, and circumstance of glorious war!

The constant and permissive fact behind the development of these imaginary wars from 1871 to 1914 was the customary consideration of war as normal and romantic. The few Europeans who campaigned in the cause of world peace, like Bertha von Suttner and Norman Angell, knew very well that the great arguments in favour of war were the traditional heroics of literature—'the heroic poems and heroic histories by means of which our schools bring us up to be warriors'—and the worship of success that turns war-leaders into national heroes, so that 'when any one comes out of a war as conqueror the guild of historical scribblers fall in the dust before him, and praise him as the fulfiller of his mission of educative culture'.[5] With these ideas in mind Bertha von Suttner published *Die Waffen Nieder!* in 1889 with the intention of bringing war down from the level of epic history and romantic literature to the real world of human suffering and misery. She knew that in the usual literary treatment of war the deed of courage was always the main act in the great drama of the nation in arms; but it was generally presented in isolation, separated by its own grandeur and dedication from the real boredom and terror of war. In describing the experiences of her characters in the wars from 1859 to 1870 Bertha von Suttner concentrated on what the historians and the novelists so often omitted: the fact of death and disease, the sorrow of wives and parents, the blood and vomit of the casualty clearing station. It was shock treatment for a society that could accept Prince Kraft zu Hohenlohe's idealization of the officer as a man 'influenced only by his desire for fame and glory, and by the high position which the spotlessness of his true honour wins for him in the society of all men'.[6]

The many tales of future warfare and the occasional anti-war story show that until 1914 most Europeans believed that they could have their wars and enjoy them. The error lay both in fact and in fiction. The first mistake was the widespread failure to anticipate the scale and duration of the next great war.* It was generally expected that it would be a swift affair, over by Christmas as the Press announced in 1914. The second mistake was in the

* In 1906 General Bonnal stated in *La Prochaine Guerre:* 'The outcome of the next war will be decided in less than a month after the opening of hostilities.' In 1912 Commandant Mordacq thought that another war might last 'about one year'. He told the politicians that it was their duty—for reasons of national morale—'to prevent the idea spreading that the next war will certainly end after the first great battle' (*La Durée de la prochaine guerre*, p. 32).

continuation of a romantic attitude to war beyond the point when it had ceased to be an affair of the thin red line, of cavalry charges, and hand-to-hand encounters. This was the target-area for Shaw's anti-romantic comedy of 1894, *Arms and the Man*. Shaw turned glory upside down and made very effective fun of the stage soldier with the matter-of-fact behaviour of Bluntschli, the professional, and the high comedy of Sergius, who saved the day by winning the battle the wrong way after two Cossack colonels had lost their regiments according to the best tactical principles. But Shaw's attack was a forlorn hope at that time and in that climate of opinion. In face of the combined forces of tradition, Jingoism, and the nationalistic Press, the advocates of peace had little hope of success. It is evident from a reading of the few anti-war stories of this period, like *Das Menschenschlachthaus* by Wilhelm Lamszus and *War* by Douglas Newton, that the authors knew their most difficult task was to demonstrate the gap between the imagined glories and the bitter realities of war. As Norman Angell put the matter in the *Great Illusion*, the idea of war had everything in its favour except death and destruction. Angell was clear-sighted enough to accept the fact that 'a sedentary, urbanized people find the spectacle of war even more attractive than the spectacle of football. Indeed, our Press treats it as a sort of glorified football match.' The language of sport was often the language of war. Captain Guggisberg, for instance, in his *Modern Warfare, or How our Soldiers Fight* found the perfect analogy in the game of football. He saw nothing incongruous in stressing what for him were the obvious similarities between the great games of peace and war:

An army, in fact, tries to *work together* in a battle or a large manoeuvre in much the same way as a football team *plays together* in a match; and you need scarcely be told what an important thing that is if you want to win. The army *fights* for the good of its country as the team *plays* for the honour of its school. Regiments *assist* each other as players do when they *shove together* or *pass the ball* from one to another; exceptionally gallant *charges* and heroic *defences* correspond to brilliant *runs* and *fine* tackling. All work with one common impulse, given to the army by its general, to the team by its captain.[7]

The subject-matter of the imaginary wars supports Angell in his claim that before 1914 war seemed to be regarded as a natural activity of nations. So many forces and ideas worked in its favour. The economic advantage of new markets and the success-story of Great Power status, the Darwinian doctrine of the struggle for existence and the political fact of imperialist expansion, the immensely powerful influences of tradition, the new Press and the Jingoistic sentiments it inspired—these were some of the factors working to demonstrate Karl Pearson's contention that 'the path of progress is strewn with the wreck of nations'.[8] Nature's first law seemed to corroborate the facts of international politics—kill or be killed. Translated into military language, and put in the words of Kaiser Wilhelm II to the German troops embarking for action against the Boxers in China, the idea became the simple command—'No quarter will be granted, no prisoners taken.'

And yet, after everything has been said about the forces of Darwinism, tradition, and imperialistic ambition that played upon the mind in those days, there still remained the hard facts of real antagonism between European countries. They are to be found in any history of the period from the start of the great change in the European power system after the German victory of 1870 to the Franco-Russian Alliance of 1894. The chapter headings give the sequence of events that led to the great world war so long foretold in fiction: the German Navy Bill of 1900; the entry of the United Kingdom into an alliance with Japan in 1902; French reconciliation with Britain and the beginning of the *Entente* in 1904; the Moroccan crisis of 1905; then the arrival of the *Panther* at Agadir on 1st July 1911; and so it runs from alarm to alarm until the record begins to reach its end with the assassination of Francis Ferdinand on 28th June 1914, which was followed by the ultimatums and finally by the proclamations of war to cheering crowds in the capital cities of Europe.

Nowadays it is a commonplace remark in the history books that the crowds were cheering for a war that never came. All but a very few expected a swift campaign on land and the destruction of the German Fleet in a North Sea engagement. No one could have foreseen that there would be four years of killing and the end of the European domination of the world. The ease and celerity with which most authors of imaginary wars had conducted their fictitious operations reflected the general view, based on the experiences of 1870 and the Balkan wars, that a decisive battle or two would quickly end hostilities. This attitude of mind had much to do with the many social and traditional factors examined earlier in this chapter. And when they combined with the wrong deductions made by the general staffs of the European powers, they could not fail to carry over the ideas of 1870 into the new age of machine-guns and submarines. No one seems to have planned or thought in terms of the extraordinary forecast first made by Ivan S. Bloch that 'everybody will be entrenched in the next war. It will be a great war of entrenchments. The spade will be as indispensable to a soldier as his rifle.' When he said that in 1900, Bloch had just completed twelve years of work on a statistical and practical examination of the nature of modern warfare, and he had come to conclusions very different from those of the military experts. Bloch had grasped the central fact that the destructiveness of the new armaments and the intricate organization of contemporary society had entirely altered the scale of warfare. His forecast was an epitaph written in full anticipation of the millions who would fall in the next great war. It looked forward to that clash between expectation and event out of which would later come the anger and sense of profound shock that characterized European thinking after 1918:

> At first there will be increased slaughter—increased slaughter on so terrible a scale as to render it impossible to get troops to push the battle to a decisive issue. They will try to, thinking that they are fighting under the old conditions, and they will learn such a lesson that they will abandon the attempt for ever. Then, instead of a war fought out to the bitter end in a series of decisive battles, we shall have as a substitute a long period of continually increasing strain upon the resources of the combatants. The war, instead of being a hand-to-hand contest in which the combatants measure their physical and moral superiority, will become a kind of stalemate, in which neither army being able to get at the other, both armies will be maintained in opposition to each other, threatening each other, but never able to deliver a final and decisive attack.[9]

This was a remarkable prediction of what came to pass in the winter of 1914. In contrast to the imaginary wars with their constant visions of fleet encounters and swift land campaigns, there were no decisive victories. Both the French on the Marne and the Germans at Tannenberg won famous battles, but they did not finish the war. It dragged on. Instead of the expected sequence of great battles the armies stopped moving; and after the French and British general staffs had, so Haldane reports, reduced their quota of heavy artillery and machine-guns because they believed that speed of manœuvre would determine the outcome, the allied armies found that they had been entrapped in a new and quite unexpected form of siege warfare in which the machine-gun proved to be the king of battle. The figures for French weapons in 1914 and 1918 make this only too clear: although the number of men under arms remained the same, the total of heavy machine-guns increased by a factor of five and the numbers of light machine-guns rose from zero to fifty thousand. That was the last devastating comment on all that had been written about the shape of future warfare since 1870. Machine-gun fire and massive artillery concentrations along the Western Front suddenly terminated the long argument for more ships, better equipment, and universal compulsory conscription that had run its course from Chesney's *Battle of Dorking* in 1871 to Saki's account of the German conquest of Britain, *When William Came*, in 1913. The armies had obtained all they had asked for, but they could not win the swift victory they had anticipated.

There can be no doubt that the authors of the many tales of future warfare shared in the responsibility for the catastrophe that overtook Europe. Men like Danrit, Le Queux, and August Niemann helped to raise the temperature of international disputes. And many others played their part in helping to sustain and foment the self-deception, misunderstanding, and downright ill will that often infected relations between the peoples of Europe. During the forty-three years from 1871 to the outbreak of the First World War the device of the imaginary war had become an established means of teaching every kind of aggressive doctrine from the duty of revenge to the need for a bigger fleet. It flourished on considerable ignorance and on the constant animosity that encouraged hundreds of writers at every level of ability and intelligence to relate what would happen in the next war. The best that can be said of them is that they often stood for high patriotic ideals at a time when few had realized how technological innovations would totally transform the nature of modern warfare. Their stories represent the last stage in the brief honeymoon between science and humanity, before the military technologies of poison gas, barbed wire, and tanks had shown what could be done with war, given the science to do it. At their worst they perpetuated an archaic attitude to war by helping to maintain the belief that another war would not cause any profound changes in the state of the world. The most effective proof of this can be seen in the stories of the coming conflict between Britain and Germany that were turned out during the peak period of this literature from 1900 to 1914. It is particularly instructive to note how during this period all the varieties, techniques, and extravagances of the tale of the war-to-come can be seen at work in the mass of literature that grew out of the increasingly bad relations between Britain and Germany. When Guy du Maurier's *An Englishman's Home* could play to packed houses in London and the German Press could make fun of British invasion scares, it is clear that the device of the imaginary war had begun to affect international relations in a way never known before.

It is important to recognize that during the first few years of the twentieth century a change began to appear in the pattern predicted for the wars of the future. Although the French continued for a time to pursue the struggle against Britain in stories like *La Guerre avec l'Angleterre* and Danrit's *La Guerre fatale*, the beginning of the Anglo-French *Entente* in 1904 left Germany as the only enemy of France. This had a curious result. There was an immediate decline in the numbers of the more aggressive fictions of the type produced by Capitaine Danrit. The French production returned to less spectacular and more professional forecasts of a future conflict, all devoted to a detailed account of the coming defeat of Germany: *Le Débacle de l'Allemagne dans la prochaine guerre*, *Une Guerre franco-allemande*, *La France victorieuse dans la guerre de demain*, *L'Offensive contre l'Allemagne*, *La Fin de la Prusse et le démembrement de l'Allemagne*. The ending of the disagreement between Britain and France had at once cut off the source of the hectic fantasies about the invasion and conquest of Albion that had been appearing since the eighteen-eighties. The *Entente* left French writers with only the traditional task of *la revanche*; and since this was a straightforward military affair, without any opportunity for exciting but improbable stories about the destruction of a great enemy fleet, their production of future war-stories became for the most part a humdrum business of adding realistic details to what were little more than staff appreciations. The difference in attitude between two stories of this period, one published in 1900 and the other in 1913, will serve to illustrate the change that took place. The first, *La Guerre avec l'Angleterre*, was the work of an anonymous French naval officer; and it was considered to be so representative of French thinking that the Admiralty Intelligence Department had it translated 'For the use of Her Majesty's Officers Only'. The anonymous author, Lieutenant X, put the French position somewhat more cautiously than Danrit had done in *La Guerre fatale*: 'As regards France, there can be but one such war to be considered, and that is against England.

It must not, however, be inferred from this that France ought to make this war, or that she has greater interests in bringing it about than in preserving peace. Still less is it to be imagined that she desires war. On the contrary the condition of our Navy makes it advisable that France should so dread making such a war as to persistently avoid it.' The *Entente* quickly put an end to this type of French prediction. The new expectations can be seen in a story of 1913, *La Fin de la Prusse et le démembrement de l'Allemagne*. The book lives up to its title. War breaks out as a result of a dispute between France and Germany. Three hundred thousand British troops speed through the newly constructed Channel Tunnel to take up their positions on the French left; the Russians attack in the east; the Royal Navy wipes out the whole German Fleet in a single great encounter in the North Sea. Germany is invaded; Kaiser Wilhelm II is taken prisoner; the Reich is divided into petty kingdoms and Poland is restored.

The same change from one enemy to another can be discovered in English fiction. Between the outburst of pamphlets about the dangers of the Channel Tunnel in 1882 and the *Entente* in 1904 France had always figured as the chief enemy, usually in combination with Russia. Whilst the French were turning out their last stories of a successful invasion of the British Isles during the first four years of the twentieth century, writers on this side of the Channel were still describing the menace from France and in particular from a Franco-Russian alliance. In 1900 Colonel Maude, as the anonymous author of the *New Battle of Dorking*, described a French invasion attempt with the customary announcement of his intention of 'calling the public attention to this vitally serious danger'. His proposition was no more than the old case against the French: 'There are three months in every year—July, August, September—during which the French Army is fit for immediate warfare. And every year during these months there is a constantly recurrent probability of a surprise raid on London by the 120,000 men whom they could without difficulty put on board ship, land in England, and march to within a dozen miles of London in less than three days from receipt of the order to move.'*

Propaganda of this kind continued into a series of anti-French

* Shaw read the book and at once wrote to the publisher, Grant Richards: 'Who wrote the *New Battle of Dorking*? Not Arnold Forster surely? Only a professional soldier could be so ignorant of warfare.' Grant Richards, *Author Hunting*, 1934, p. 156.

stories between 1900 and 1904: *The Sack of London in the Great French War of 1901, The Coming Waterloo, A New Trafalgar, Pro Patria, The Invaders, Seaward for the Foe, Starved into Surrender, Black Fortnight.* All of them presented variations on the single theme that, as one author put the issue, 'Great Britain stood face to face with allied France and Russia for the death-grip.' And then, with the appearance of the *Riddle of the Sands* in 1903 and the translation of Niemann's *Der Weltkrieg* in 1904 as the *Coming Conquest of England*, the great war between Britain and Germany began. For the first time in the course of this literature the Germans started on the large-scale production of stories like *Der deutsch-englische Krieg, Die 'Offensiv-Invasion' gegen England, Die Engländer kommen, Mit deutschen Waffen über Paris nach London.* Crisis by crisis they mirrored the state of relations between the two countries, as British writers in their turn described a future conflict with Germany in which every device from the use of spies to a successful invasion was employed to argue the case for conscription or for more dreadnoughts. The brief interlude of simple interest in the new ships and the romance of the torpedo fleet ended abruptly. During the ten years before the First World War the growing antagonism between Britain and Germany was responsible for the largest and most sustained development of the most alarmist and aggressive stories of future warfare ever seen at any time in European history.

In both countries the new phase in the tale of imaginary warfare turned on the question of naval supremacy. As a result of the construction programmes of 1898 and 1900 the German Fleet had entered on a period of rapid expansion, and already some had begun to suspect that the real intention was not to protect German commerce, as Prince Hohenlohe had told the Reichstag, but to challenge the Royal Navy. After the serious deterioration in relations between the two countries caused by the German attitude during the Boer War, the new and very real dislike of Germany grew into a widespread belief that the great menace of the future was the German Fleet. At the beginning of 1901 the editor of *Black and White* wrote on the subject of 'The German Navy' in a way that was typical of the Press at that time: 'Nothing speaks more strongly of the growth of Germany's power than the rapid strides her navy has made in recent times. It is only quite a few years ago that the idea of an important German navy would have seemed as incongruous as would the notion of a great Swiss fleet.

Then suddenly one day the world awoke to the fact that Germany was a great maritime power, and from that day to this, through the tireless exertions of the energetic and far-sighted Kaiser, she had gone steadily forward towards the fulfilment of her dream as the premier naval Power of the world.'[10] There was much to feed the suspicion that Germany had hostile intentions. In 1900 the first German fantasies in support of the naval construction programme had appeared. The author of *Wehrlos zur See* described the coming destruction of Germany in order to demonstrate the case for a continued expansion of the Fleet; and in *Die Abrechnung mit England* of 1900 the same argument was presented in the more encouraging form of a successful war against Britain. Enemy cruisers inflict immense damage on British shipping and after a humiliating defeat Britain has to surrender Gibraltar and all her African territories. At the same time some German service writers were beginning to discuss the possibility of using the German Fleet to invade Britain. In the many editions of the *Nation in Arms* that tedious militarist, Baron Colmar von der Goltz, had never tired of proclaiming the urgent need to prepare against the day when the nation would have to face 'a final struggle for the existence and greatness of Germany'. His solution was a plan for war:

Bearing this constantly in mind, we must work incessantly, by example, by word, and by our writings towards this end, that loyalty towards the Emperor, passionate love for the Fatherland, determination not to shrink from hard trials, self-denial, and cheerful sacrifice may wax ever stronger in our hearts and in those of our children. Then will the German army, which must be and shall ever remain, the German nation in arms, enter upon the coming conflict with full assurance of ultimate victory.[11]

In 1900 von der Goltz had begun to argue that an invasion of Britain was possible on the grounds that 'the distance is short and can easily be traversed by an enterprising admiral who succeeds, by the excellence of his fleet and by his audacity, in obtaining for a short time the command of the sea'. In 1901 similar views of other German service writers began to receive considerable attention from the British Press. One of them, Freiherr von Edelsheim, discussed plans for a descent on the British Isles in his *Operationen zur See*. His conclusions were, in effect, advance notice of a naval war; for Edelsheim declared that 'it is necessary to have our battle fleet so strong that it will be in a position to assist materially in

Two books from the German side about a future war. This copy of *Der deutsch-englische Krieg* published in 1906 is already marked '7th edition';

Europa in Flammen. Der deutsche Zukunftskrieg, 1909 by Michael Wagebald was published in 1908.

any undertaking of our troops'. When arguments of this nature coincided with news of the construction of new docks at Emden and of plans for still more warships, then the Government came to agree with the Press that the Kaiser might really intend to live up to his new title of Admiral of the Atlantic. An immediate consequence of the growing anxieties about the nature of German naval intentions was the demand early in 1903 for a naval base on the east coast and for the establishment of a North Sea squadron.

The contrived nightmare of the *Battle of Dorking* now seemed far closer to realization than ever it had been in 1871 when Chesney had argued the case for military improvements. In fact, the circumstances of 1871 were in many ways repeated in the excitement caused by the appearance of the *Riddle of the Sands* in 1903. Like Chesney before him, that brave and chivalrous yachtsman, Erskine Childers, had devised the perfect myth in which to convey the anxieties and anticipations of a people beginning to be alarmed at the new menace from overseas. The exciting detective work in the stage-by-stage account of the unravelling of the German invasion plan was admirably calculated to express contemporary fears for the future. The rapid narrative, the constant mystery and adventure, the excellent sailing episodes, and the appearance of the All-Highest himself combined the advantages of realism and romance. The story seemed as if it ought to be true; and for this reason it caused a sensation when it came out. Several hundred thousand copies of the cheap edition were sold and the Germans ordered the book to be confiscated. The *Riddle of the Sands* was undoubtedly the best story of its kind since the *Battle of Dorking*. It inaugurated a new and even more sensational fiction about German intentions which was developed in many later works, especially in Le Queux's notorious *Invasion of 1910*, Guy de Maurier's *An Englishman's Home*, and Saki's *When William Came*. Erskine Childers presented the first stage of a legend that was taken up and enlarged by his successors. This started from the final chapters of the *Riddle of the Sands*, after the hero had hidden himself on the German tug and so had discovered the secret of the mysterious operations off the East Friesland coast:

The course he had set was about west, with Norderney light a couple of points off the port bow. The course for Memmert? Possibly; but I cared not, for my mind was far from Memmert tonight. *It was the course for England too.* Yes, I understood at last. I was assisting at an experimental rehearsal of a great scene, to be enacted, perhaps, in the near future—a scene when multitudes of sea-going lighters, carrying full loads of soldiers, not half loads of coal, should issue simultaneously, in seven ordered fleets, from seven shallow outlets, and under escort of the Imperial Navy traverse the North Sea and throw themselves bodily upon English shores.

Here, then, was a renewal of the ancient anxiety for the survival of an island people in the face of an attempt at invasion by a great overseas military power. For those who wanted evidence of Germany's aggressive intentions there were the new stories of a future war in which the Germans inflicted a swift and humiliating defeat upon the British. One of the earliest was August Niemann's *Der Weltkrieg* of 1904, a highly optimistic and amateur attempt to rearrange the world to suit German pretensions. The book was immediately translated into English as a warning of what the Germans had in mind. Niemann's ideas were somewhat over-optimistic, since amongst other things they called for a combination of France, Russia and Germany against Britain. Nevertheless, the attitude he revealed in his preface was enough to convince many readers that the Germans meant what he said:

> Almost all wars have, for centuries past, been waged in the interests of England, and almost all have been incited by England. Only when Bismarck's genius presided over Germany did the German Michael become conscious of his own strength and wage his own wars. Are things come to this pass that Germany is to crave of England's bounty —her air and light, and her very daily bread? . . . My dreams, the dreams of a German, show me the war that is to be, and the victory of the three great allied nations—Germany, France and Russia—and a new division of the possessions of the earth as the final aim and object of this gigantic universal war.

After Niemann's declaration of the war-to-come between Britain and Germany stories of the future conflict appeared every year in the two countries until a real war put an end to this literature. For the first time in the history of international politics, as a direct result of universal literacy and mass journalism, the writing of popular fiction had begun to have a recognizable effect on the relations between countries, since these tales of the war-to-come encouraged British and Germans to see themselves as inevitable enemies. Most of these stories were written by earnest men with the best of patriotic motives. One of the more striking examples of this general high seriousness can be seen in the work of Charles

Doughty, the author of the classic *Travels in Arabia Deserta*, who wrote two verse plays to warn his countrymen of the German peril. In the first play, *The Cliffs*, he outlined what he considered were the German plans for an invasion of the British Isles:

> . . . given a clear Coast,
> And half-a-week before them, they'd cut off
> Scotland, and raid Newcastle and the Forth:
> And landing in poor disaffected Ireland,
> Promise her irrevocable Home Rule;
> And a Protectorate over her proclaim.
> Tardy or quickly, the Admiralty might enclose
> Both Portland and wide Plymouth Sound with booms.
> But such then might an Enemy's diving ships
> Stoop under; and with contact-mines by night-
> Time sow the field. Some even might, stealing forth,
> Torpedo at their anchorage drowsing Dreadnoughts.
> Moreo'er, they'll seize our great commercial ports,
> Burn British shipping in them and destroy
> All coaling stores.

The first major increase in production took place in 1906, a bumper year which saw the appearance of several notorious books: *Völker Europas, Hamburg und Bremen in Gefahr, 1906: der Zusammenbruch der alten Welt, The Shock of Battle, The Enemy in our Midst, The North Sea Bubble, The Writing on the Wall, The Invasion of 1910.* They were all written at a time when international relations had deteriorated perceptibly after Bülow had staged the Tangier incident in March 1905 in the hope of detaching France from her new relationship with Britain. Again in 1905 both the Admiralty and the War Office had begun to consider the possibility of a war between Germany and the Anglo-French powers; and in 1906 the new thinking in Britain became more obvious when the first of the dreadnoughts was launched and a start made with the establishment of a Home Fleet.

In March 1906 the *Daily Mail* declared war on Germany in a serial story which proved to be the most sensational of all the pre-1914 imaginary wars. It was written by Queen Alexandra's favourite novelist, William le Queux; and his account of the German descent on Britain, *The Invasion of 1910*, aroused such intense interest throughout the world that it was translated into twenty-seven languages, including Arabic, Japanese, and Chinese. The story sold over a million copies throughout the world when it was published as a book. It was immediately translated into German, given a different ending, and sold in a special edition for boys under the title of *Der Einfall der Deutschen in England.* The cover of this edition carried a magnificent drawing of the German troops entering the smoking ruins of a thoroughly demolished London.

The story began in 1905 as another of Harmsworth's ideas for the *Daily Mail.* He commissioned Le Queux to do the writing, and after four months spent in touring the invasion area of south-east England, Le Queux started on the serial, in which he had help from H. W. Wilson, the naval writer, and from that untiring champion of Army expansion, Lord Roberts. Le Queux and the Field-Marshal worked out the most likely plan for a German invasion, but when the scheme was presented to Harmsworth they were told that, although the strategy might be faultless, it would be bad for circulation. 'Bobs' or no 'Bobs', the Germans had to pass through every sizeable town, 'not keep to remote one-eyed country villages where there was no possibility of large *Daily Mail* sales'.[12] In the interests of circulation the invasion plan was altered to allow ferocious Uhlans to gallop into every town from Sheffield to Chelmsford. And, still with an eye to the sale of the *Daily Mail,* Harmsworth placed special advertisements in the London dailies and many of the provincial newspapers. These carried a map showing the district the Germans would be invading next morning in the *Daily Mail.* Another publicity trick was to send sandwich-men, dressed as German soldiers, to parade through London with notices of the revelations to be read in the *Daily Mail.* An eye-witness has described the scene when 'the startling portent was seen of a long file of veterans in spiked helmets and Prussian-blue uniforms parading moodily down Oxford Street . . . They carried sandwich boards to inform all whom it might concern that the great William Le Queux, already famous as the historian (in 1894) of the Great War in England (in alliance with Germany against France and Russia) in 1897, was now about to add to his laurels by reporting day by day in the columns of England's most wide-awake newspaper the progress of her great Invasion (by Germany) in 1910. And didn't he just.'[13]

But Le Queux had little to reveal. The German forces assembled for the invasion behind the Frisian Islands, where Erskine Childers had described the first experiments for the descent upon Britain. Thereafter, as Le Queux wrote, the whole campaign went with

THE INVASION OF 1910

WITH A FULL ACCOUNT OF THE SIEGE OF LONDON

BY

WILLIAM LE QUEUX

NAVAL CHAPTERS BY H. W. WILSON

INTRODUCTORY LETTER BY
FIELD-MARSHAL EARL ROBERTS, K.G., K.P., ETC.

LONDON
EVELEIGH NASH
1906

Title-page of William Le Queux's story *The Invasion of 1910* as issued in book form in 1906.

R

Speaking in the House of Lords on the 10th July 1905, I said :- "It is to the people of the Country I appeal to take up the question of the Army in a sensible practical manner. For the sake of all they hold dear, let them bring home to themselves what would be the condition of Great Britain if it were to lose its wealth, its power, its position." The catastrophe that may happen if we still remain in our present state of unpreparedness is vividly and forcibly illustrated in Mr Le Queux's new book which I recommend to the perusal of every one who has the welfare of the British Empire at heart.

29. Nov: 1905

Roberts. F.M.

Letter from Lord Roberts commending *The Invasion of 1910*.

the regularity of a clockwork machine. Cliché by cliché he enlarged on the arguments in Lord Roberts's call for conscription: distressing news—complete bewilderment—hopeless defence—scowling Uhlans—desperate fight—our own dear London—shot without mercy—literally a shambles—sad page of history. And it would never have happened, said Le Queux, if the feckless inhabitants of Great Britain had not closed their ears to Lord Roberts's warning that the country was not prepared for modern warfare; 'for had we adopted his scheme for universal service such dire catastrophes could never have occurred'. And how he rubbed in the disaster: repulsive Prussian troopers shoot down helpless women; terrified Londoners dig their graves under the eyes of German firing squads; brutal proclamations commanded the requisitioning of everything from private possessions to country houses. The biggest blow, however, was left for the editor of the German translation to arrange. He removed about two hundred pages of the narrative covering the time between the fall of London and the ending of the war, since these described the British counter-attack and the massacre of the Germans in London. The efforts of the French to intervene between the two countries were ascribed to the United States in the German text; and whereas Le Queux ended with a peace treaty that gave Holland and Denmark to Germany, the translator saved his readers any possible embarrassment by reporting that 'in the German peace terms there was no question at all of any surrender of territory or populations whether in Europe or in other parts of the world'.

The great popularity enjoyed by the *Invasion of 1910* and the *Riddle of the Sands* had the double effect of spreading the idea of a German invasion and of presenting a stereotype of German methods and intentions, since the prediction made by Erskine Childers in 1903 was shown to be true by the events of Le Queux's invasion in 1910. The two books and many others of the same kind played a part in increasing national anxieties. Le Queux was particularly active in developing the legend of the ubiquitous German spy. He took over and improved on the old story of the disguised enemy soldiers first reported in the Channel Tunnel pamphlets of 1882. According to Le Queux 'advance agents' of the German forces played an important part in the successful invasion. For years the Germans had kept a civilian army in Britain: 'Most of these men were Germans who having served in the army, had come over to England and obtained employment as waiters, clerks, bakers, hairdressers, and private servants, and being bound by their oath to the Fatherland had served their country as spies. Each man, when obeying the Imperial command to join the German arms had placed in the lapel of his coat a button of a peculiar shape, with which he had long ago been provided, and by which he was instantly recognised as a loyal subject of the Kaiser.'

The legend was omitted from the German translation, but it had a considerable vogue in Britain. Other writers added to it, and eventually the story became embalmed in the folklore of the First World War. In another invasion story of 1906, *The Enemy in our Midst*, the author described the operation of a 'Committee of Secret Preparations' which directed the work of Germans resident in Britain:

Every registered alien was an authority on the topography and resources of the district in which he dwelt. If there was a *cul-de-sac* into which an enemy could be driven, or trapped and butchered, he knew of it; if there were mews, or garages, he was acquainted with them and their accommodation for horses and vehicles; he knew the resources of every grocer's shop, every public-house, every dairy, every fruiterer's, every butcher's, and every telephone call office. The capacities of the railways were known to a truck; the tubes were understood throughout every yard of their length, and their possibilities for an appalling sacrifice of English people calculated and put down on paper.

This nonsense was the source of many yarns about the German military bands that spent their time in laying secret concrete foundations for siege guns in the London suburbs, and about the even more sinister characters with tell-tale sabre cuts on their cheeks who were for ever rowing round key ports on the east coast. One indication of the widespread Germanophobia appeared in a letter to *The Times* from the positivist philosopher, Frederick Harrison. He warned his countrymen that the German Army had been 'trained for sudden transmarine descent on a coast; and for this end every road, well, bridge, and smithy in the east of England and Scotland had been docketed in the German War Office'.[14] This was pure William Le Queux and it was widely believed. At this time, for instance, questions were asked in the Commons about the existence of enemy agents in the London area. Sir John Barlow asked Haldane for information on the 66,000 German reservists reputed to be living in the Home Counties. Did they maintain a secret arms dump near Charing Cross? Another Member of Parliament, Colonel Lockwood, acting on information from

STATE OF SIEGE DECLARED

NOTICE.

TO ALL GERMAN SUBJECTS RESIDENT IN ENGLAND.

WILHELM.

To all OUR LOYAL SUBJECTS, GREETING.

We hereby COMMAND and enjoin that all persons born within the German Empire, or being German subjects, whether liable to military service or not, shall join our arms at any headquarters of either of our Army Corps in England within 24 hours of the date of this proclamation.

Any German subject failing to obey this our Command will be treated as an enemy.

By the EMPEROR'S Command.

Given at Beccles, Sept. 3rd, 1910.

VON KRONHELM,
Commanding the Imperial German Army in England.

FACSIMILE OF A PROCLAMATION POSTED BY UNKNOWN HANDS ALL OVER THE COUNTRY.

Two pages from Le Queux's book of 1906: German proclamation of 3 September 1910 calling out their 'fifth column' in England; and British proclamation of the following day, authorized by the Secretary of State for

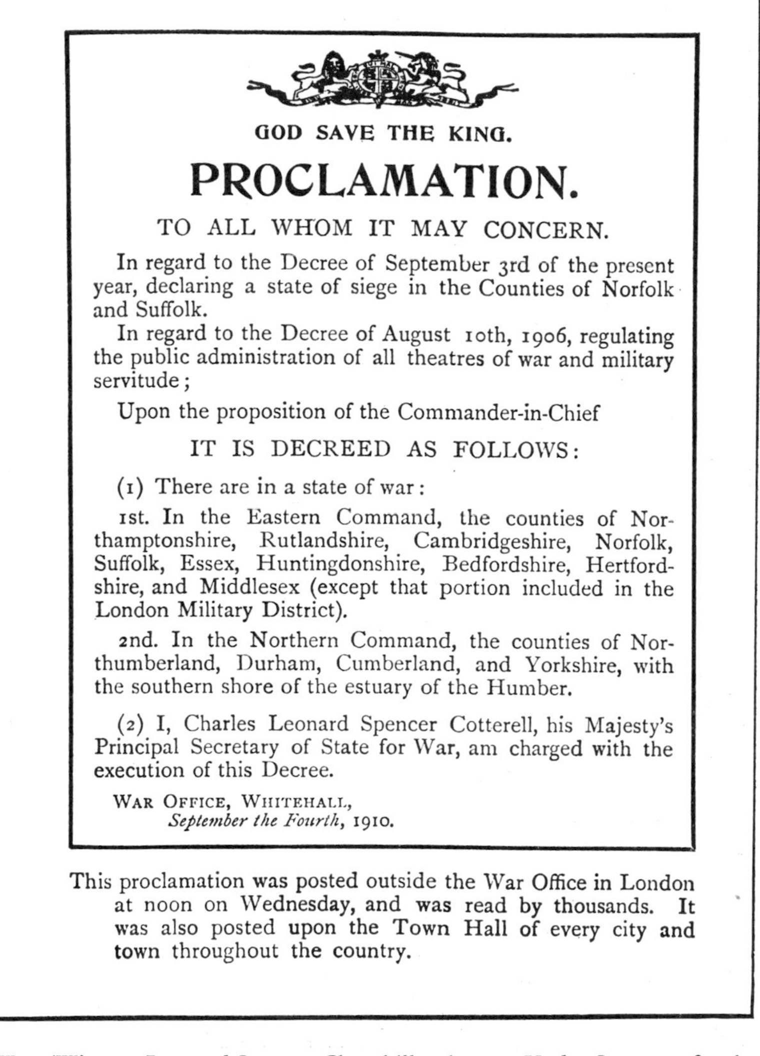
HOW THE ENEMY DEALT THE BLOW

GOD SAVE THE KING.

PROCLAMATION.

TO ALL WHOM IT MAY CONCERN.

In regard to the Decree of September 3rd of the present year, declaring a state of siege in the Counties of Norfolk and Suffolk.

In regard to the Decree of August 10th, 1906, regulating the public administration of all theatres of war and military servitude;

Upon the proposition of the Commander-in-Chief

IT IS DECREED AS FOLLOWS:

(1) There are in a state of war:

1st. In the Eastern Command, the counties of Northamptonshire, Rutlandshire, Cambridgeshire, Norfolk, Suffolk, Essex, Huntingdonshire, Bedfordshire, Hertfordshire, and Middlesex (except that portion included in the London Military District).

2nd. In the Northern Command, the counties of Northumberland, Durham, Cumberland, and Yorkshire, with the southern shore of the estuary of the Humber.

(2) I, Charles Leonard Spencer Cotterell, his Majesty's Principal Secretary of State for War, am charged with the execution of this Decree.

WAR OFFICE, WHITEHALL,
September the Fourth, 1910.

This proclamation was posted outside the War Office in London at noon on Wednesday, and was read by thousands. It was also posted upon the Town Hall of every city and town throughout the country.

War. (Winston Leonard Spencer Churchill, who was Under-Secretary for the Colonies 1906–8, was not, in fact, Secretary for War in 1910, but the name of the imaginary holder of the office is notable.)

Le Queux, asked the sorely tried Haldane about 'the military men from a foreign nation who had been resident for the last two years on and off in the neighbourhood of Epping, and who had been sketching and photographing the whole district and communicating their information directly to their own country'. Haldane thought that the spies could find all the information they wanted in an Ordnance Survey map. In fact, Haldane was very worried at the extent of the spy mania. And he had good reason, for after Le Queux had done his work in the *Daily Mail* in 1906 anxious citizens began to discover enemy agents in every part of the country. What they feared was explained in a letter to *The Times* by a Colonel Lonsdale: '. . . there exists in the country at the present moment what some people would call a "spy scare" . . . I hold, as many do, that the cause is very serious and the alarm well grounded.'[15] Reports poured into the War Office of German plans to seize dockyards and put the Fleet out of action in preparation for an invasion. Robert Blatchford, the Socialist writer, used to lie awake at night thinking of the coming invasion and saying to himself: 'My God! This horror is marching steadily upon us and our people will not believe it.' And according to Wilfred Scawen Blunt's diary for August 1908 even the King was talking of Kaiser Wilhelm's plan to throw 'a *corps d'armée* or two into England, making proclamation that he has come, not as an enemy to the King, but as the grandson of Queen Victoria, to deliver him from the Socialistic gang which is ruining the country'.[16] Behind all these anxieties was the one dominant fear that, in the words of a *Quarterly Review* article on the German peril, 'what the Spanish danger was to the Elizabethans, what the Gallic danger was to their posterity, that and nothing less nor other is the German danger to this generation'.[17]

There can be no doubt, therefore, that by 1906 and certainly by 1908 these anxieties and forecasts about German intentions had become a recognizable and potentially dangerous element in the European situation. The propaganda of one country attracted attention in another. One side blamed the other. The English writer, P. A. Hislam, in his *Admiralty of the Atlantic*, complained that 'the adolescent maritime instinct and ambitions of Germany have been fed by innumerable books in which the main theme has been a war with England. These works range from the wholly fanciful and impossible stories of the type of *Die Abrechnung mit England*, in which the German Navy successively destroys the fleets of Japan, England, and the United States . . .'[18] On the German side, in 1906, Carl Siwinna gave a survey of the major errors perpetrated by British and German authors of imaginary wars in his book, *Vademecum für Phantasiestrategen*. In 1908—and this was more serious—the important German naval journal, *Marine Rundschau*, had a special article on the invasion literature then appearing in Britain.[19] One of the points made for the attention of German naval officers reflects on the damage done by William Le Qucux and others like him:

Invasion is still a word that today fills the average Englishman with a more or less vague sense of terror. Is it really possible? Or is it only a tale of terror like the *Invasion of 1910*—read by hundreds of thousands in the *Daily Mail*—a horror story like so many similar stories of recent years?

There can be no doubt at all that just now in England they are once more troubled by the idea of invasion—naturally by German armies only. German espionage is almost a standard feature of one section of the press. Never before has hatred of Germany generated such widespread alarm in Britain. The German fleet, which is less than one third of the British in tonnage, is supposed to be able to clear the way across the North Sea for the unconquered German Army; and this fleet is being built with the express intention of seizing the mastery of the world for ever from the island kingdom! In the English press and in personal contacts with earnest and thoughtful men this idea of invasion is for ever emerging, in spite of the fact that in the German press and by word of mouth assurance is constantly being given that a German invasion of Britain is a chimera; that such an invasion would be contrary to the elementary principles of the efficient use of military power; and that it would be made void by the doubtlessly permanent and marked preponderance of the British Fleet.

The German author was right. Fears of an invasion were widespread. During the summer of 1908, for example, national anxieties came close to panic when the Navy began extensive manœuvres in the Channel and the North Sea with the evident intention of practising methods for dealing with an attempt at invasion.[20] When a German torpedo boat on fishery protection duties appeared off the Tyne in the middle of local manœuvres, there was a flood of letters and articles in the Press on the single topic of German intentions. And out of this and the Bosnian crisis of 1908 came another crop of invasion stories: *The Swoop of the Vulture, When England Slept, The Invasion that did not come off, An Englishman's Home, The Great Raid, The Swoop*.

On 23rd November 1908 Lord Roberts returned to the theme of the invasion and asked the House of Lords to consider the case for conscription. Two months later he had dramatic support in the sensational success of *An Englishman's Home*, which opened at Wyndham's Theatre on 27th January 1909. The play was by Guy du Maurier, then second-in-command 3rd Battalion The Royal Fusiliers, and it sprang from a deep anxiety in him that Germany meant to make war. His brother, Gerald du Maurier, produced the play without the knowledge of the author, who was then in South Africa. The plot dealt with a thinly disguised invasion by the forces of 'the Emperor of the North', and it so caught the public mood that a special recruiting office was set up in the theatre to deal with the rush of volunteers to join the newly formed Territorial Force. Photographs from scenes in the play and excerpts from the dialogue appeared throughout the Press; letters from Lord Roberts, Haldane, and others congratulated the author on the finest piece of propaganda they had seen; a gramophone company turned out special recordings from the more important episodes in the play; and as a result of the uproar it caused about the state of the nation's defences there was a considerable rise in recruiting for the Territorials.

Throughout 1909 and into 1910 the flood of invasion stories continued. Some began as serials like *The Great Raid*, which started in *Black and White* in February 1909 and continued every week until 15th May, complete with illustrations of enemy troops in Britain. One double-page drawing showed artillery, cavalry, and infantry marching through Central London as the Union Jack was lowered on public buildings. The text below carried the message that 'nearly all the chief authorities, including Mr. Haldane, the Minister of War, agree that our present means of home defence are inadequate, and it is hoped that the present outburst of public interest in the subject will lead to the general filling up of the ranks of the Territorial Army'. One promising young writer was at that time taking an unusual interest in the matter. He seized on the stock device of the German attack on Britain and turned it upside down for his own tale of the great invasion, *The Swoop! or How Clarence Saved England*. The young writer was P. G. Wodehouse.*

Wodehouse had set out to make fun of the invasion scare. He

* Wodehouse was beginning his career as a writer. The story is now a rare piece that has escaped the attention of many collectors.

opened after the fashion of the propagandists by addressing a letter to his readers from The Bomb-proof Shelter, London W.

It is necessary that England should be roused to a sense of her peril, and only by setting down without flinching the probable results of an invasion can this be done. This story, I may mention, has been written and published purely from a feeling of patriotism and duty. Mr. Alston Rivers' sensitive soul will be jarred to its foundations if it is a financial success. So will mine.

The story mocks the invasion legend by a process of inversion and comic inflation. In the first chapter Wodehouse converts Guy du Maurier's theme into the comedy of 'An English Boy's Home'. The patriot who warns an indifferent and bored family of the nation's peril is the hateful boy, Clarence MacAndrew Chugwater, one of General Baden-Powell's Boy Scouts. The news of the German landing reaches an equally indifferent public in the small print of the Stop Press; 'Fry not out, 104. Surrey 147 for 8. A German army landed in Essex this afternoon. Loamshire Handicap: Spring Chicken, 1; Salome, 2; Yip-i-addy, 3. Seven ran.' The rest of the tale deserves its mention in any history of imaginary wars, if only for the solitary element of comedy it brings into such a solemn form of fiction. In the manner of the later master Wodehouse crams the plot with a great variety of incidents. The invasion is no simple affair of a single German army. Everybody joins in: 'No fewer than eight other hostile armies had, by some remarkable coincidence, hit on that identical moment for launching their long-prepared blow.' The invaders advance in their thousands across the golf courses of southern England. As the bored inhabitants play on, hordes of Germans, Russians, Swiss, Chinese, Young Turks, and Moroccan brigands advance in company with the forces of the Mad Mullah and the Prince of Monaco. And so it went on, but to no effect. The book was not a success. After such a heavy diet of war stories and appeals to join the Territorials, the public was not likely to be amused by such frivolity.

The excessive nervousness revealed in the many tales of invasion had become the object of inquiry at home and abroad. In January 1910 Charles Lowe had a long article on the subject of these stories in the *Contemporary Review*. His views give an indication of the scale of publishing in this field:

Among all the causes contributing to the continuance of a state of bad blood between England and Germany, perhaps the most potent is the

W. Heath Robinson, like P. G. Wodehouse, made his comments on the theme of a German invasion in two drawings published in *The Sketch*, 22 June 1910. The captions are (*left*): 'Farewell, a long farewell, to all our greatness": a German officer is removed from the sphere of action on a

detachable cliff-edge near Hove'; (right): ' "Uh-land". Capturing Uhlans in the Westminster Bridge Road, with the kind cooperation of the spiked helmets of the foe'.

baneful industry of those unscrupulous writers who are for ever asserting that the Germans are only awaiting for a fitting opportunity to attack us in our island home and burst us up. . . . Thus it is that one of the most remarkable signs of the times is the number of works of fiction dealing with the invasion of England—works in which pen and pencil vie with each other in the production of luridly life-like pictures of aggression from across the German Ocean. . . . Such pernicious works of fiction have been positively pouring from the press for the last few years.[21]

Part of the attack was directed against William Le Queux, who had described the German espionage organization, but had not produced 'one tittle of evidence in support of his allegation'. At the end the author demonstrates the basic contradictions in the various accounts of German espionage activities by listing the different totals given by persons who claimed to know the numbers of German spies and agents at work in the United Kingdom:

GERMANS IN ENGLAND	
Major Reed's spies	6,500
Sir John Barlow's 'trained soldiers'	66,000
Lord Roberts's 'trained soldiers'	80,000
Colonel Driscoll's 'trained soldiers'	350,000

These extraordinary figures underline the state of widespread alarm that produced the tale of invasion. The mixture of patriotism, political opportunism, militarism, and derivative writing behind this outburst of fiction gives emphasis to the complaint by another writer in the *Contemporary Review* that 'in no country in the world is more heard of the invasion peril than in England at this moment'.[22] But in many ways the most telling indication of the extent of this nervousness about invasion is to be seen in the verdict from abroad. In 1910 there appeared in Paris a book on the subject of the *Fictions guerrières anglaises*, in which the author reviewed the course of imaginary wars from Chesney's day down to the alarms of 1909. His verdict was that 'this fear of invasion, which is endemic in England, shows itself at times in the form of crises the most recent of which, during last Spring, was exceptionally severe. And if one had listened to the alarmists, one would have concluded that the inviolability of Britain had never been so seriously endangered as during the first months of 1909, in the course of which they reported dangers in every direction—at sea, in the air, and even in the bowels of the earth.'[23] According to the Frenchman, beneath the apparently phlegmatic British attitude there was a deep-seated and permanent anxiety which had been exploited 'by many writers who had described the feared invasion usually in the darkest colours'. Another indication of French interest—or was it compassion?—appeared in *Black and White* exactly eleven months after the magazine had started one more alarmist tale of invasion on its way. On this occasion the editor showed a full-page drawing of the British lion with shield and trident stretched in symbolic fashion across a view of the countryside. Above were the words of an editor who had conveniently forgotten that he had published *The Great Raid*: 'Paul Thiriat's view of the situation. He has profound confidence in the British Lion'. And beneath the drawing by the French artist were the words: 'From his studio in Seine-et-Marne, M. Paul Thiriat, the well-known French artist has sent this sketch to "Black and White" as an expression of his own independent opinion upon the situation. In an accompanying letter he says: "Everything looks calm; England is at peace; her factories in full work, her trade prosperous, her beloved soil breathing fertility. Suddenly the alarmists conjure up the Invasion spectre. But the British Lion is calm and proud. He seems to say to all the subjects of King Edward, 'Don't trouble yourselves. Live in peace. I am here to guard you.' "

After that there is little left to say about the progress of these stories of imaginary warfare before 1914. In Germany they continued, not so numerous but just as outrageous as many of the British productions. In the *Weltkrieg in den Lüften,* for example, Britain is defeated by fleets of airships because she had been foolish enough to ally herself with the French. Again, in Adolf Sommerfeld's notorious account of France defeated by Germany, *Frankreichs Ende in Jahre 19??*, there is the savage forecast that 'all clemency, it must be understood, was entirely out of the question, and this not only because of Germany who might be excused since self-preservation had long been admitted as the first law of existence, but because it was necessary to crush for ever the sole disturber of the peace of Europe'. And finally, in the early months of 1915, the history of these tales of war and invasion came to a full stop with Paul Georg Münch's account of the conquest of Britain in *Hindenburgs Einmarsch in London*. This was in its own way as complete a fantasy as Machen's legend of the English bowmen; and, as in so many of the British invasion stories, the exaggerated sense

THE PEOPLE KNEW THE ANSWER OF VON HINDENBURG. THEY HAD READ IT, AS HAD ALL THE WORLD FOR MILES AROUND, IN THE CATACLYSM OF THE PLUNGING TOWERS. NEW YORK MUST SURRENDER OR PERISH!

There were very few American forecasts of future wars until after 1914, when American patriots followed the Chesney technique of predicting disaster: 'The people knew the answer of von Hindenburg. They had read it, as had the world for miles around, in the cataclysm of the plunging towers. New York must surrender or perish!' Illustration from J. Bernard Walker, *America Fallen*, 1915.

of absolute right that shapes Münch's denunciation of enemy wickedness is a clear sign of repudiated feelings of guilt. For here one can see how the entire literature of imaginary warfare is in the last analysis a myth-world created out of animosities and anxieties, and the whole projected into a fantasy of the future where only the worst or the best can come to pass. Hence, the last of the old-style German forecasts closed with Hindenburg's address to his victorious troops in London. He told them to go back to Germany and tell their children of the great events they had seen, so that in the years to come their grandsons could say that 'a grandfather of mine camped in front of Buckingham Palace after he had helped to clear the world of our enemies'.

The optimistic account of *Hindenburgs Einmarsch in London* was the last of the many tales of war between Britain and Germany that had derived from the political situation. Stage by stage the nations moved towards the war so many writers had tried to describe. As Austria became ever more deeply entangled in the Balkan situation, it seemed to be only a matter of time before the alliance with Germany would lead to a great conflict. And then war came, in the words of the *Spectator*, 'exactly as all sensible people knew it would come—very suddenly, without apparent reason, or, at any rate, without apparent reason in the least proportionate to the event'.[24] Somewhere in the Balkans an Archduke had been assassinated, and out of that came war, unprecedented killing and the end of European supremacy in the world. But at first few realized that Gavrilo Prinćip had touched off the long-anticipated explosion. Sarajevo seemed yet another episode in the constant upheavals in the Balkans. Hilaire Belloc has related how he was one of the many who had no idea that war would come. And then, as he sailed down the Channel in the *Nona*, he found the answer to what was happening when he saw that away across the water 'like ghosts, like things themselves made of mist, there passed before me and the newly risen sun, a procession of great forms, all in line, hastening east-wards. It was the Fleet, recalled. The slight haze along that distant water had thickened, perhaps, imperceptibly; or perhaps the great speed of the men-of-war buried them too quickly in the distance. But, from whatever cause, this marvel was of short duration. It was seen for a moment, and in a moment it was gone. Then I knew that war would come, and my mind was changed.'[25]

Chapter Five

From the Nations in Arms to the Post-Warfare State, 1918–1984

DURING the half-century that has passed since 1914 the literature of imaginary warfare has seen a constant retreat from the old, heroic, and aggressive attitudes. The chief enemy is no longer some foreign power; it is the immense destructiveness of modern weapons. War itself and not an enemy nation is the target for attack. Since 1918 the intention behind the story of the conflict-to-come has ceased to be an argument for conscription, for new weapons, or for new ships. Long before the British Foreign Secretary announced in 1963 that it was no longer possible to say that war is simply an extension of politics by other means, a new race of propagandists had converted the device of the imaginary war into a straightforward plea for peace by demonstrating the horrors, the uselessness, and the murderous consequences of technological warfare. In the new stories endurance and indomitable courage are the great virtues. The Othello Syndrome has vanished along with all 'the pride, pomp, and circumstance of glorious war'. Editors no longer commission stories like *The Great War of 1892* in the hope that they will attract new readers with 'a full, vivid and interesting picture of the GREAT WAR of the future'. Although the device of projecting contemporary possibilities into an imagined future remains the same, the code has been largely rewritten.

This radical change in the tale of the war-to-come has developed through two principal phases; and these are no more than stages in the dialogue about the conduct of international affairs and the increasing menace of armed conflict that has been going on ever since the end of the First World War. In the opening period, before 1939, the central theme was the argument for peace by the revelation of the terrors to be expected from gas and air attacks on cities. The second stage began with the explosion of the first atomic bombs; and, as might be expected, the main purpose of the post-1945 stories has been to display the post-warfare condition of mankind in such warning visions as *Ape and Essence*, *On the Beach*, *Le Diable l'emporte*. What they all say can be best conveyed in the concluding sentences of Hans Kirst's *Keiner kommt davon*. After describing the first and last nuclear war upon the planet Earth, the narrator ends his account with the brief statement: 'Germany no longer existed. And so ended the sixth day. Europe did not survive the seventh day. The last hours of the human race were running out.'

Fact and fiction are at last in complete agreement. The brief history of imaginary warfare and the even briefer history of the swift advance from high explosives to atomic bombs now teach the one lesson: the deliberate application of technology to the waging of war will undoubtedly achieve the final logic of absolute success by causing the destruction of mankind. This conviction, expressed in hundreds of books and many international conferences, marks the final stage in the century-long discussion about armaments that began in 1862 when Ericson's *Monitor* started off the arms race. In the words of an editorial in the *Illustrated London News* for 5th April 1862: 'We may depend upon it that we are now entering upon a race in which success will no longer be achieved by wealth or material resources, under merely ordinary conditions of skilful development, but that skill, science, and individual energy will need only moderate means to obtain the greatest triumphs.' The editor was wrong about the cheapness of the new ironclads, but he was unhappily accurate about the effectiveness of calling in science to adjust the balance of war. His views were a paraphrase of what John Ericson had told Lincoln: 'The time has come, Mr. President, when our cause will have to be sustained not by numbers, but by superior weapons . . . if you apply our mechanical resources to the fullest extent you can destroy the enemy without enlisting another man.'[1]

Ericson's views seemed tenable enough one hundred years ago, when war was still a continental affair, a confrontation between relatively small groups. But ever since the episode of the *Monitor* and the *Merrimac*, the constant development of new military technologies and of completely new weapons has more and more threatened to involve the entire world in war. The Cuban crisis of 1962 made it only too obvious that the scale of conflict is no longer continental but world-wide. And in this swift change that has come upon the world since the construction of the *Monitor* the year 1914 marks the great divide between the old Tennysonian delight in 'all the wonder that would be' and the realization that war can no longer be considered both natural and inevitable. For this reason the tales of future wars that have appeared during the past half-century serve as epigraphs on the social consequences of scientific advance. They reflect the many problems thrown up by the almost catastrophic increase in population throughout the world, by the rapid development of terrestrial communications which have made the world one small place, and above all by the urgent need to create a new attitude of mind in place of the traditional belief that war is a satisfactory means of solving differences between nations.

The two principal phases in the fiction of future warfare—after 1918 and after 1945—manifest the shock, dismay, and disillusionment that have overtaken the Western world. It is essentially the literature of a time of troubles. All that has been written about future wars since Hiroshima merely repeats and amplifies what was said between the two world wars. The only difference is the change of scale; for both periods reveal an initial sense of shock, which can be examined in many visions of a ruined world; and both reflect profound anxieties about the political changes of their time. Since 1945 this literature has taken the familiar form of tales about a Communist-dominated world in the manner of Orwell's *Nineteen Eighty-Four*; but immediately after 1918 they were still local and national projections about the peril of a workers' rising and the establishment of a British Soviet Republic.

From 1919 onwards a series of stories appeared, all of which were devoted to the horrors of revolution. The titles indicate the intentions of their authors: *London Under the Bolshevists, The Red Fury, The Battle of London, The Red Tomorrow, Against the Red Sky, Revolution*. Their forecasts of a mass rising by the workers show clearly how this kind of story is parasitic upon the contemporary mood. For the fear of insurrection owed as much to the dread example of the Russian Revolution as it did to the wave of postwar strikes and to the growing strength of the Labour Party. To the more timorous in 1919 it seemed that the country was on the verge of a Bolshevist uprising. According to the authors of the new tales of a future civil war, this danger was the immediate consequence of a widespread sense of disillusionment. Men had expected too much, wrote the author of *Anymoon*. During the war 'the minds of all mankind had been seeking new ideals, searching frantically for some universal panacea that would bring security and happiness . . . All confidently expected a new heaven and a new earth to arise almost spontaneously, with the aid of a little coaxing by mortal hands, directly the war had ended.' This view was common ground with the authors of imaginary revolutions of the future. They all traced the origins of the disaster to the anger of the masses when they found that there was to be no perfect world for them after the long agony of trench warfare. There is an example of this in J. D. Beresford's *Revolution*, when the embittered ex-Serviceman, a stock character in these stories, explains the resentment that made him take up arms against the Government of the day: 'Some of us over there thought we were coming back to a wonderful fine place after it was all over. We believed it was all going to be different, sort of Utopia, short hours, and good pay, and everybody pals with everybody else.' The contrast between the promise and the fulfilment had made the ex-Servicemen angry. After the slogans about 'the War to end War' and 'the War to make the World safe for Democracy' they had returned to find that their country was certainly not 'a place fit for heroes to live in'. This fact coincided with the spread of revolutions throughout Europe. It made some think that Britain might go the way of Russia if the middle classes did not act in time. This was the simple philosophy presented by the author of *The Battle of London*. He explained the purpose of his story in a foreword:

The Battle of London was written with the frank intention of shocking what the friends of Red Russia call the *bourgeoisie* into a realisation of the only means of meeting revolution if and when it should arise. It is to be hoped, and is indeed most likely, that a Liberty League, or something like it, will never be called upon to save England as the Fascists saved Italy. But nobody can say to-day that all danger is absolutely over, so that a consideration of how to meet it is not merely academic. Should the catastrophe of a Labour Government ever arrive—and futile dissension between the main body of the middle classes may some day bring it about—we know in advance what is the minimum tyranny the milder Labour Leaders would inflict upon us, and may be certain that the wilder spirits would soon be clamouring for more. Fortunately we now have the example of the Fascists—and the Liberty League—to show us what to do in a real crisis.

It is clear that the centre of anxiety has shifted within the tale of the war-to-come. All the unquestioned certainties of the self-righteous nation have vanished.* No one now sets out to write a twentieth-century version of *Blake of the 'Rattlesnake'*. The handful of stories that continue to put forward arguments for new equipment are survivals from an earlier and more innocent age. This appears most clearly in the propaganda of three stories published in 1926 and 1927—*The Broken Trident, The Naviators*, and *The Harbour of Death*. The author—E. F. Spanner, Royal Corps of Naval Constructors (Retired)—had taken to print in order to prove that 'the Navy, as it is at present, is entirely useless to prevent this Country from being defeated by a Continental Power possessing a strong Air Force'. But this use of the device of the imaginary war was most unusual. From 1918 to 1939 the mood shaping most of this fiction was a profound sense of anxiety and doubt about the future which came out in many tales describing the end of mankind and in admonitory visions of terrible disasters still to come.

For the first time since the eighteenth century, when the practice of projecting ideas of every kind into an imaginary future period began to appear in European fiction, there has been a succession of stories about the destruction of civilization. In fact, during the last forty years many writers have helped to develop a form of fiction devoted solely to the last days of the human race and the experiences of the Last Man. The stereotype was established in 1920 with the publication of the *People of the Ruins* by Edward Shanks; and it has now reached the point when the world-wide success of *On the Beach* has made it a myth for our time. The only real variation in these stories is that in the nineteen-twenties men feared that war might wipe out most of mankind. Today we know how this could come about.

The literature of imaginary warfare since 1918 is, therefore, almost entirely the history of an obsession engendered by a loss of faith in the grand old doctrine of inevitable progress. Most of the stories are apprehensive. They reflect a general fear that men have unleashed forces beyond their control, a fear that—as it has been said—'men have brought their powers of subduing nature to such a pitch that by using them they could now very easily

* During the period 1920–3 some stories of a triumphant Germany appeared—*Deutschlands Auferstehung, Bismarck II, Die rächende Stunde, Der zweite Weltkrieg*. They attracted no attention in Germany.

exterminate one another to the last man'.[2] This theme runs through many tales of the future from the first statement by Edward Shanks in the *People of the Ruins* in 1920 to the moral lesson in Alfred Noyes' story of *The Last Man* in 1940. Stories like *Theodore Savage, The Collapse of Homo Sapiens, Last of my Race, Ragnarok, At the End of the World, Day of Wrath, The World Ends,* and others of the same kind all condemn a civilization that has not yet learnt how to make wise use of its powers over nature. The Last Man theme runs through the European fiction of the nineteen-twenties. The Germans coined the term *Weltuntergangsroman* to describe stories like *Der Bazillenkrieg Der Pestkrieg, Gletscher über Europa.* In the French stories of this period—*La Guerre microbienne* and *Le Napus,* for example—mankind has been destroyed by its own folly and the wild beasts have inherited the earth. British, French, and German authors made the same points: that the human race must find a way of adapting itself to the new environment created by science or it will perish. To this end Edward Shanks described the desolate England of the year 2074, a land in ruins, split into small barbarian principalities, where the few brutalized inhabitants scratch a wretched existence in the shadows of their ruined factories. The folly of men in waging war has brought about the cataclysm; for the moral Shanks reveals is that the disaster was the immediate consequence of man's inability to put an end to war. And so, he writes, 'it kept on breaking out again, first in one country and then in another. For fifty years there was always war in some part of the world.' This view is typical of post-1918 stories. Like the author of *The Collapse of Homo Sapiens,* the new writers look forward to 'a succession of bloody, ruthless, annihilating wars'. The details might vary, but the result described is generally the same. Britain, Europe, and sometimes most of the human race have been destroyed. The familiar world of the twentieth century is obliterated; and the time-traveller to the London of the future can only report that St. Paul's is a heap of rubble, the bridges over the Thames have vanished, the great crowds have shrunk to the few stunted half-animal inhabitants of 'a little settlement containing all that was left of the civilisation of the British Empire'.

The theme of the Last Man was, however, but one of several reactions to the First World War that found expression within the tale of the future. Whilst the stream of cataclysmic after-the-disaster stories was moving forward to its natural conclusion in the apocalyptic end-of-the-world theme described by Alfred Noyes in *The Last Man*, another series of quite different stories began in the nineteen-twenties. Although the point of origin for these is not the fact of some imaginary future war, their common theme of the Arcadian blessedness reserved for a surviving few is so closely related to the anger and dismay behind the future war stories that they call for some comment. Where the imaginary war stories find the source of disaster in man's failure to limit the destructiveness of modern weapons, these parallel visions of the simple Arcadian life take the argument one stage farther. They represent in its most extreme form the sense of frustration and discontent caused by the complexities and difficulties of an urban and technological civilization. Since science alone is to blame for the unhappy state of the world, the simple solution is to destroy the machine and return to a state of nature. So, the terrors of modern society are released by the vision of the primitive and peaceful life of the future. In the *Secret of the Desert*, for example, urbanized man's feeling of helplessness in a dangerous and difficult world is exorcized by a return to the simple, self-explanatory cycle of an agricultural society. The contrivance that brings about this desirable state is always some natural disaster—a great wind, a flood, a plague—that destroys all but a chosen few of the human race. It is indicative of the mood and the intention in these stories that the survivors show no desire to play heir to all the ages. For them the industrial world is well lost. The complex society of the twentieth century is reduced to the scale of the individual. The human termites of the great cities find a personal significance and a sense of individual value in the close relationships described in future Arcadias like *Tomorrow*, *And a New Earth*, *Unborn Tomorrow*, *Deluge*, *Dawn*, *The Machine Stops*, *Three Men Make a World*, *Gay Hunter*. Here at last in an archaic world of the future the human mind can once again comprehend its environment. The multiplex becomes simple, understandable, manageable; and society is now a community in which all men have their recognized and respected functions. One example can speak for all these stories. In *Three Men Make a World* a scientist's discovery of petrol-destroying bacteria is the means of freeing the world from the Old Man of Industrialism. Mechanical transport breaks down everywhere, and after a period of famine and disease Britain becomes a land of small kingdoms. The machine is the symbol and the cause of evil according to the author:

It has added little to knowledge, and the application of that knowledge has been most damnable. It's given us a new range of brutality, but little happiness. We grow more miserable as the machine grows more perfect, for it is supplanting us. It has killed the craftsman, the man who moulded things with his own hand and brain. The individual, the man long tempered by his work, is gone, the man with a shop of his own, the worker with a lathe or a plough or a shovel. He's dead. That is the one thing the machine has done for us.

The argument belongs to the great debate of the 'thirties on the place of man in a highly organized society which reached its most sophisticated form in Huxley's *Brave New World*. The conflict between the Savage and the world of Our Ford, between individual values and the advantages of a planned economy, produced the characteristic anti-utopia of the period. The paradox was that, although *Brave New World* had all the signs of the ideal state as it had been described by Bellamy, Wells, and scores of other optimists, it could not find a place for a man who wanted God, poetry, freedom, danger, and sin. To recover his lost liberties the rebel would have to choose: either destroy the complex society that caused so much pain or retreat from it entirely; either build an Arcadia in the blank spaces of the future or find a Shangri-La in the remotest corner of the earth. This dilemma explains why the characteristic ideal state of the 'thirties was Hilton's sentimental *Lost Horizon*. The great success of the book, and the film of the book, depended to a great extent on the way Hilton succeeded in reducing the vast problem of war and peace to the comfortable but cloudy philosophizing of Father Perrault. The only point in the story was that Shangri-La would be a sanctuary for the things of the spirit that could not hope to survive in 'a time when men, exultant in the technique of homicide, would rage so hotly over the world'. Father Perrault's belief that 'the Dark Ages that are to come will cover the whole world in a single pall' was also the dominant fear in the many tales of future wars that came out during the nineteen-thirties.

It is noteworthy that the large-scale production of tales of future wars did not begin until 1931; and although as time went on many authors came to expect that Germany would start another war, the social and human consequences of modern warfare engaged their attention far more than the political dangers of a resurgent Germany.* So, in *The Gas War of 1940*, published in 1931, the

* The exceptions are significant of the state of Europe. In the early

author put forward a thesis that was common to most of these stories: 'Man has created a peril which he must at all costs avoid. That peril is the perfection of instruments of destruction. If man cannot so adapt himself, shall I say re-make himself, so that he can live in amity with man, he is lost.' The author's message is delivered by means of a world conflict which breaks out on 3 September 1940. He describes a German blitzkrieg: 'Poland was attacked from the air, and its bloody ruins occupied by tanks. Alsace and Lorraine were invaded after punishment from a German air-fleet that left alive a mere handful of their people. The great forts, the network of trenches and gun-emplacements on which France had spent labour and treasure so lavishly, were battered and pulverised into tumbled heaps of earth and steel and concrete.'

All the great cities of the world experience the terrors of poison gas and high explosive. Governments collapse and fearful pestilences afflict the wretched survivors of the shattered cities. London is smashed by a succession of air raids:

And then, in a moment, the lights of London vanished, as if blotted out by a gigantic extinguisher. And in the dark streets the burned and wounded, bewildered and panic-stricken, fought and struggled like beasts, scrambling over the dead and dying alike, until they fell and were in turn trodden underfoot by the ever-increasing multitudes about them. . . . In a dozen parts of London that night people died in their homes with the familiar walls crashing about them in flames; thousands rushed into the streets to be met by blasts of flame and explosion and were blown to rags; they came pouring out of suddenly darkened theatres, picture-houses, concert and dance halls, into the dark congested streets to be crushed or burnt or trodden to death.

This vision of a desolate city and its mutilated inhabitants was the image of a contemporary fear. Peace and not politics was the aim of stories like *The Poison War, The Black Death, Menace, Empty Victory, Invasion from the Air, War upon Women, Chaos, Air Reprisal, What Happened to the Corbetts*. The authors all described war in order to preach peace. For example, in *The Black Death* the narrative begins with an account of poison-gas clouds that kill off the entire population of the United Kingdom except for a holiday

'thirties a few stories like *Bomben auf Hamburg* and *Luftkrieg 1936* put out propaganda for Germany. In 1939 there were half a dozen French stories (*Maginot Siegfried, Batailles pour la mer, L'Afrique en flammes*, and others), all by a Commandant Cazal who reverted to the pre-1914 tradition with forecasts of Allied victories in the near future.

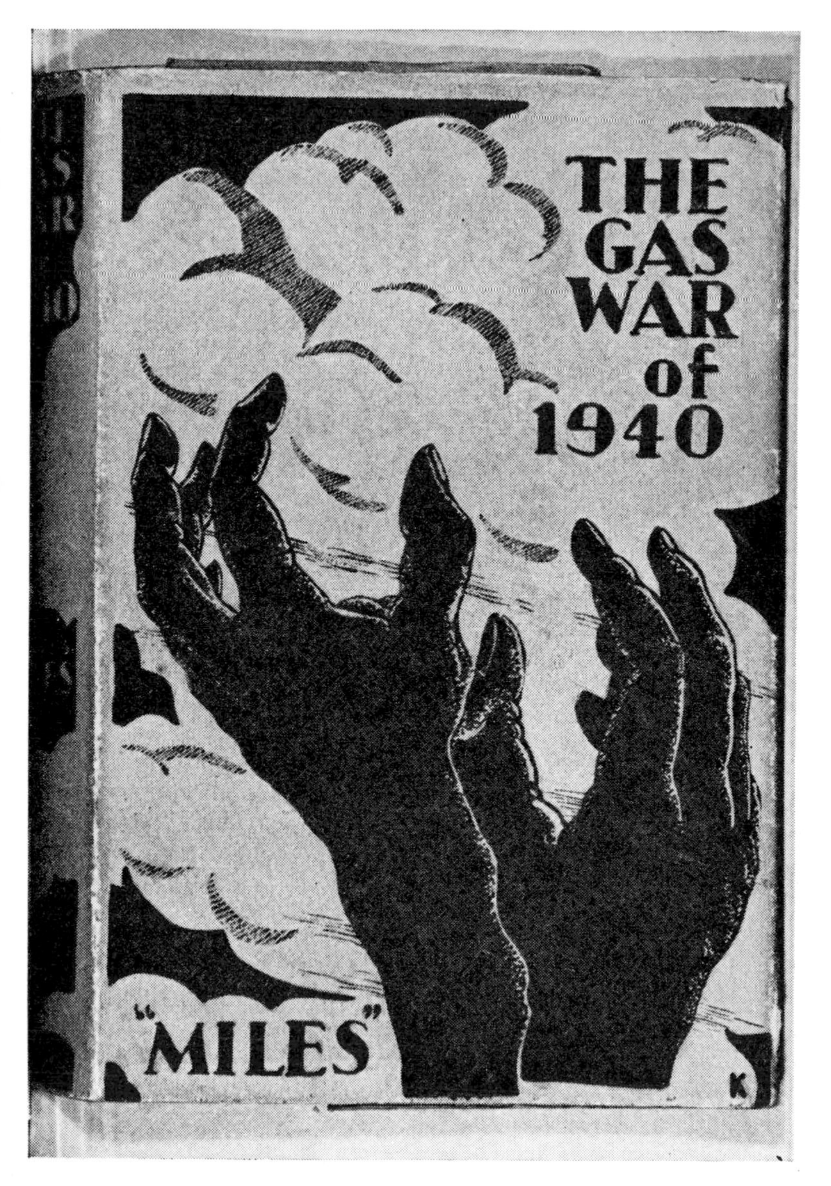

The Gas War of 1940 by 'Miles' (S. Southwold): book published in 1931.

group stranded in the Cheddar Caves at the time of the air raids. Their experiences on returning to the surface are used to bring out the devastation of modern warfare. An enemy airman delivers the author's message to the reader:

Your factories made poison gas, too, but you shilly-shallied. You would and you would not. Compromise. The middle way. You thought there might be something between our will to power and the Sermon on the Mount. Well, you have found the road between. You must not blame us.

How, then, shall civilization be saved? According to a story published in 1934, *North Sea Monster*, salvation can only come from closer international relationships. For the purposes of the demonstration it is imagined that an earthquake has created a new island, Aphroditeland, in the North Sea. Since it is unusually rich in minerals, it becomes the object of ferocious international disputes. In this there is a lesson for the time:

To think that the appearance of a spot of land in the North Sea had aroused the old national rivalries and seemed about to plunge Europe into the vortex of war! And why so, when the average citizen in the countries concerned would affirm that he did not want to go to war over a coalfield? Was it not due to the fact that states still strove to maintain their isolation; that they had not learned the lesson of the last war and its aftermath? Instead of tackling fundamental problems which were crying out for solution they spent the intervening period in bickering over trivialities and trying to run a modern state by antique political methods. What could be more obvious than that the complex economic life of today demanded the closest co-operation between nations and governments.

But how shall civilization be saved? The solution seems to vary in direct proportion to the strength of a writer's desires. The majority favour the method outlined in the preface to *Invasion from the Air:* they write books which are of set purpose 'neither anti-German, nor pro-French, but anti-war'. Their hope is that a vision of the horrors-to-come will make the reader ponder the consequences before it is too late. Others create extraordinary wish-fulfilment fantasies in which some danger to the world causes all the nations to unite, or in which some form of international police force prevents the outbreak of war. The most interesting, however, are stories like *The Woman who Stopped War* by Cornwallis-West and *The Impregnable Women* by Eric Linklater in which

Phantom Victory: A Fictional History of the Fourth Reich, 1945–1960 by Erwin Lessner, published in 1944.

the completely new figure of a redemptive Aphrodite appears to save men from their own folly. For the first time in the fiction of future warfare the realization of the terrors at man's disposal touches off an attack on man himself. In these stories the warrior, the central figure of innumerable imaginary battles, has ceased to count. Indeed, man himself no longer matters. In *The Woman who Stopped War* the masculine world is shown to be morally bankrupt; in the face of male destructiveness the women are everywhere constructive, positive, and hopeful. Whilst the women of Europe and the world work together to prevent the outbreak of war, the men bumble on in the old way and in every capital city politicians work day and night to extricate themselves from a situation for which they alone were responsible. The heroine preaches the same lesson everywhere: 'It is the men and only men who make war, and they will continue to make it until women use the weapon men put into their hands when they made the greatest war of all.' Their secret weapon is a world-wide strike; and they use it to give peace to a world dominated by man-made instruments of destruction.

These ideas reveal the great change in attitude that has affected European thinking since the brave days at the end of the last century when Lord Wolseley, the conqueror of the Ashanti and the Egyptians, could say that 'all other pleasures pale before the intense, the maddening delight of leading men into the midst of an enemy, or to the assault of some well-defended place'. But now that the majesty and glory have gone out of war, only the misery and horror remain to give point and purpose to the tale of imaginary warfare in its newfound task of compelling men to take an unblinkered look at their world. For some writers, like Eric Linklater in *The Impregnable Women*, the true enemy was the folly of Political Man:

In the second decade of the century there had been created a huge nexus of treaties and covenants, by which everyone agreed to abjure and renounce war as an instrument of policy, and protect his neighbours from unwarranted aggression. But this admirable machinery had never been given engineers to work it. As often as the signatories were called on to implement their pledges—in plainer language, to keep a promise—they declined to do so, but dressed their refusal in such a way as to make it seem they were activated by some higher motive than self-interest. A breach of contract, thus ingeniously phrased, was known in diplomatic cant as a formula, and by so-called democratic governments the formula was much esteemed.

After this prelude to a twentieth-century version of *Lysistrata*, a war breaks out in Europe. The comedy develops when a group of women—the wives of Cabinet Ministers and distinguished soldiers—decide with admirable common sense that they must end

From the film of H. G. Wells's *Shape of Things to Come* (1936). There are no more newspapers nor radio, and on a board attached to some ruins is chalked up 'NATIONAL BULLETIN: MAYDAY 1970: THE PESTILENCE HAS CEASED THANKS TO THE DETERMINED ACTION OF OUR CHIEF IN SHOOTING ALL WANDERERS'.

the fighting in order to bring their men home. Their reasons for stopping the war are an attack on the validity of the wholly male world of politics and warfare:

Politics are a male invention. When men have interests which must be defended, they contrive a screen of words which they call a policy, and if they can persuade a few simple people that their screen is of general value, then they are ranked as politicians. But we are women, and our concern is not the defence of any clique or faction or vested interest. It is the defence and happiness of all humanity.

The date of that was 1938, close to the end of an anxious and terrible decade. What followed is too familiar for repetition. It is enough to say that the tale of imaginary warfare kept pace with the mood of the period; and as Europe drew nearer to the Second World War, the new stories became more fearful. In 1939 R. C. Sherriff brought out *The Hopkins Manuscript* which looked forward to a time when the nations of western Europe have been wiped out and the world is ruled by coloured peoples. Then in 1940 in *The Twenty-Fifth Hour* the tale relates the almost total destruction of the human race and the rebirth—for man must always have hope—of civilization in the Nile Valley. And finally, just before the full terror of total war had burst upon Europe, Alfred Noyes produced the last commentary on the period in *The Last Man*. He began the book in 1939 with the intention of showing how the complicated modern world had hampered the true development of the human being. Noyes has the doubtful distinction of having written the first account of instant warfare in the history of this literature, for he begins with the invention of an 'all pervasive ethereal wave' that can stop the beating of the human heart. Of course, the lunatic governments use the invention and in the space of half an hour they kill every human being on earth save for a single couple. After this the story becomes a moral tale, as the new Adam and Eve journey through Italy to Rome. In contrast to the many solutions put forward by authors of imaginary wars, in Noyes's view there can be no easy solution to the spiritual problem at the heart of war and political folly. A ban on bombing planes, the control of machinery, even a return to a state of nature have nothing to do with the problem. Man has to reform himself from within according to the ideal pattern of Christianity. 'The most tragic thing of all', he writes, 'was that the complete answer to all those tragic disputations and conflicts was there, all the time, in the *philosophia perennia* of Christendom.'

Shortly afterwards the realities of the blitzkrieg in France and the Low Countries abruptly ended the practice of predicting the shape of the war-to-come. What happened after the panzers and the dive-bombers began their work was often far worse than anything forecast in fiction. In the abominations of modern warfare, in the inhumanity of Dachau, Buchenwald, and Oswiecim, in the mass extermination of millions of Jews, and in all the brutalities of a new iron age, men were forced to recognize a capacity for evil that had, so it was thought, vanished for ever from the earth. As the war spread across the continents until almost the entire human race had been drawn into the conflict, a feeling of the unprecedented and the unpredictable grew out of the events of a war that was everywhere destroying long-accepted ideas and revealing more and more opportunities for destruction. The speed of development from aeroplanes to ballistic missiles, and the immense range of operations from the Don to North Africa, from the Arctic Circle to the Pacific, demonstrated the lethal capacities of applied science. And then, after all the changes and disasters of the first really world-wide war in human history had had their effect upon the mind, the imagination had somehow to find a place and an explanation for the last news of all. Shortly after 09.00 hours on the morning of 6th August 1945 the United States aeroplane *Enola Gay* began its bombing run over a Japanese city. At 09.15 hours the first nuclear bomb exploded over Hiroshima at a height of 31,000 feet and ended life for 80,000 men, women, and children.

The Lord President of the Council, Sir John Anderson, found the exact words for what had happened at Hiroshima when he said: 'This is not a mere development of something already known. It is something quite outside all human experience; and this is only the beginning.' The mushroom cloud above Hiroshima was at once a symbol and a cause. It started off a new dialogue of the Western mind with itself and its achievements that is still going on today. For those who had known the golden epoch before 1914 this took the form of endless lamentations for the fate of Europe and its sad fall from the mastery of the world. The atomic bomb, then the hydrogen bomb and the development of the intercontinental missile, added to the anxieties caused by the division of world power between Russia and the United States, and the rapid abandonment of great colonial empires. To the old the years after Hiroshima seemed a decadent, perverted, desperate time. Looking at the postwar world through the memory of what he believed to be a happier age, Lord Vansittart had said that 'it almost breaks my heart when I think that I started life in a world inhabited by hope and am ending it in one inhibited by doubts of its own duration'.[3] In like manner, as H. G. Wells saw how the war had smashed his hopes for the future, and had given the lie to all his predictions of limitless progress and happiness for all, the last years of the ageing visionary grew increasingly gloomy. After so many years spent in promising new worlds for old the end of his life had been embittered by a sense of frustration and by doubts about the future of mankind. After so many prophetic tales of the paradise just ahead for all men, it is ironic that his last book, *Mind at the End of its Tether*, should carry the despairing message that 'this world is at the end of its tether. The end of everything we call life is close at hand and cannot be evaded.'

But Wells was wrong. He had shed an old man's tears over the end of things, when it was only his own period and the once glorious idea of progress that had passed away. For the young the world still continued on its difficult and dangerous way. One age had died, but another had been born with different problems and different anxieties. It was the Age of Longing according to Arthur Koestler, and the Age of Anxiety according to Wystan Auden. The deliberate choice of special titles with which to name our epoch was no more than the writers' shorthand way of saying that we live in a troubled period, when so many of the ideas and attitudes that came in during the first industrial revolution can no longer fit the greatly changed condition of the world since 1945. We are caught, they say, between anxiety at the immense problems that call for a solution and a longing to break through into a more settled and peaceful time. As Auden wrote in the *Age of Anxiety* in 1948, the way ahead is dark and difficult:

> Both professor and prophet depress,
> For vision and longer view
> Agree in predicting a day
> Of vast convulsion and vast evil,
> When the Cold Societies clash
> Or the mosses are set in motion
> To overrun the earth,
> And the great brain which began
> With lucid dialectics
> Ends in a horrid madness.

Without knowing it, Wystan Auden had foretold the main developments still to come in the field of predictive fiction. The years since the end of the Second World War have been notable for the largest number of books ever published in the history of the genre, as well as for the range and for the frequently high quality of the writing. The Western world is now so obsessed with the future condition of mankind that at times it seems as if the state-of-society question has become the most favoured collective neurosis; for most writers now seem to realize with final and complete clarity the truth of those words of Leibniz that the present is pregnant with the future. In the course of this postwar flood of publications more stories than ever before have appeared about future warfare, and about future tyrannies, invasions from space, and other disasters that put an end to the human race; but at the same time there has been a comparable increase in the number of non-fictional examinations of the immense opportunities for good or evil that now lie before the great technological societies of the world. Put briefly, this means that the main body of the new literature has moved from the extremes of despair and dismay in the late nineteen-forties to the present phase of renewed delight in the marvels of technology and a qualified optimism that men will solve the problems of peace and war. On one side there are the new myths like *Nineteen Eighty-Four* and *Ape and Essence* that have sought to demonstrate an unquestioned human capacity for evil. At the same time straightforward attempts to forecast the future, like the Russian account of *Life in the Twenty-First Century* and the American prediction in *The Shape of Tomorrow*, have concentrated on describing the benefits technology could bring to humanity, provided that men can make right use of the gifts of science. It all depends, say the Russian forecasters, on the promotion of 'peace, friendship, mutual understanding among the peoples of the world'. Translated into the American idiom this reads as the warning at the end of *The Shape of Tomorrow* that 'failure to control for humane ends the mastery over nature which technology has given us could lead to disaster, either through war or through a robotized society which erased individual independence'.

Although the talk is of science and mankind, the abiding issue is the question of war. What the tale of imaginary warfare began to say in the nineteen-twenties has become an item on the agenda of international assemblies today. The old fantasies of shattered cities and an empty world were a means of warning the reader before 1939 that war is too dangerous a custom to remain the last argument between nations. On the occasion of the Ciba Foundation symposium, *Man and his Future*, in 1962, the former Director of the World Health Organization, Dr. G. B. Chisholm, put this problem very clearly:

Right up to the present time the ancient belief that: 'The welfare, prosperity and power of the group into which I happened to be born is more important than the welfare, prosperity, power, or even the lives of the members of any or all other groups' has been held by most of the human race. Along with that faith is also held another: 'Whenever we are frightened or feel threatened, the right, effective and virtuous thing to do is to increase our ability to kill other people.' That was our normal method of ensuring the survival of our group in the past, but its success depended on the defensibility of our group or its ability to overcome the defences of competing groups. No group can any longer defend itself against death from attack from outside, nor can it effectively attack other groups without great risk of complete destruction of its own people. It is no longer possible to 'win' a war. The whole method of survival by groups in competition to the death with other groups has broken down. The survival group, for the first time in human experience, has become the human race itself. From now on we will survive as members of the human race or not at all, but we have no previous experience of this situation and no traditional concern or education for survival of the human race. The occasion for such concern had not arisen until about fifteen years ago and was not foreseen or provided for by our parents or ancestors. Now we are all threatened with extinction by our own traditional survival patterns, a position which most of us still find impossible to accept as real, because we have been taught from infancy to depend on our 'conscience' values, and even to consider changes in them is commonly felt to be immoral and disloyal.[4]

This discussion of war is simply the problem of human conduct; it is at the centre of the argument about behaviour and belief, about the gap between principle and practice, that has developed since 1945. The feeling that the human being, certainly the human group, is morally weaker and far less civilized than had been imagined in the past has been very characteristic of postwar thinking. Much has been said about the split personality of Western man and the need for a new synthesis of religion, science, and philosophy. Looking back on the melancholy history of the years since 1914, the late Dr. Joad lost faith in the old liberal and progressive view of man and ended by agreeing with the Ninth of the Thirty-Nine Articles that original sin 'is the fault and corruption of every man that naturally is engendered of the offspring of Adam'. When man became lord of the thunderbolt, with powers of life and death over the world, it seemed in those early years after Hiroshima and Nagasaki that mankind had reached the point of no return.

But even if the dangers have increased immeasurably since 1918, only the scale has changed in the tales of imaginary warfare. Most of this literature since the end of the Second World War has repeated on a world scale and in far more urgent language all that was said after the First World War. Then, the example of the Russian Revolution had acted on anxieties caused by social unrest in Britain to produce frightening tales of a workers' rising. Since 1945 the experience of the police state and the extension of Russian power into Europe have generated still more frightening tales of Britain, or France, or even the United States under enemy occupation. Indeed, the appearance of American tales about the desperate days ahead shows how a common fear has united the Western world. Like the Europeans, the American writers described the future in the idiom of the post-warfare state of *Ape and Essence* or the perpetual warfare state of *Nineteen Eighty-Four*. The whole intent of this type of fiction in both continents is satirical and corrective. Both forms deal with man: with his responsibility for the disaster as taught by Huxley, or with his helplessness in the iron grip of the police state according to Orwell.

Orwell's satire gave shape to one of the familiar terrors of our time: the opportunity that technology provides for achieving the complete domination of human beings. The logic of the Party's desire for absolute power can only lead to the conquest of the world. Consequently the three super-states of Eurasia, Oceania, and Eastasia must be organized to wage a war without end, for the great advantage of war is that by using up the products of technology it most effectively keeps down the standard of living. In this way it is possible for the totalitarian state to maintain an unshakeable hold on its helot subjects. Here is the iron future of the new iron age:

> In one combination or another, these three super-states are permanently at war, and have been so for the past twenty-five years. War, however, is no longer the desperate, annihilating struggle that it was in the early decades of the twentieth century. It is a warfare of limited aims between

combatants who are unable to destroy one another, have no material cause for fighting and are not divided by any genuine ideological difference. This is not to say that either the conduct of war, or the prevailing attitude towards it, has become less bloodthirsty or more chivalrous. On the contrary war hysteria is continuous and universal in all countries, and such acts as raping, looting, the slaughter of children, the reduction of whole populations to slavery, and reprisals against prisoners which extend even to boiling and burying alive, are looked on as normal, and, when they are committed by one's own side and not by the enemy, meritorious.

In a mood of black and bitter idealism Orwell had set out to show the evils as yet only latent in the admired world of democracy and technology. His method was to invert contemporary values and give the lie to all former hopes of continuous improvement in the condition of humanity. The point of reference for his attack was the past, the realization within the reader that, as Goldstein had written, 'in the early twentieth century the vision of a future society unbelievably rich, leisured, orderly, and efficient—a glittering antiseptic world of glass and steel and snow-white concrete—was part of the consciousness of nearly every literate person'. Thus, the story gains much of its effect from the difference between hope frustrated and fear completely realized, between the heaven that might have been and the hell that is sure to come. In *Nineteen Eighty-Four* Orwell had created a myth for the epoch of Himmler and Beria. It is the story of a secular fall and the consequent expulsion from the promised paradise of everlasting progress. By means of memorable slogans—'progress in our world will be progress towards more pain'—and by his ability to convey meaning through symbolic situations—Winston in the Ministry of Love—Orwell was able to present our world with the image of its fears. The real terror in the story, however, was that Orwell promised no hope of any redeemer. Man is completely and irrevocably a fallen creature. Orwell's projection of the seemingly inevitable into a certain future was an unconditional and, in the last analysis, a nihilistic and despairing vision.

Since Orwell had merely drawn his own conclusions from the common experience of recent European history, it was inevitable that his successful exercise in terror should start off a fashion for stories of the tyrannies-to-come. In the era of the Iron Curtain and the spread of police states throughout eastern Europe, of the Berlin Blockade and the Korean War, Orwell's *Nineteen Eighty-*

Four became a sacred book in the religion of democracy and the pattern for many similar projections. These appeared year by year until 1960, when the beginnings of more liberal government in Russia and the growing hope of an agreement between East and West began to show their effects in a decline in this form of fiction. All of these stories dealt with the common theme of human misery in a regimented world of thought-detection and secret police; and most of them made their point by describing the new war of the state against the citizen. A series of these stories—*Born in Captivity, Night in Babylon, A Sign of the Times, The Bright Phoenix, Up Jenkins!* —revealed a general refusal to go to the full extent of the Orwellian rigour. After describing the essential features of the struggle between men and tyranny, they end with the act of rebellion or the civil war that will restore the citizen to his rightful place in a just society. One of the best of these stories was *Facial Justice* by L. P. Hartley. It combines Orwell with Huxley to produce an account of life in the rigidly organized New State that came into existence after World War III. Here, in an era of regimentation, there is hope in the adventure of Jael 97, the first of the revolutionaries in the fight to be oneself.

The most important aspect of these Orwellian stories, however, is that they are much more than the immediate result of postwar anxieties in a Europe emerging from a long night of tyranny and war. The myth of Winston and O'Brien became a Western literary and political convention. As part of the contemporary political vocabulary it has been equally relevant to the assessment of society in the United States. The course of development has been the same there: immediate recognition of *Nineteen Eighty-Four* as a singularly effective tale-for-the-times and a swift follow-on of derivative stories. When it burst upon the reading public as the American Book-of-the-month choice for July 1949, it was at once proclaimed the complete commentary on the condition of modern technological society. In a review of the book *Time* declared that Orwell had no need for someone to explain or interpret his story—'for the simple reason that any reader in 1949 can uneasily see his own shattered features in Winston Smith, can scent in the world of 1984 a stench that is already familiar'.

The stench betrays its origin in the best of the American variations on Orwell's theme—*Player Piano* by Kurt Vonnegut and *Fahrenheit 451* by Ray Bradbury. These like the rest of this form of fiction describe the workings of an all-powerful unitary society in a future United States and in both of them there is rebellion for the sake of individual freedom. The argument against a regimented world is stated by Dr. Paul Proteus in *Player Piano* when he is charged with conspiracy and sabotage: 'Machines and organization and pursuit of efficiency have robbed the American people of liberty and the pursuit of happiness.' This fear has been growing in the Western world ever since the steam engine revealed the powers of applied science and its capacity to change the condition of human society. The early manifestations appear in Mary Shelley's *Frankenstein; or, a Modern Prometheus*. The new creature brought into existence by reason of 'the improvement which every day takes place in science and mechanics' turns out to be a destructive monster. Daedalus, it seems, had released the Minotaur from its labyrinth.

The point was made more clearly by Samuel Butler half a century after Byron and the Shelleys during that rainy summer in Switzerland had thought of passing the time by writing a ghost story. Surveying the vast development that had taken place during the central period of nineteenth-century expansion, Butler was able to state clearly what had merely been hinted by Mary Shelley. In an essay written for a Christchurch newspaper in 1863, 'Darwin among the machines', he dealt both earnestly and playfully with the idea of a gradual evolution of increasingly complex machines. These, he imagined, might one day develop a consciousness of their own, as the higher animals had done, and in consequence might come to dominate their creator. He returned to the idea when he started to write *Erewhon* and made it one of the central features of his attack upon Victorian values. After the narrator had crossed over the range into Butler's imaginary nowhere, he set about the usual business of his kind by investigating the state of man in the new-found commonwealth. He discovered a museum in which cylinders, pistons, and fragments of advanced contrivanced were preserved. The Erewhonians had experienced and rejected all the marvels of technology four hundred years before the industrial revolution had begun in Europe, because they had discovered that machines were destined to supplant the race of man. Butler had put forward one of the arguments in the now too familiar debate about the effects of science on humanity which has thrown up several classic Luddite visions like W. H. Hudson's *A Crystal Age*, William Morris's *News from Nowhere*, and E. M. Forster's *The Machine Stops*. Another and more important side of this debate has been developed in a number of even more famous discussions of the conflict between man and modern technological society. These begin with two works of 1920, Zamyatin's *We* and Karel Čapek's *R.U.R.* They continue through *Brave New World* and *Nineteen Eighty-Four* and reach their present state of discussion in the situation as seen through American experience in *Player Piano* and *Fahrenheit 451*. All of them place the action in a future period, for what is under examination in these projections is a social malady that must be shown fully formed so that the danger can be realized before it is too late.

Ever since the discussion of the prospects before mankind established the tale of the future as a recognizable literary form in the second half of the nineteenth century, a whole range of criticisms relating to the state of society has gradually narrowed down into the single statements of *Nineteen Eighty-Four* and *Ape and Essence*. They sum up the progress of a technological society and emphasize the problems that have grown from it these past hundred years. They force the issue on the reader as a choice between the final triumph of technological man in the annihilation of atomic warfare or in the total subjection of the citizen. This is the present stage in the argument that Samuel Butler set in motion; for one of the main dilemmas of scientific development according to Orwell and Huxley is that either war will finish off most of mankind or war will become a permanent institution of the new servile state. And here come together all those different statements about the condition of man that have followed on Butler's *Erewhon* and Bulwer Lytton's *Coming Race*. These are the questions of affluence and freedom, progress and stability, peace and war that could only come under discussion after nineteenth-century science had multiplied populations, annihilated distance and increased disastrously man's power to destroy his own species. Before the First World War the answers to these questions had been equal and opposite: destruction or construction, the arcadian delights of William Morris's rural paradise or the full rigours of organization and technology in the steel-and-concrete worlds of Edward Bellamy and H. G. Wells. But no matter what was said about the effect scientific developments might have on society, it was most rare to find anything but interest—and often delight—in an account of the probable consequences of applying science to the traditional business of war. For this reason the tales of future wars, as they grow in number from 1871 onwards, are important for the way they can help to explain the change in the Western attitude to the future. And in this the decisive date is 1914 and the most important period begins after 1945. The First World War revealed the great problem of the humane use of science and the Second World War demanded a solution before disaster overtook the human race. What could happen is now the subject of sombre forecasts by eminent scientists:

Suppose that one of the contending groups in a nuclear war is victorious in the sense that half its population and an organized government survive, this government would inevitably attempt to conquer the rest of the world to prevent future nuclear wars, and might well succeed. A few centuries of Stalinism or technocracy might be a cheap price to pay for the unification of mankind. Such a government would perhaps take extreme precautions against the outbreak of war, revolution, or any other organized quarrels. It might be thought necessary to destroy all records of such events; and the successors of Lenin or Washington, as the case might be, would not be permitted to learn of the deeds of these great men. Most of literature, art, and religion would be scrapped.[5]

It is evident that the present state of scientific development finds our world poised unhappily between past intuitions and present premonitions. It faces a possible future disaster which an eminent biologist can only describe in the catastrophic vocabulary of *Nineteen Eighty-Four*. This present stage in the dialogue between man and science marks the end of a Renaissance dream. It opened with Bacon's hope that the single-minded pursuit of science would result in 'the enlarging of the bounds of human empire, to the effecting of all things possible'. But evil was present from the beginning in the paradise of the *New Atlantis*. Towards the end of his catalogue of the marvels to be seen in Solomon's House, Bacon mentions 'ordnance and instruments of war and engines of all kinds; and likewise new mixtures and compositions of gunpowder, wildfires burning in water and unquenchable'. Accustomed to the advantages of a superior military and maritime technology, which had enabled the Europeans to overrun the world and conquer ancient empires, Bacon naturally saw no signs of danger in the improvement of instruments of war. How could he have foreseen the scourge man would fashion for himself? Like the rest of his civilization Bacon imagined that science would work solely for 'the endowment of human life with new inventions and riches'. That single vision found fulfilment in the smoke and steam of the nineteenth century. The lesson of technological advance grew into the Victorian dogma of continuous social and moral improvement. By the evidence of its own great achievements science had brought about a decidedly new attitude to time, since the realization of the human capacity for 'the effecting of all things possible' changed the direction of the imagination. At the moment when the discoverers were completing the exploration of the world, the fact of progress from steam-engine to steamship brought in an awareness of new horizons in time, the beckoning mirage of continents still to be discovered in a golden future. As the power of science to change the world grew more evident decade by decade, the progressive ideal state of time-to-come became the characteristic utopia of Western civilization. It was an article of faith that, as Gladstone once remarked, 'the world grows better from century to century'; and this belief shaped the expectations of generations of volunteer world-improvers from Fourier to Edward Bellamy and H. G. Wells. The hopes of the age appear most strikingly in the unqualified optimism of an American work of 1833 by J. A. Etzler, *The Paradise within the Reach of all Men*. He begins by stating what could be achieved by the powers of science: 'I promise to show the means for creating a paradise within ten years, where everything desirable for human life may be had for every man in superabundance . . . he may lead a life of continual happiness, of enjoyments unknown yet; he may free himself from almost all the evils that afflict mankind, except death, and even put death far beyond the common period of human life, and, finally, render it less afflicting: mankind may thus live in, and enjoy a new world far superior to our present, and raise themselves to a far higher scale of beings.'

Because this form of expectation was entirely feasible in the Baconian sense of the simple material improvement of mankind, the thinking behind it gave rise to a one-track idea of progress. It was imagined that the world would go on for ever advancing from improvement to improvement. 'Let the great world spin for ever down the ringing grooves of change,' cried Tennyson. For the Victorians the future was an area of unlimited opportunity and unqualified advantage. In the ideal states of the future there was no place for war. It had vanished, because the brotherhood of man, or better social organization, or the simple effects of abundance had expelled the ancient evil. As Dr. Leete explains to the astounded survivor from the past in *Looking Backward*, 'we have no wars now, and our governments no war powers'. Here it is possible to observe how the process of self-deception started from an uncritical attitude to the results of applied science. The immediate consequence was the development of two totally distinct areas of activity within the Western imagination. As writers contemplated the shape of things to come, two separate streams of thought emerged and advanced in parallel with each other down to the outbreak of the First World War. Most of the fiction of the future produced before 1914 discussed either war in the future or the world in the future. But the dangerous and concealed dilemma of the Western world was the mental habit of seeing the future in terms of the mutually exclusive categories of ideal states and ideal wars. And this habit persisted on those very rare occasions when a perceptive and imaginative writer like H. G. Wells thought of the form a technological war might take, as in *The World Set Free*. Even there the old optimism was strong enough to create a perfect world-state out of an atomic war.

In one way this was no more than the most recent stage in the Baconian programme for 'the effecting of all things possible', since the progressive ideal state of the future carried on more effectively than ever the great war against nature in the interests of mankind. The agreed formula was more organization and more technology. In another way, however, a failure in imagination had set the Western mind in conflict with itself, since that second and opposite field of the imaginary wars of the future was no more than a military extension of the doctrine of progress. In various ways the tales of future warfare preached the single lesson of preparedness for the war of nation against nation. Their simple solution was more men, more equipment, and better organization. Only on rare occasions did a writer attempt to imagine what a full-scale technological war might mean to civilization. The paradox was that, whereas the ideal state of the future prescribed for the improved condition of mankind, the tale of imaginary warfare had nothing at all to say about the future state of mankind. The one lesson in all this literature before 1914 was that men went to war to defend and extend the nation-state.

It was the great age of the unprecedented. For the first time in human history the generations of the period from Waterloo to the Marne had been called on to make an entirely original and sustained adjustment to the extraordinary process of constant change brought about by the applied sciences. They met the challenge in all its obvious and immediate demands: factory acts, universal elementary education, a trained bureaucracy, new universities, new professional institutes, and all those many answers to the problems of the epoch that go from the foundation of the Fabian Society to the campaign for the Promotion of Technical Education. And yet men failed for the most part to detect the still hidden challenge of war and science. Compare, for example, the striking difference between the accuracy of so many forecasts in the utopian tales of the future and the almost total failure to foresee the economic and social consequences of a technological war. Was it simple ignorance, or complacency, or a decline in moral sense? Or was it a surfeit of the unprecedented, or the direct result of living through a century of peaceful progress which had been interrupted by brief but by no means destructive wars? All these factors had a part in causing men to miscalculate both the scale and the duration of a technological war. For in the nineteenth-century book of nature it was written that man's path was ever onward, that the wars between nations were natural and could be profitable.

Kierkegaard had divined the way things were going. Surveying the nineteenth century, he remarked that 'he who fights the future has a dangerous enemy. The future is not, it borrows its strength from the man himself and when it has tricked him out of this, then it appears outside of him as the enemy he must meet.' And this was what later came to pass in the slaughter of trench warfare, for Western society found out too late that the great campaign for the conquest of nature could cause unheard-of destruction and misery. A once beneficent scientific knowledge had laboured prodigiously so that men might slaughter one another more speedily and on a far greater scale than had ever been possible before. As Wilfrid Owen said, 'the poetry is in the pity':

> What passing-bells for these who die as cattle?
> Only the monstrous anger of the guns.
> Only the stuttering rifles' rapid rattle
> Can patter out their hasty orisons.

The same sense of anger and consternation runs through *Die letzten Tage der Menschheit* by the Austrian poet and dramatist, Karl Kraus. He looks at the First World War and sees in the struggle between man and technology all the deadly complications of abnormality. This was the new attitude that grew out of the consternation caused by the First World War—the sense of irrational destruction, of collapse, and the end of all order. The new symbols are related to the end of the world, or the end of man, or the collapse of order. In Yeats's phrase it was 'the centre cannot hold', and for T. S. Eliot it was a wasteland:

> What are the roots that clutch, what branches grow
> Out of this stony rubbish? Son of man,
> You cannot say, or guess, for you know only
> A heap of broken images, where the sun beats,
> And the dead tree gives no shelter, the cricket no relief,
> And the dry stone no sound of water.

In many ways the most profound and far-reaching result of the First World War was that such a demonstration of the destructive potential of science induced a change in attitude to the future. Writing in the nineteen-thirties, Jung pointed out that 'modern man has suffered an almost fatal shock, psychologically speaking, and as a result has fallen into profound uncertainty'. The course of the tale of the future from the end of the First World War to the present day confirms the diagnosis. The most telling sign of the new uncertainty has been the virtual disappearance from fiction of the once dominant utopian vision of the well-ordered state of the future. At the same time the tale of the war-to-come has changed into a demonstration of the folly of modern warfare. In fact, the period since 1918 has seen a steady increase in the anxieties about the future of mankind which the Second World War and the invention of nuclear weapons have brought to a head. In the purposive tale of the future this has meant that a variety of different lines of development have converged, as the statements about the shape of the future have grown clearer and more detailed. Before 1939 these principal tendencies could be summed up in the menace of man's total control of man as it was demonstrated in *Brave New World* and in the menace of annihilation as it was demonstrated in Alfred Noyes' *The Last Man*. These fears are no longer European. The world that science has joined together is united even in its nightmares. Today the issue before the technological societies of the world is that organization plus technology can equal tyranny, and that technology plus war may very well mean extinction. The warning set out in the fiction of Huxley's *Brave New World* was expanded by the American, James Burnham, in his analysis of *The Managerial Revolution*. He reasoned that 'in the case of the United

Mobile warfare of the future: tanks with detachable jet-propelled turrets are presented in an illustration in *Army Information Digest*, official U.S. Army Magazine, October 1963.

States, just as with the rest of the world, we may conclude that the direction toward managerial society is irreversible'. It followed that the new society of the United States would curb the masses, and that out of the Second World War would come a division of global power between three super-states.

Although Burnham undoubtedly gave Orwell some of the ideas that later went into *Nineteen Eighty-Four*, the two men were continuing along lines first revealed after 1918. Like the rest of the world, they had technology in common. For this reason Orwell seemed to Americans no more than the natural continuation of Burnham's argument; and out of Orwell and Burnham came American fantasies of an oppressive future in *Player Piano* and *Fahrenheit 451*. For similar reasons the fear inspired by the first atomic bombs, and by the later development of even more lethal means of destruction, established the Huxleyan end-of-civilization projection as the other and complementary situation facing our world. The anger and anxiety of Huxley and Orwell issued into visions of the future that were immediately accepted as symbolic of the dilemma before modern man. The two writers had presented the problem as a double danger—either the tyrant state or no state at all, either Big Brother or The Thing. Like Orwell and his American successors, Huxley spoke to all men under the universal shadow of a destructive technology. The lesson is that, in Huxley's phrase, we all get precisely what we ask for; and in *Ape and Essence* he composed a homily on the danger of confusing ends and means. In the entirely logical lunacy of total warfare he described the final triumph of scientific method and political opportunism. The text came straight from Pascal: 'We make an idol of truth; for truth without charity is not God, but his image and idol, which we must neither love nor worship.' The proof is drawn from the facts of science and of politics. There are the scientists in their government institutes all over the world—biologists, pathologists, physiologists. They are kindly men, good fathers and devoted husbands, who come home of an evening for a quiet dinner followed by chamber music and intelligent talk with friends. And then in the morning, 'after orange juice and Grapenuts, off they go again to their job of discovering how yet greater numbers of families precisely like their own can be infected with a yet deadlier strain of *bacillus mallei*'. Again, there are the politicians and the political theorists who represent the collective madness of the modern world. So, Gandhi stood for the eternal opposite of the political creeds, but his tragedy was that 'this man who believed only in people had got himself involved in the subhuman mass-madness of nationalism, in the would-be superhuman, but actually diabolic, institutions of the nation-state. He got himself involved in these things, imagining that he could mitigate the madness and convert what was satanic in the state to something like humanity.' But nationalism and politics, said Huxley, proved too much for Gandhi; and they would be too much for our world, so ran the lesson of *Ape and Essence*, if men did not mend their ways.

By the device of a film-script Huxley introduces the reader to the world of A.D. 2808 some time after the atomic bombs and the man-made plagues of the Third World War have destroyed most of mankind. In southern California, and in what used to be the City of the Angels, Huxley seeks to prove Pascal right by describing an unbelievably degraded community in which the pursuit of truth without charity has ended in the religion of Moloch. The survivors worship Belial, the Lord of Flies, to whom they sacrifice the children deformed by gamma radiation. The script cuts from scene to scene: a chorus of young voices repeats the new catechism answer that 'the chief end of Man is to propitiate Belial, deprecate his enmity and avoid destruction for as long as possible'; and in the interior of the Los Angeles Coliseum by the intermittent light of torches a massed audience of the faithful chant monotonously 'Glory to Belial, to Belial in the lowest'. The Arch-Vicar of Belial in the usual manner of major characters in imaginary future worlds talks freely of all that has happened. He explains the operation of Belial in the world and conveys to the reader Huxley's own *argumentum ad mundum*:

Progress and Nationalism—those were the two great ideas he put into their heads. Progress—the theory that you can get something for nothing; the theory that you can gain in one field without paying for your gain in another; the theory that you alone understand the meaning of history; the theory that you know what's going to happen fifty years from now; the theory that, in the teeth of all experience, you can foresee all the consequences of your present actions; the theory that Utopia lies just ahead and that, since ideal ends justify the most abominable means, it is your privilege and duty to rob, swindle, torture, enslave and murder all those who, in your opinion (which is, by definition, infallible), obstruct the onward march to the earthly paradise. Remember that phrase of Karl Marx's: 'Force is the midwife of Progress'? He might have added—but, of course, Belial didn't want to let the cat out

'Landwalkers, now on the [U.S.] Army's test program, might be used for transportation of personnel and cargo in areas where terrain or deep debris would make ground travel by other means impracticable . . . and where weather conditions or hostile air activity would preclude the use of aircraft.' Movement of vehicle's arms and legs will correspond to arm and leg movements of its driver. From a U.S. Army exhibit 'Army Mobility looks to the Future' at the New York World Fair, 1964–5.

'Cargo rockets may provide an answer for delivery to areas inaccessible to land approach or denied conventional air approach by the weather or hostile air activity. Travelling at extreme speeds they would be brought in by electronic homing devices with their impact cushioned by parachutes or jet retardation combined with a long take-up spear on the nose.' From the same U.S. Army exhibit as the previous picture.

of the bag at that early stage of the proceedings—that Progress is the midwife of Force. Doubly the midwife, for the fact of technological progress provides people with the instruments of ever more indiscriminate destruction, while the myth of political and moral progress serves as the excuse for using those means to the very limit.

Huxley's admonitory vision of a catastrophic future is very much a period piece. It derived from the immediate postwar feeling that the world was facing the end of things, that civilization had come perilously close to dissolution. It is an unhappy book, the product of contradictory moods. Huxley alternates between indicating the path of salvation and attacking humanity for its failures with a bitterness he had not previously shown. *Brave New World* is almost idyllic in comparison with the often unrestrained savageness of *Ape and Essence*. But then, the gap between the two satires is more than a mere hardening of mood; it is the measure of a civilization's advance in the self-conscious realization of its own defects and dangers. Huxley is no longer concerned with the effects of a rigidly controlled society upon its members. His theme deals with the heart of the matter as he saw it. He examines the collapse of civilization as a result of the spiritual and moral failings of men. Here, for example, is the Arch-Vicar summing up the case against the modern world; he describes how the success of the industrial revolution made men lose all sense of reality:

'And remember this,' he adds, 'even without synthetic glanders, even without the atomic bomb, Belial could have achieved all His purposes. A little more slowly, perhaps, but just as surely, men would have destroyed themselves by destroying the world they lived in. . . . From the beginning of the industrial revolution He foresaw that men would be made so overwhelmingly bumptious by the miracles of their own technology that they would soon lose all sense of reality. And that's precisely what happened. These wretched slaves of wheels and ledgers began to congratulate themselves on being the Conquerors of Nature. Conquerors of Nature, indeed! In actual fact, of course, they had merely upset the equilibrium of Nature and were about to suffer the consequences. Just consider what they were up to during the century and a half before the Thing. Fouling the rivers, killing off the wild animals, destroying the forests, washing the topsoil into the sea, burning up an ocean of petroleum, squandering the minerals it had taken the whole of geological time to deposit. An orgy of criminal imbecility. And they called it Progress.'

These ideas have been familiar patter in innumerable lay sermons ever since Hiroshima; and the reasons advanced for the present dilemma of a technological civilization have been both numerous and varied. The malady of our time, so the charges run, is that Western man has been too greedy, too witless, too lacking in self-control, or simply not far-sighted enough to anticipate the consequences of unrestrained development in the applied sciences. In general terms this malady is a major topic in the now fashionable discourse concerning the impact of science on society. In particular, it reflects the anxieties that have grown with the invention of more and more deadly instruments of war. Most of all the discussion concerns the Bomb. It speaks menace to mankind through the new and terrible vocabulary of explosions in the megaton range, pre-emptive strikes, Polaris submarines, hardened bases, the process of escalation, the crunch, megadeath and overkill, the dead man's revenge and the Doomsday tape. Huxley's object lesson of *Ape and Essence* in 1949 has found support in scientific papers and cold-blooded calculations like the *Rand Corporation Report* of 1959. The facts that now shape the tale of the future come straight from the missile sites and the computing laboratories. Today a single Victor bomber has a capacity for destruction greater than all the high explosive dropped by all the air forces during the Second World War. Tomorrow, according to Mr Khrushchev, three fifty-megaton bombs would be enough to wipe out the entire United Kingdom. And according to the defence analysis made by the Rand Corporation, if nuclear missiles hit 150 cities in the United States there would be 160,000,000 casualties out of 180,000,000 Americans. *Finis Americae.*

With these fearful possibilities the brief history of the imaginary wars of the future comes to an end. As long as nuclear weapons continue to exist, nation will speak to nation in terms of the common fear that unites the peoples of this planet. The future described in the poetry of Edwin Muir is the picture of a world that has returned to zero:

> On the second day
> The radios failed; we turned the knobs; no answer.
> On the third day a warship passed us, heading north,
> Dead bodies piled on the deck. On the sixth day
> A plane plunged over us into the sea. Thereafter
> Nothing. The radios dumb;
> And still they stand in corners of our kitchens,
> And stand, perhaps, turned on, in a million rooms
> All over the world. But now if they should speak,

We would not listen, we would not let it bring
The bad old world that swallowed its children quick
At one great gulp.

There is now nothing left that the imagination can do with the shape of the total war-to-come except to describe the end of civilization. For this reason the film of *On the Beach* had considerable effect throughout the world, since it told its story to audiences from Washington to Moscow in images that required no interpretation. Because words can no longer hope to convey what could burst upon the continents, the mind has had to derive a new language out of what might come to pass. The symbols of our present predicament are the flash in the sky, the mushroom cloud, the dead city, the submarine voyaging the oceans in search of human beings, and the little group of survivors from the world catastrophe. These are the present signs of future disasters. They provide a code by which it is possible to picture the situation before mankind—a situation in which it seems to matter little whether the forecast derives from the computers of the Rand Corporation or from the many recent fantasies of nuclear wars. For, following on the example set by *Ape and Essence*, during the past fifteen years writers have described the course of the last great war on this planet or they have considered—and these are the majority—the Huxleyan state of the degenerate and desperate survivors from the Thing. Thus, in Hans Kirst's *Keiner kommt davon* there is a detailed account of the six-day war that destroys Europe and the world; and in Jens Rehn's *Die Kinder des Saturns* the story begins when two men and a woman emerge from a fall-out shelter to find that they are sole heirs to a shattered world. Similar visions of the death and desolation waiting for mankind appear in French tales like Réné Barjavel's *Le Diable l'emporte* and Marcel Bouquet's *Et ce fut la guerre atomique*. In English only minor differences distinguish the American from the British versions of the cataclysm that awaits the world. There is little to choose from in any of these new tales. They might be a history of the survivors, as set down in *The Long Tomorrow, The Fallen Sky, The Chrysalids, The Long Way Back, Alas! Babylon*; or they might describe the last days of humanity as related in tales like *On the Beach* and *A Canticle for Leibowitz*. The choice, all these writers say, is between the mutations and miseries of a broken world or those flashes at the end of Ray Bradbury's *The Martian Chronicles* that tell the universe—'No more Minneapolis, no more rockets, no more Earth.' *Finis mundi*.

As long as science makes it possible for men to change their environment, there will be no end to the making of models of the future. So, these pessimistic visions of the post-warfare state of human history receive their contradiction in disastrous but finally more hopeful accounts of what might lie before mankind. Some of the new after-the-disaster stories end with the better days to come when a purged and regenerate race has learnt the lesson the Old People failed to understand in time. Hope for the sake of hope keeps on breaking in with a vision of renewal. For instance, in *The Chrysalids* an ideal community of beneficent telepaths has emerged from the ruins; and in one of the most recent stories in this field, *Midge* by Paul MacTyre, there is every hope that the remnants of mankind may learn brotherhood and wisdom from swarms of intelligent, telepathic, and highly moral insects. The tale of imaginary warfare has become a parable for the times. The issue is set in terms of black pessimism and a somewhat subdued optimism. One view can be seen in the gloomy allegory, *Aniara*, which was first produced in 1956 by the Swedish poet, Harry Martinson. This long poem describes an incident in the far-off future when the goldonda, 'Aniara', is engaged on the routine business of conveying passengers to Mars from radiation-poisoned Earth. An accident sends the space craft off course, speeding for ever towards the distant constellation of Lyra. The message for the day is that modern civilization is going the same way; and unless it can get back on to the right course, the end is certain. The narrator speaks for the dead space travellers, but the message is for today:

> I had coveted a Paradise for this race
> but since we left the one we had destroyed
> the Zodiac's lonely night became our only home,
> a gaping chasm in which no god could hear us.
>
> The eternal mystery of Heaven's stars,
> the miracle of the celestial mechanism,
> is the law but not the Gospel.
> Mercy can only thrive where there is life.
>
> We failed to grasp the true meaning of the Law,
> and found an empty death in Mima's hall.
> The God on whom we fixed our final hopes
> lay wounded on the plains of Douris.[6]

The other side of the future is not quite so hopeless. Once more the experience of the period after the First World War has been repeated in new tales about the end of civilization. The disaster begins tomorrow after a virus epidemic, a world-wide earthquake, the sudden onset of a new ice age, or some other natural catastrophe has destroyed most of mankind. The action starts in the recognizable contemporary world; for the authors have transposed the anxieties aroused by the Bomb to a setting in which man will eventually triumph over almost total catastrophe. Their stories are defiant myths designed for a time of doubt and anxiety. They describe the worst that could happen and then show how there is every reason to hope that man's indomitable spirit will be equal to the most terrible adversities. And—most important fact of all—this type of fiction is common to Western society today. There are American, English, French, and German versions that all tell the same tale of catastrophe and survival. After floods and earthquakes have destroyed the continents in Van Holk's *Weltuntergang*, a new primal pair restores the race of man. In that very successful story *Earth Abides* by the American writer, George Stewart, the few survivors of a world-wide virus epidemic (Americans, of course) revert to the original state of mankind and become a tribe of hunters.

All these tales have the same theme of destruction and rebirth. They describe disasters as great as any nuclear war but controllable because the earth has not been poisoned, and some human beings, sound in mind and body, have survived. They represent a powerful demand for a second chance, for a fresh start. This has the effect of returning the human race to the Promethean stage of a desolate world and the solitary group destined to start off once more the whole sequence of development from tribe to nation. So, the return to an aboriginal or to an uncomplicated pastoral condition throws up archetypal images of survival and achievement. A new Adam and Eve walk the earth again. The child becomes the symbol of renewed hope for the human race. And the Aeneas theme of perilous adventures and the foundation of the city brings comfort to an anxious world. For example, in *The Death of Grass* the message comes through clearly in the last line of all. As the hero goes out to the settlement, he turns to the heroine. 'There's a lot to do,' he said. 'A city to be built.'

The most revealing indication of the present demand for these survival myths is the world success of John Wyndham's admirable epic, *The Day of the Triffids*. It is undoubtedly the best of its kind since Wells wrote the *War of the Worlds*. As a work of fiction it belongs to the imaginative pondering of scientific possibilities that began with Mary Shelley's *Frankenstein*. In fact, there is a connexion between the two stories. Both tell of the disasters that follow when man loses control over his creation, and between them they reveal the extent of the change that has taken place in the general attitude to science. But in 1816 Mary Shelley could only think of science as a private pursuit for a gentleman, and this had purely personal and family consequences. It is very different today. The new fiction of the coming disaster, in all its many forms from Huxley to Wyndham, has established a modern version of the Faustus legend. The different varieties are all contained within the two extremes of the man-made catastrophe that either follows on the use of nuclear weapons, as in *Ape and Essence*, or on the 'ingenious biological meddlings' that produce the monstrous Triffids. Civilization has assumed the role of Frankenstein. Hence, the importance of tales like *The Day of the Triffids*, because by means of a fantasy they give dramatic point to a contemporary neurosis. The Triffids awaken ancient fears of the unchained monster set free by the folly of man. Like those other symbols of deep-seated anxieties, Big Brother and the Thing, the Triffids reveal the fear that man's mastery of nature may lead to his undoing. But, since there must always be hope, at the end of a black tale like *Ape and Essence* there is the incident when the lovers escape from the land of Belial, and Dr. Poole scatters the fragments of the eggshell over the grave. The same message occupies most of *The Day of the Triffids*. At the end the certainty that man will regain his lost place in the world sounds through the final lines: '. . . when we, or our children, or their children, will cross the narrow straits on the great crusade to drive the triffids back and back with ceaseless destruction until we have wiped the last one of them from the face of the land that they have usurped.'

These epics of survival and the Huxleyan myths of the final catastrophe show that the tale of imaginary warfare as it used to be has vanished almost completely. Even the now rare military forecast of the next war, like *War—1974* by an American officer, is based on the supposition that nuclear weapons will not be used in a new war. In February 1963, for example, the Vice-Chief of Staff, United States Army, introduced a study of the U.S. Army in 1970 with the doctrine that 'tactical nuclear war and large-scale non-nuclear war will be subject to increasing restraints on both sides because of the danger of escalation into a general nuclear exchange'. But this prospect has not so far encouraged writers to write an account of the limited warfare that might develop. Instead, the modern stories of the war-to-come are either extraordinary fantasies set far away in deep space, or they take the form of a tale told at one remove. In contrast to the pattern adopted for most of these stories before 1939 and for all of them before 1914, the present form is notable for the absence of the old stage-by-stage description of war in the future. Although the dangers represented by the hydrogen bomb are still at the centre of contemporary anxieties, the shape of the war-to-come no longer provides a satisfactory subject for the tale of imaginary warfare. Because it is no longer possible to describe the indescribable, a wholly new practice has grown up within this field of fiction since 1945. Furthermore, because the psychopathology of these stories is deeply rooted in the individual psychology of writers who are particularly sensitive to the mood of their society, they are striking evidence of the tensions within the Western world. They show the many efforts made by the imagination to absorb and contain within itself the dreadful possibility that all life could come to a sudden end on our planet.

Whilst the old didactic, aggressive, or romantic drives continue unchecked, the relationships between them and the new forms are less obvious but more revealing. Thus, the didactic urge to warn the nation of imminent danger, the inspiration of so many stories from the *Battle of Dorking* to *On the Beach*, has taken a new direction. The description of a possible war of the future begun by Chesney has become a tale that looks either backward or forward. The perils of war now appear as a tale told after the event in the manner of Huxley, or the reader is brought to the edge of disaster in tales like *Fail-Safe, Two Hours to Doom, Two Hours to Darkness.* Although the imagination can find no place for a detailed description of the Thing, it will go as far as playing the game of anticipations and consequences. This process of turning away from the contemplation of the war-to-come has continued into the more romantic areas of the new fiction. The end-stage of Chesney's innovation can be seen in the present vogue for the cold-war spy story and for the even more romantic and extravagant yarns of interplanetary conflicts in the far-off future. The spy stories, especially the James Bond cycle, show how the facts of the confrontation between East and West have reduced the old-style tale of imaginary warfare to the level of the possible. Since it is no longer possible to repeat the old tales in a modern setting, the aggressive drive behind the desire to defeat the enemy now finds an outlet in a cold-war conflict. Smersh and the apparatus of international espionage provide the background of the struggle between nations against which the tale of violence and of triumph can be told. Once the hero in the tales of imaginary warfare was a fearless subaltern, a captain of destroyers, an officer of Zouaves. Now the professional warrior in the struggle between East and West is the secret agent, licensed to kill, whose only connexion with real life is the fact of the cold war. The rest is literally out of this world—a tale of constant violence, frequent cruelty, instant sex, and the final triumph of the nation's defender.

The imagination has transformed the dangers of a nuclear war into a secret battle between the rival champions of East and West. This change reflects most faithfully the efforts of diplomacy in the present epoch of the Hot Line between Washington and Moscow. The policy of seeking to limit a war in Korea and to contain the danger of a war over Cuba has clear parallels in a field of fiction that has sought to convert war into a simple ritual. There is, in fact, a new principle at work within the tale of imaginary warfare. The further these stories move away from the task of admonition and warning, the less they have to do with the real shape of a future war as we expect it would be. Today, the deciding factor is that a writer can never hope to describe another *Trafalgar Refought*. It is not possible to have the ambition 'to produce a vivid picture', as Alan Burgoyne wrote in 1905, 'of likely happenings at sea had Nelson lived in this present year of grace'. And so, although the old delight in technological marvels and the taste for aggressive adventure stories continue, there is no place left for them in our world. Before 1914 it had been the universal practice in this type of fiction for writers to project the possibilities of one year into the next; but nowadays the work once done by the old-world tales of destroyers and airships in action is carried on in totally changed circumstances. The modern jargon of blaster guns, power fields, atomic weapons and space ships is the military language of an unrecognizable future. In science-fiction magazines and in many tales of the future that came out during the nineteen-fifties the description of imaginary wars has nothing whatsoever to do with the condition of our time. Here, at the point where purposive fiction gives way to the tale of wonder and adventure, the wars of the future reach their most fantastic development. In the remote epoch of the galactic civilizations, when man has penetrated to the farthest regions of the universe, the tale of war becomes a ritual game in which it cannot possibly matter to the reader how many millions are snuffed out. Once more the great fleets advance through the endless seas of intergalactic space; and in the imagined world of the hundredth millennium, as related by Asimov in *Foundation and Empire*, 'far, far in the future, out in the Milky Way among a million worlds two mighty movements clash over the destiny of the Universe, grappling for control amidst the chaos of the stars—and only one can survive'. The tale of imaginary warfare in its final state brings comfort to our time with stories that exorcise the real horrors only by ignoring them.

During the past fifteen years a new popular literature has brought science, war, and Utopia together in the conventions of space adventure. The new fiction has the great advantage of being able to offer a means of escape from a perplexed and troubled time, since many tales of interplanetary adventure establish a fantastic world of the future in which the cold war, Communist China, and other problems of the day have been forgotten. The circumstances of our world dissolve into the encouraging pattern of a new age of discovery, when vast machines voyage through infinite space and the White Man—especially *Homo americanus*—is for ever triumphant, for ever dominant in a future that knows no insurmountable problems. Many of these stories offer man his heart's desire far away in the galaxies: peace, prosperity, highly advanced technologies, uncomplicated adventure, perpetual wonder, and wars so far away in time that they have no menace in them. Most of them read like a nightmare by Zane Grey out of Edgar Rice Burroughs. The cowboys of the western frontier now thunder through the interstellar ranges of the galaxies. What happens has little to do with science, although the fantastic wars and adventures are often presented with all the minutiae of an absurd pseudo-scientific jargon.

And with that there is now nothing remaining to be said about the history of the tale of imaginary warfare. The very rapid growth of this new form of fiction since the publication of the *Battle of Dorking* in 1871 is in part a record of the immense changes wrought by the applied sciences. Only two centuries have passed since the unknown author of the *Reign of George VI* produced the first ideal state of the future ever to be published in English. His forecast for the early decades of the twentieth century contained no fundamental changes in the organization and composition of society. The idea of the future, as understood by the author in 1763, was an area of insignificant change. Science could not have any effect on the course of civilization; and to judge from his prediction of pike-and-musket battles in 1917, science could be expected to be always divorced from the conduct of war. And yet during that same winter two hundred years ago, when the *Reign of George VI* was spreading its message of no change among the reading public, the great drama of scientific change had already begun. A young instrument mechanic employed by the University of Glasgow had been at work repairing a defective model of the Newcomen steam engine. James Watt soon realized that, if he could improve the thermal efficiency of the Newcomen engine, he would tap an enormous source of power. His discovery was the invention of the separate condenser and the application of steam power to industry. By 1780 all Britain was entranced with the wonder of the new steam-mill; and after 1783, when news of the first balloon ascents had swept across Europe, the spectacular demonstrations of the great powers of science in the steam engines and the first balloons made men realize that the future was going to be very different from the past.

A century later the practice of trying to imagine the shape of things to come had grown into a European habit. It was the age of the first ironclads and the first wonder tales of science as narrated by Jules Verne. But the pursuit of science and the waging of war were still separate activities in the general thinking of that time. War was a function of politics and governments; science was a business for engineers and laboratories. Chesney, for example, could imagine the invention of 'the fatal engines which sent our ships one after the other to the bottom'; but this was a purely literary contrivance that had nothing to do with the facts of real warfare. Like most of the writers who followed his example, Chesney was the prisoner of his age; for all the evidence of the tale of the war-to-come shows that it was standard practice to think of war in terms of the conventions of literature and national history. In the periodicals it was habitual for review articles to describe a tale of future war, like *The Coming Waterloo* by Captain Cairnes, as 'a very engrossing as well as a plausible picture of the next great war'.[7]

One of the central doctrines of nineteenth-century science was the principle of evolution in organic nature. Unfortunately the process of natural selection conveyed no lessons of adaptation to a civilization that was content to explain social change by reference to an unqualified idea of automatic progress. In the period before 1914 H. G. Wells was one of the few writers who persisted in proclaiming the fact that the rapid growth of technology had profoundly affected both the rate and the scale of social development. In 1905, for instance, he described the dangers of constant change with an understanding unusual at that time:

The almost cataclysmal development of new machinery, the discovery of new materials, and the appearance of new social possibilities through the organised pursuit of material science, has given enormous and unprecedented facilities to the spirit of innovation. The old local order has been broken up or is now being broken up all over the earth, and everywhere societies deliquesce, everywhere men are afloat amidst the wreckage of their flooded conventions, and still tremendously unaware of the thing that has happened.[8]

Nowadays we know very well what has happened. Two world wars have taught the lesson that modern warfare is by far the most dangerous manifestation of the powers of science. The inhuman logic of science now confirms the analysis made by Wells in 1905; if men want the benefits of technology, they must adjust themselves to meet its dangers. This implication explains an extraordinary reversal of roles that has taken place within Western society during the last half-century. Formerly it was left to poets like Tennyson and to the many designers of ideal states to describe the glories still to come. Since the First World War, however, the vision of the future created by the artist has been the ominous prediction in *Brave New World, Ape and Essence*, and *Nineteen Eighty-Four*. In a period when the idea of time-to-come is at once the terror and the delight of Western society, the imaginative writer insists that man must continue to be in control of all things, or else he will have to fit the environment he has created out of science. At the same time a new conclave of professors and research workers has taken up the business of prophecy and exhortation. By means of books and international conferences they announce that science is the basis of our civilization and adjustment is the way to peaceful change. So, the Professor of Applied Electron Physics in the Imperial College of Science and Technology tells his readers that: 'Technology, allied to nationalism, and to the imperfectly controlled economic forces in our complicated society, may still be a demonic force, but technologists are no longer demons. An enlightened society could easily redirect them from the multiplication of gadgets and of labour- and thought-saving devices to the really great problems of the future. These are of quite novel kind. Man must be brought into equilibrium with his new environment. He must be adapted to leisure, and his work must become *occupational therapy*.'[9]

At times it is difficult to distinguish the scientist from the philosopher. Many physicists, biologists, and economists now demand that men and nations should practise the virtues of prudence, wisdom, and forbearance taught by the higher religions. The Director of the Institute for Research in World Economics at Kiel has foretold the paradise the world could have, if only men would be wise: 'But greater still than the miracle of freedom from hunger and poverty will be the freedom from fear. Radical disarmament, and consequently the abolition of war, will give the people the sort of security which they are all now longing for—freedom from the threat of mass annihilation.'[10] To the sceptic, Sir Julian Huxley answers that the present situation is both an encouragement and a challenge: 'The challenge is man's obvious imperfection as a psychosocial being; both individually and collectively, he is sadly in need of improvement, yet clearly improvable. The encouragement derives from the fact of past improvement.' And how will the improvement come about? Man must save himself by every prudent measure possible—even to the point of developing new social institutions to deal with the problems of a world-wide society. The former Director of the World Health Organisation states the problem and supplies the answer: 'Because our ancestors did not develop any concern for the survival of the human race, no occasion having arisen until about fifteen years ago, we have no national institutions entrusted with or designed for that purpose. . . . This system and situation represent an extensive malfunctioning of human minds which is very dangerous. It appears that the next step in social responsibility and organization is biologically necessary in the interests of human survival as a form of life. The transcendence of world values over local and national values is overdue and essential to survival. Its delay is, in the most literal sense, endangering all mankind.'[11] The jargon of science conceals a rudimentary application of the Sermon on the Mount.

The message of science, these writers say, is that men must unite or perish. They describe the prospect of peace before the world. They emphasize the great work to be done in feeding and organizing the growing millions throughout the world. They know that after two hundred years of technological development the effect of science has been to offer mankind a degree of peace and plenty that would appear unbelievable to the utopian visionaries of the past. But now that the laboratories of the world have brought the issues of peace and war together in a choice between possible utopia and probable extinction, one can see what in the nineteenth century was obscure—that peace and war are different functions of science. For this reason the tale of imaginary warfare can no longer describe the great conflicts of the nations. If men do not find ways of abolishing or limiting war, it is claimed, the description of the war-to-come will be a programme for annihilation. The choice is still with men and nations. If men can live up to the high demands of science, then they may well enter into the terrestrial paradise foretold by the new prophets. If they do not, then the course of history may well follow the great cycle of destruction and restoration described in *A Canticle for Leibowitz*. After a devastating nuclear war a new monastic order keeps the ancient learning alive through the dark ages of a broken world. A renaissance follows, science is rediscovered, the secrets of the atom are tracked down, and the world once more comes to the brink of destruction. As a nuclear war begins, a space ship takes off for the planets with a party of children in accordance with the papal instructions contained in *Quo peregrinatur grex*. Whatever may happen to the world, the race of man must not die out. As the horizon becomes a red glow, the children climb into the ship. Then the monks enter: 'The last monk, upon entering, paused in the lock. He stood in the open hatchway and took off his sandals. "*Sic transit mundus*," he murmured, looking back at the glow. He slapped the soles of his sandals together, beating the dirt out of them. The glow was engulfing a third of the heavens. He scratched his beard, took one last look at the ocean, then stepped back and closed the hatch. There came a blur, a glare of light, a high thin whining sound, and the star-ship thrust itself heavenward.' *Resurgemus*.

Notes

Chapter 1

1 Professor Oskar Morgenstern, *The Question of National Defense*, 1959. Quoted by John Strachey, *On the Prevention of War*, 1962, p. 11.
2 François Mallet, *La conquête de l'air et la paix universelle*, 1910, p. 73.
3 Anon., *The Reign of George VI, 1900–1925*. Reprinted with preface and notes by C. Oman, 1899, pp. 46–47.
4 J. Coriande Mittié, *La Descente en Angleterre: Prophétie en deux actes et en prose; représentée pour la première fois le 4 nivose, an 6, au Théâtre de la Cité-Variétés*, Paris, 1798, pp. 12–14.
5 William Burke, *The Armed Briton*, 1806, pp. 32–34.
6 *The Anti-Gallican*, 1804, p. 132.
7 Robert Southey, *Sir Thomas More; or, Colloquies on the Progress and Prospects of Society*, 1829, 2 vols. Vol. 2, p. 77.
8 *Hansard*, 3rd Series, lxxii, 1223–34.
9 General Sir R. Biddulph, *Lord Cardwell at the War Office*, 1904, p. 47.
10 *Illustrated London News*, 5 April 1862, p. 328.
11 A. C. Benson (ed.), *The Letters of Queen Victoria*, 1907, 3 vols. Vol. 2, p. 473.
12 Anon., *A History of the sudden and terrible Invasion of England by the French in the month of May, 1852*, 1851, pp. 10–11.
13 David Urquhart, *The Invasion of England*, 1860, p. 11.
14 Captain H. M. Hozier, *The Invasions of England*, 1876, 2 vols. Vol. 2, p. 86.
15 Admiral Colomb, *Essays on Naval Defence*, 1896, p. 138.
16 *Hansard*, cliv, 623.
17 George W. E. Russell (ed.), *Letters of Matthew Arnold*, 1895, 2 vols. Vol. 1, p. 96.

Chapter 2

1 For a full discussion see: Basil L. Crapster, 'A. B. Richards (1820–76): Journalist in defence of Britain', *Army Historical Review*, Vol. xii, No. 166, June 1963, pp. 94–97.
2 *All the Year Round*, 22 April 1871, p. 498.
3 *Annual Register*, 1871, Part 1, p. 2.
4 Anon., *The Fox's Prophecy*, 1914, p. 3.
5 Anon., *The Battle of Dorking*, 1871, p. 7.
6 Ibid., pp. 34–35.
7 *Annual Register*, 1871, Part 1, p. 108.

8 *Daily News*, 23 September 1871.
9 Clarendon Macaulay (Walter Marsham Adams), *The Carving of Turkey*, 1874, p. 15.
10 Stochastic (*pseud.*), *The Stricken Nation*, 1890, p. 10.
11 Quoted by Percy Dunsheath, *A History of Electrical Engineering*, 1962, p. 77.
12 Alexis de Tocqueville, *Democracy in America* (ed. H. S. Commager, 1946, p. 16.
13 M. de Lamartine, *France and England: a Vision of the Future*, 1848, p. 138.
14 *Saturday Review*, 11 April 1868.
15 Viscount Wolseley, *The Story of a Soldier's Life*, 1906, 2 vols. Vol. 2, p. 232.
16 Anon., *Plus d'Angleterre*, 1887, p. 11.
17 William Delisle Hay, *Three Hundred Years Hence*, 1881, pp. 235–6.

Chapter 3

1 E. S. Turner, *Boys will be Boys*, 1948, p. 173.
2 Kennedy Jones, *Fleet Street and Downing Street*, 1920, p. 198.
3 Quoted by Robert Routledge, *Discoveries and Inventions of the Nineteenth Century*, 1876, p. 1.
4 Samuel Smiles, *Lives of the Engineers,* 1874, 5 vols., Vol. 1, p. xxiv.
5 Francis Bacon, *Essays and New Atlantis* (ed. Gordon S. Haight), 1942, p. 288.
6 Julius von Voss, *Ini*, 1810, pp. 88–89.
7 Robert Fulton, *Torpedo War and Submarine Explosions*, 1810, p. 40.
8 Quoted by Charles H. Gibbs-Smith, *Sir George Cayley's Aeronautics*, 1962, p. 83.
9 *Colloquies on the progress . . . of society*, p. 224.
10 James Burnley, *The Romance of Invention*, 1886, p. 317.
11 Anon., *A History of Wonderful Inventions*, 1862, p. 37.
12 Robert Routledge, p. 118.
13 H. O. Arnold-Forster, *In a Conning Tower*, 1891, p. 11.
14 General Prince Kraft zu Hohenlohe-Ingelfingen, *Letters on Strategy*, 2 vols, 1897. Vol. 1, p. 266.
15 General Prince Kraft zu Hohenlohe-Ingelfingen, *Letters on Cavalry*, 1899, p. 72.
16 H. G. Wells, *The World Set Free*, Atlantic Edition, 1926, p. 91.
17 Quoted by Bernard Bergonzi, *The Early H. G. Wells*, 1961, p. 124.
18 Quoted by Kenneth Allott, *Jules Verne*, 1940, p. 223.
19 H. G. Wells, *The War of the Worlds*, 1926, p. 11.
20 H. G. Wells, *Anticipations*, 1902, p. 212.
21 Ibid., p. 204.
22 H. G. Wells, *The War in the Air*, 1926, p. 246.

23 H. G. Wells, *The World Set Free*, 1926, p. 116.
24 The opinions of many experts were printed at the end of Conan Doyle's short story under the heading of 'What the Naval Experts Think', *Strand Magazine*, July 1914, pp. 20–22.
25 Arthur Machen, *The Bowmen and other Legends of the War*, 1915, pp. 34–35.

Chapter 4

1 Georges Valbert, *Hommes et choses*, 1883, p. 303.
2 *The Channel Tunnel and Public Opinion*, 1882, p. 1. Reprinted from the *Nineteenth Century*, April 1882.
3 Capitaine Danrit, *La Guerre de forteresse*, 1893, 2 vols. Vol. 2, pp. 126–7.
4 Arthur J. Marder, *British Naval Policy, 1880–1905*, 1940, p. 233.
5 Bertha von Suttner, *Lay Down Your Arms*, 1892, p. 212.
6 Prince Kraft zu Hohenlohe-Ingelfingen, *Letters on Cavalry*, 1892, p. 93.
7 Ubique, *Modern Warfare; or, how our Soldiers fight*, 1903, p. 94.
8 Quoted by William L. Langer, *The Diplomacy of Imperialism*, 1935, 2 vols. Vol. 1, p. 88.
9 Ivan S. Bloch, *Modern Weapons and Modern Warfare*, 1900, p. xvi.
10 'The German Navy', *Black and White*, 19 January 1901.
11 Baron Colmar von der Goltz, *The Nation in Arms,* 1887, p. 391.
12 Bernard Falk, *Bouquets for Fleet Street*, 1951, p. 65.
13 Esmé Wingfield-Stratford, *Before the Lamps Went Out*, 1945, pp. 209–10. Two questions were asked in the Commons about this incident on 13 March and 14 May 1906.
14 *The Times*, 17 July 1908.
15 *The Times*, 17 July 1908.
16 *My Diaries*, p. 624.
17 *Quarterly Review*, July 1908, p. 268.
18 P. A. Hislam, *The Admiralty of the Atlantic*, 1908, p. 216. See also this report by the same author: 'Briefly, the British Government, by those means which are always open to the Power ready to pay for information, came into possession of a matured scheme for the invasion of this country which had not only been submitted to the German Government, but had been adopted as a plan of campaign that could be put into operation at almost any moment with the minimum of ostentation and the maximum probability of success. While British naval forces nominally in home waters were at some distance from their stations—at Lagos or Gibraltar, for instance, or even in the western end of the Channel—a military force was to be embarked in the numerous liners and trading steamers that are always to be found in the German North Sea harbours. This

invasion flotilla was to make for the Humber, and at the same time the whole German fleet was to seize the Straits of Dover' (pp. 75–76).

19 v. R., 'Die Invasion Englands in englischer Beleuchtung', *Marine Rundschau*, November 1908, pp. 1246–58.
20 Élie Halévy, *A History of the English People, 1905–1915*, 1934, p. 387.
21 Charles Lowe, 'About German Spies', *Contemporary Review*, January 1910, pp. 42–56.
22 A. Hurd, 'England's Peril', *Contemporary Review*, April 1910, p. 679.
23 Louis C., *Fictions guerrières anglaises*, 1910, p. 7.
24 *Spectator*, 8 August 1914, p. 185.
25 Hilaire Belloc, *The Cruise of the Nona*, 1925, p. 150.

Chapter 5

1 Quoted by T. K. Derry and Trevor Williams, *A Short History of Technology*, 1960, p. 706.
2 Sigmund Freud, *Civilization and its Discontents*, 1929, p. 144.
3 *The Times*, 11 June 1947.
4 J. F. Brock and G. B. Chisholm, 'Future of the Mind', *Man and his Future*, 1963, p. 319.
5 J. B. S. Haldane, 'Biological possibilities in the next ten thousand years', *Man and his Future*, p. 340.
6 Harry Martinson, *Aniara*, adapted from the Swedish by Hugh MacDiarmid and Elspeth Harley Schubert, 1963, p. 129.
7 *Spectator*, 26 January 1901, p. 145.
8 H. G. Wells, *A Modern Utopia*, Atlantic Edition, 1925, pp. 37–38.
9 Dennis Gabor, *Inventing the Future*, 1963, pp. 125–6.
10 Fritz Baade, *The Race to the Year 2000*, 1963, p. 205.
11 *Man and his Future*, pp. 320–1.

BIBLIOGRAPHIES

A. *Principal Works Consulted*

ALLOTT, KENNETH. *Jules Verne* (1940).

ANON. *A History of Wonderful Inventions* (1862).

ANSTEY, F. *A Long Retrospect* (1936).

ARNOLD-FORSTER, MARY. *The Life of H. O. Arnold-Forster* (1910).

ARON, RAYMOND. *The Century of Total War* (1954).

BAADE, FRITZ. *The Race to the Year 2000* (1963).

BALFOUR, MICHAEL. *The Kaiser and his Times* (1964).

BARDOUX, JACQUES. *Essai d'une psychologie de l'Angleterre contemporaine* (1906).

BAXTER, J. P. *The Introduction of the Ironclad Warship* (1933).

BEALES, A. C. F. *History of Peace* (1931).

BENSON, A. C. (ed.). *Letters of Queen Victoria, 1837–1861* (1907).

BERESFORD, J. D. *H. G. Wells* (1915).

BERESFORD, LORD CHARLES. *Memoirs* (1914).

BIDDULPH, GEN. SIR R. *Lord Cardwell at the War Office* (1904).

BIRKENHEAD, LORD. *The World in 2030 A.D.* (1930).

BLATCHFORD, ROBERT. *My Eighty Years* (1931).

BLUNT, WILFRID SCAWEN. *My Diaries, 1888–1914* (1932).

BOULGER, D. C. *England's Arch-enemy* (1914).

BOWLE, JOHN. *Politics and Opinion in the Nineteenth Century* (1954).

BREX, TWELLS. *'Scare-mongerings' from the Daily Mail 1896–1914. The paper that foretold the War* (1914).

BROGAN, D. W. *The Development of Modern France* (1940).

BROME, VINCENT. *H. G. Wells* (1952).

BURNLEY, JAMES. *The Romance of Invention* (1886).

BURY, J. B. *The Idea of Progress* (1920).

BURY, J. P. T. (ed). *The Zenith of European Power*. Vol. X, *The New Cambridge Modern History* (1960).

C., LOUIS. *Fictions guerrières anglaises* (1910).

CAZAMIAN, MADELEINE L. *Le Roman et les idées en Angleterre* (1923).

CHATFIELD, LORD. *The Navy and Defence* (1942).

CLODE, CHARLES. *Military Forces of the Crown* (1869).

COLLINGWOOD, R. G. *The New Leviathan* (1942).

CONNELL, JOHN. *W. E. Henley* (1949).

CRAIG, GORDON A. *The Politics of the Prussian Army, 1640–1945* (1955).

CRAMB, J. A. *Germany and England* (1914).

CRAMB, J. A. *Origins and Destiny of Imperial Britain* (1900).

CRUSE, AMY. *After the Victorians* (1938).

DEHIO, LUDWIG. *Germany and World Politics in the Twentieth Century* (1959).

DE LA GORCE, PAUL-MARIE. *The French Army* (1963).

DÉROULÈDE, PAUL. *Poésies militaires* (1896).

DERRY, T. K., and WILLIAMS, TREVOR I. *A Short History of Technology* (1960).

ENSOR, SIR ROBERT. *England, 1870–1914* (1936).

ERDMANN, G. A. *Deutschlands Seeherrschaft im XXen Jahrhundert* (1900).

EVANS, B. IFOR. *English Literature between the Wars* (1948).

EYCK, ERICH. *A History of the Weimar Republic* (1962).

FALK, BERNARD. *Bouquets for Fleet Street* (1951).

FALLS, CYRIL. *A Hundred Years of War* (1961).

FLEMING, D. F. *The Cold War and its Origins, 1917–1960* (1961).

FLEMING, PETER. *Invasion, 1940* (1958).

FLOWER, NORMAN (ed.). *The Journals of Arnold Bennett* (1932).

FOORD, E., and HOME, G. *England Invaded* (1913).

FREUD, SIGMUND. *Civilization and its Discontents* (1929).

FYFE, HAMILTON. *Northcliffe* (1930).

GABOR, DENNIS. *Inventing the Future* (1963).

GLEASON, J. H. *Genesis of Russophobia in Great Britain* (1950).

GRETTON, R. H. *A Modern History of the English People* (1913).

HALDANE, RT. HON. R. B. *Before the War* (1920).

HALÉVY, ÉLIE. *A History of the English People, 1905–1915* (1934).

HAMMANN, OTTO. *The World Policy of Germany, 1890–1912* (1927).

HANCOCK, W. K. *Four Studies in War and Peace* (1961).

HANKEY, LORD. *The Supreme Command* (1961).

HARRISON, A. *England and Germany. Essays republished from 'The Observer'* (1907).

HAUSSER, O. *Deutschland und der englisch-russische Gegensatz, 1900–1914* (1958).

HERZ, JOHN H. *International Politics in the Atomic Age* (1959).

HOWARD, MICHAEL. *The Franco-Prussian War* (1961).
HINSLEY, F. H. (ed.). *Material Progress and World-Wide Problems, 1870–1898*. Vol. XI, *New Cambridge Modern History* (1962).
HINSLEY, F. H. *Power and the Pursuit of Peace* (1963).
HOBSON, J. A. *The Psychology of Jingoism* (1901).
HUNTINGTON, SAMUEL P. *The Soldier and the State* (1959).
JAGOW, DR KURT (ed.). *Letters of the Prince Consort* (1938).
JERROLD, DOUGLAS. *Georgian Adventure* (1937).
JONES, KENNEDY. *Fleet Street and Downing Street* (1920).
JUNG, C. G. *Modern Man in Search of a Soul* (1933).
KENNEDY, J. M. *English Literature, 1880–1905* (1912).
KNOWLES, JAMES (ed.). *The Channel Tunnel and Public Opinion* (1883).
LAMOND, JOHN. *Arthur Conan Doyle* (1931).
LANGER, WILLIAM L. *The Diplomacy of Imperialism* (1935).
LEWIS, T. C. *Heroes of Science* (1884).
LUCE, SIR HENRY. *The Diary of a Journalist, 1890–1910* (1922).
MALLET, FRANÇOIS. *La Conquête de l'air et la paix universelle* (1910).
MANSERGH, NICHOLAS. *The Coming of the First World War* (1949).
MARCKS, ERICH. *England and Germany* (1900).
MARDER, ARTHUR J. *The Anatomy of British Sea Power: a history of British Naval Policy, 1880–1905* (1940).
MARDER, ARTHUR J. *Fear God and Dread Nought* (1952–9).
MAURICE, MAJ.-GEN. SIR FREDERICK. *Haldane, 1856–1915* (1937).
MAUROIS, ANDRÉ. *Poets and Prophets* (1936).
MONTAGUE, C. E. *Disenchantment* (1922).
MULLER, H. J. *Out of the Night: a Biologist's View of the Future* (1936).
MUMFORD, LEWIS. *Technics and Civilization* (1924).
MACKENZIE, SIR COMPTON. *Literature in my Time* (1933).
NEF, JOHN V. *War and Human Progress* (1950).
NEWBOLT, SIR HENRY. *My World as in My Time* (1932).
NICOLSON, HAROLD. *King George V* (1952).
NOYES, ALFRED. *Two Worlds for Memory* (1953).
PLAYNE, CAROLINE E. *The Pre-War Mind in Britain* (1928).
PONSONBY, SIR FREDERICK. *Recollections of Three Reigns* (1951).
PORTER, MRS GERALD. *William Blackwood and his Sons* (1898).
PUTNAM, G. H. *Memories of a Publisher* (1915).
ROSE, J. H., and BROADLEY, A. M. *Dumouriez and the Defence of England against Napoleon* (1909).

ROUTLEDGE, ROBERT. *Discoveries and Inventions of the Nineteenth Century* (1876).

ROWAN, R. W. *Spy and Counter-Spy* (1928).

RUSSELL, BERTRAND. *The Impact of Science on Society* (1953).

SCHWEITZER, ALBERT. *The Decay and Restoration of Civilization* (1923).

SEELEY, JOHN. *Greater Britain* (1870).

SEELEY, JOHN. *The Expansion of England* (1883).

SIMPSON, F. A. *The Rise of Louis Napoleon* (1950).

SLADEN, NORMAN ST BARBE. *The Real Le Queux* (1938).

SOROKIN, PITIRIM. *Social Philosophies of an Age of Crisis* (1952).

SOULE, GEORGE. *The Shape of Tomorrow* (1958).

SUTTNER, BERTHA VON. *Memoirs. The Records of an Eventful Life* (1910).

SWINNERTON, FRANK. *The Georgian Literary Scene* (1938).

TAYLOR, A. J. P. *The Course of German History* (1961).

TAYLOR, A. J. P. *Rumours of Wars* (1952).

TAYLOR, A. J. P. *The Struggle for Mastery in Europe* (1954).

VAGTS, ALFRED. *A History of Militarism* (1959).

VALBERT, G. (CHERBULIEZ, V.). *Hommes et choses* (1883).

VASSILIEV, M., and GOUSCHEV, S. (eds.). *Life in the Twenty-First Century* (1960). (Translated from the Russian.)

WALTZ, K. N. *Man, the State and War* (1959).

WARD, A. C. *The Nineteen-Twenties* (1930).

WELLS, H. G. *Anticipations* (1902).

WELLS, H. G. *The Discovery of the Future* (1902).

WELLS, H. G. *The Fate of Homo Sapiens* (1939).

WELLS, H. G. *Mind at the End of its Tether* (1945).

WEST, G. *H. G. Wells* (1930).

WHITESIDE, THOMAS. *The Tunnel under the Channel* (1962).

WILLIAM II, KAISER. *Comparative History, 1878–1914* (1922).

WILLIAMS, HAROLD. *Modern English Writers, 1890–1914* (1918).

WINGFIELD-STRATFORD, ESMÉ. *Before the Lamps Went Out* (1945).

WOLSELEY, VISCOUNT. *The Story of a Soldier's Life* (1906).

WOODHOUSE, C. M. *British Foreign Policy since the Second World War* (1961).

WOODWARD, E. L. *The Age of Reform* (1958).

WOLSTENHOLME, GORDON (ed.). *Man and his Future* (1963).

B. *Select List of War Studies, 1770–1964*

(i) *1770–1870*

ANDERSON, J. *System of National Defence* (1853).

ANON. *Great Britain. The Danger of Invasion and means of Defence, fairly estimated: with a few remarks, submitted to the consideration of Government and of the public* (1803).

ANON. *Lettre à un ami sur l'utilité des globes volants de M. de Montgolfier et sur la possibilité de la prise de Gibraltar* (1783).

ANON. *Speculative Ideas on the Probable Consequences of an Invasion, on our late encampments, and on the state of some of the seaports in England* (1782).

BIRCH, CAPT. JOHN FRANCIS. *Memoir on the National Defence* (1808).

BLUNT, H. *Perils and Panics of Invasion, in 1796–7–8, 1804–5, and at the present time* (1860).

BOWLES, REAR-ADML. W. *Thoughts on National Defence* (1848).

BRERETON, MAJ.-GEN. W. *Measures for the Defence of England* (1859).

BRIALMONT, GEN. A. *A French (or rather a Belgian) Officer's Ideas upon the Defence of England. (Système de défense de l'Angleterre) Edited by A. Kinloch* (1860).

BRUCE, J. *Report on the Arrangements which were made for the Internal Defence of these Kingdoms, when Spain, by its Armada, projected the invasion and conquest of England; an application of the wise proceedings of our ancestors to the present crisis of public safety* (1798).

BURGOYNE, GEN. SIR JOHN FOX. *Military Opinions* (1859).

BURGOYNE, GEN. SIR JOHN FOX. *Observations on the Possible Results of a War with France under our present system of military preparation, with remarks on the military condition of Great Britain* (1852).

A CIVILIAN. *Hints for a Volunteer Coast Defence* (1853).

CREASY, E. S. *The Invasions and the Projected Invasions of England* (1852).

CROWE, JOHN WILLIAM. *A Few Words on the Militia Question* (1853).

DIROM, LT.-GEN. A. *Plans for the Defence of Great Britain and Ireland* (1797).

DOUGLAS, GEN. SIR HOWARD. *On the Defence of England: naval, littoral and internal* (1860).

FERGUSSON, JAMES. *The Peril of Portsmouth; or, French fleets and English ports* (1852).

FITZ-ROY, CAPT. ROBERT. *On the Application of Steam to Ships of War* (1853).

FLEMING, THOMAS WILLIS. *A Marine Militia; the country's best national defence* (1846).

FULTON, ROBERT. *Torpedo War and Submarine Explosions* (1810).

GARDINER, GEN. SIR R. *Political and Legislative Considerations on National Defence: addressed to the people of England* (1860).

GORE, M. *The National Defences* (1859).

GUSTAFSON, G. V. *Observations on the Steam Navy of Great Britain* (1847).

HALSTED, CAPT. E. P. *The Screw-fleet of the Navy* (1850).

HEAD, SIR FRANCIS B. *The Defenceless State of Great Britain* (1850).

JOINVILLE, PRINCE DE. *Note sur l'état des forces navales de la France* (1844).

JOINVILLE, PRINCE DE. *On the State of the Naval Strength of France* (1844).

KNOX, CAPT. C. *The Defensive Position of England* (1852).

LANG, J. D. *The Prospect of Australia in the event of a War with France* (1858). Sydney.

MAGRATH, LT. *An Historical Sketch of the Progress of the Art of War* (1838).

NAPIER, SIR CHARLES. *Defence of England* (1850).

NAPIER, SIR CHARLES. *A letter on the Defence of England* (1852).

POLLEXFEN, W. M. *The Unsinkable Vessel of War* (1850).

RANELAGH, LORD VISCOUNT. *Observations on the Present State of our National Defences* (1845).

A RETIRED OFFICER. *A few remarks on our present Inefficient Means of Defence against an Invasion* (1847).

RUSSELL, J. S. *The Fleet of the Future in 1862* (1862).

SALVADOR, CAPT. GABRIEL. *De l'agitation pour la défense nationale en Angleterre. Examen critique des principaux documents publiés sur cette question* (1848).

URQUHART, DAVID. *The Invasion of England* (1860).

(ii) *1870–1914*

ALDERSON, A. W. *The Extinction in Perpetuity of Armaments and War* (1908).

ANON. *The Coming War; or, England without a navy* (1875).

ANON. *Dans l'attente d'une guerre* (1887).

ANON. *Déploiement stratégique probable des forces allemandes sur la frontière française* (1881).

ANON. *Der strategische Aufmarsch der deutschen Truppen und der französischen Armee im nächsten deutsch-französischen Kriege* (1882). Translated from the French.

ANON. *Die Schweiz im Kriegsfalle* (1885).

ANON. *La Prochaine Guerre par un soldat* (1884).

ANON. *Russlands nächster Krieg. Eine strategische studie* (1888).

ANON. *Le Soldat dans la guerre de demain* (1912).

ANON. *Serons-nous vainqueurs? Quelques réflexions sur la prochaine guerre franco-allemande* (1887). Translated from the German.

ARCHEN, LT. *Les Ballons dirigeables: leur emploi comme arme offensive et les conditions du tir dirigé contre eux* (1908).

AUBOEUF, DR J. *Le Coup de massue (La prochaine guerre franco-allemande)* (1907).

ANON. (SALIS-SAMADEN, FREIHERR VON). *Ideen über unser militarisches Verhältniss bein einem Krieg mit Russland. Von einem österreichischen offizier* (1870). Vienna.

BARTHÉLEMY, H. *L'Alsace et la Lorraine; comment elles redeviendront françaises* (1887).

BARTHÉLEMY, H. *Avant la bataille* (1886).

BARTHÉLEMY, H. *La Guerre* (1888).

BARTHÉLEMY, H. *Paris en cas de guerre* (1895).

BAUMGARTEN-CRUSIUS, LT. *Der oesterreichisch-russische Zukunftskrieg. Eine studie über den wahrscheinlichen strategischen Aufmarsch der österreichischen und russischen Streitkräfte langs der galizischen Grenze* (1884). Hanover.

BERGET, A. *The Conquest of the Air* (1909).

BERNEY, REV. THOMAS. *The Battle of the Channel Tunnel and Dover Castle and Forts* (1882).

BERNHARDI, FRIEDRICH ADAM JULIUS VON. *Deutschland und der nächste Krieg* (1912).

BLATCHFORD, R. *Germany and England* (1909).

BLEIBTREU, KARL. *Deutschland und England* (1909).

BLOCH, I. S. *Modern Weapons and Modern War; being an abridgement of 'The war of the future in its technical, economic and political relations'* (1900).

BONNAL, GÉNÉ. *La Prochaine Guerre* (1906).

BOUCHER, COL. ARTHUR. *L'Allemagne en péril* (1914).

BOUCHER, COL. ARTHUR. *La France victorieuse dans la guerre de demain* (1911).

BOUCHER, Col. ARTHUR. *L'offensive contre l'Allemagne* (1911).

BRIDGE, ADM. SIR CYPRIAN A. G. *Sea-power* (1910).

BRUCHHAUSEN, MAJ. VON. *Der kommende Krieg* (1906).

CHESNEY, GEN. SIR G. T. *The 'Confusion worse confounded' at the War Office* (1891).

CLOWES, WILLIAM LAIRD. *The Royal Navy: a history from the earliest times to the present* (1897).

COLIN, COMDT. J. *The Transformations of War* (1912). Translated from the French.

COLIN, COMDT. J. *France and the next war* (1914). Translated from the French.

COLLINSON, GEN. T. B. *On the Present Facilities for the Invasion of England, and for the Defence thereof* (1876).

COLOMB, VICE-ADM. P. H. *Essays on Naval Defence* (1869).

CORNFORD, LESLIE COPE. *The Defenceless Islands* (1906).

DANIEL (Pseud.). *The Writing on the Wall* (1911).

DAUDET, LÉON. *L'avant-guerre. Études et documents sur l'espionage juif-allemand en France depuis l'affaire Dreyfus* (1913).

DAULE, S. *Der Kriegswagen der Zukunft* (1906).

DELAISI, FRANCIS. *La Guerre qui vient* (1911).

DELAISI, FRANCIS. *The Inevitable War* (1915). Boston, Mass.

DELAISI, FRANCIS. *Der kommende Krieg* (1915).

DESBRIÈRE, ÉDOUARD. *Projets et tentatives de débarquement aux Îles Britanniques, 1793–1805* (1900–2).

DEWAR, LIEUT. A. C. *Is Invasion Impossible?* (1909).

DIBOS, CAPT. M. *Les Aérostats dans leur utilisation* (1893).

UN DIPLOMATE. *La France et l'Allemagne en 1906; la guerre possible* (1906).

DUCOMMUN, ÉLIE. *The Probable Consequences of a European War* (1906).

EDELSHEIM, FREIHERR VON. *Operations upon the Sea* (1914). New York.

EDELSHEIM, FREIHERR VON. *Operationen zur See* (1901).

ELLIOTT, ADM. SIR G. *Future Naval Battles* (1885).

F. *Darf Russland einen Angriff auf den Bosporus wagen?* (1892). Vienna.

FABIUS (Pseud.). *Invasion and Defence. How a formidable invasion might be met and defeated* (1909).

FALKENHAUSEN, GEN. VON. *Der grosse Krieg der Jetztzeit. Eine studie über Bewegung und Kampf der Massenheere des 20en Jahrhunderts* (1909).

FALKENHAUSEN, GEN. VON. *Kriegführung und Wissenschaft* (1913).

FOCH, MARSHAL FERDINAND. *The Principles of War* (1918).

FRÉMY, ARNOULD. *La Guerre future* (1875).

FROBENIUS, H. *The German Empire's Hour of Destiny* (1914).

FROBENIUS, H. *Des deutschen Reiches Schicksalstunde* (1914).

GRAHAME-WHITE, CLAUDE, and HARPER, HARRY. *The Aeroplane in War* (1912).

GRANT, CAPT. J. G. *The Defence of the Tay* (1888).

GROUARD, LT.-COL. AUGUSTE. *France et Allemagne. La guerre eventuelle* (1913).

HAMLEY, GEN. SIR EDWARD. *National Defence* (1889).

HANNA, COL. H. B. *Can Germany invade England?* (1912).

HANNEKEN, GEN.-LT. H. VON. *Vorstudien für einen englisch-russischen Krieg* (1878).

HANNEKEN, GEN.-LT. H. VON. *Studies on the probable course and result of a War between Russia and England* (1878).

HEARNE, R. P. *Aerial Warfare* (1909).

HERON, ROBERT MATTHEWS. *The War Scare in Europe* (1889). (Translation and enlargement of *La question allemande*, 1888, by same author.)

HISLAM, PERCIVAL A. *The Admiralty of the Atlantic* (1908).

HISLAM, PERCIVAL A. *The North Sea Problem* (1913).

HOHENLOHE-INGELFINGEN, GEN. PRINCE KRAFT. *Letters on cavalry* (1989).

HOHENLOHE-INGELFINGEN, GEN. PRINCE KRAFT. *Letters on strategy* (1897).

HOZIER, COL. SIR H. M. *The Channel Tunnel* (1888).

HOZIER, CAPT. H. M. *The Invasions of England; a history of the past with lessons for the future* (1876).

HUGHES, NATHAN C. *The Channel Tunnel; or England in danger* (1882).

HUMBERT, COL. GUSTAVE. *La Prochaine Guerre* (1900).

HURD, A., and CASTLE, H. *German Sea-Power* (1913).

HUTCHINSON, GEN. W. N. *The Navigable Balloon in War and Peace* (1888).

ISLANDER (Pseud.). *The Naval and Military Situation of the British Isles* (1913).

JANE, F. T. *Heresies of Sea Power* (1906).

JANE, F. T. *The Torpedo in Peace and War* (1898).

KELLER, ÉMILE. *La Guerre de demain* (Extrait du *Correspondant*) (1891).

KNOWLES, J. *The Channel Tunnel and public opinion* (1883).

KOETTSCHAU, OBERSTLT. C. *Der nächste deutsch-französische Krieg. Eine militärisch-politische Studie* (1886–7).

KOETTSCHAU, OBERSTLT. C. *La Prochaine Guerre franco-allemande* (1887).

KOETTSCHAU, OBERSTLT. C. *The Coming Franco-German War* (1887).

LAUBEUF, A. M. *Les Luttes maritimes prochaines* (1908).

LAUBEUF, A. M. *Naval Supremacy* (1908).

LEA, HOMER. *The Day of the Saxon* (1912).

LEBERECHT, G. F. *Luftfahrten im Frieden und im Kriege* (1913).

LECOMTE, MAXIME, and LEVI, LT.-COL. CAMILLE. *Neutralité belge et invasion allemande: histoire; stratégie* (1914).

LENSCHAU, DR THOMAS (ed.). *England in deutscher Beleuchtung* (1906).

LE QUEUX, W. *Spies of the Kaiser, plotting the downfall of England* (1909).

LICHNOWSKY, FURST. *Gehen wir einem Kriege mit Grossbritannien entegen?* (1908).

LONGRIDGE, J. A. *The Artillery of the Future, and the New Powders* (1891).

MAITROT, GÉN. *Nos frontières de l'Est et du Nord* (1912).

MALO, CHARLES. *La Prochaine guerre* (1912).

MALTZAHN, VIZE-ADML. C. *German and British naval armaments as a product of historical development and of maritime strategy.* Translated from the *Deutsche Revue* (1911).

MARTIN, R. *Das Zeitalter der Motorluftschiffahrt* (1907).

MARTIN, R. *Deutschland und England: ein offenes Wort an den Kaiser* (1908).

MAUDE, COL. F. N. *The Invasion and Defence of England* (1888).

MAUDE, COL. F. N. *War and the World's Life* (1907).

MAURICE, MAJ.-GEN. SIR J. F. *National Defences* (1897).

MEYER, HAUPTMANN A. *Der Krieg im Zeitalter des Verkehrs und der Technik* (1909).

MORDACQ, COMDT. *Essais stratégiques. La durée de la prochaine guerre* (1912).

MOULTON, RT. HON. LORD. *Science and War* (1919).
NAQUET, GUSTAVE. *L'Europe délivrée: histoire prophetique de 1871 à 1892* (1871).
NERCY, GUSTAVE. *La Future Débâcle* (1896).
NOLTE, FRÉDÉRIC. *L'Europe militaire* (1884).
OSMAN BEY (MAJ. VLADIMIR ANDRÉJEVICH). *La Guerre à l'horizon* (1890).
PALAT, GÉN. *Les probabilités d'une guerre franco-allemande* (1913).
PAVLOVITCH, MICHEL (LAZARAVICH, MIKHAIL). *Le conflit anglo-allemand; la guerre improbable* (1912).
PINON, R. *France et Allemagne, 1870–1913* (1913).
OSTEN-SACKEN-RHEIN, OBERSTLT. *Deutschlands nächster Krieg* (1905).
R., VON. *'Die Invasion Englands in englischer Beleuchtung.' Marine Rundschau* (November 1908).
ROBERTS, FIELD-MARSHAL LORD. *National Security. Speech delivered in the House of Lords on 23rd November, 1908* (1908).
ROSS, MAJ. C. *The Problem of National defence* (1907).
ROUTIER, CAPT. FERNAND. *L'Espionnage et la trahison en temps de paix et en temps de guerre* (1914).
SCHEEBART, P. *Die Entwicklung des Luftmilitarismus und die Auflösung der europäischen Land-Heere, Festungen und Seeflotten* (1909).
SCHWARTE, M. *Technik des Kriegswesens* (1913).
SEGUIN, LOUIS. *La Prochaine Guerre* (1880).
SEGUIN, LOUIS. *Der nächste Krieg* (1881).
SIWINNA, CARL. *Vademecum für Phantasiestrategen* (1906) (Kattowitz).
SORB, CAPT. *Armée, marine, colonies* (1908).
SORB, CAPT. *La Doctrine de défense nationale . . . La prochaine guerre franco-allemande, etc.* (1912).
SUTTNER, BERTHA VON. *Lay Down your Arms* (1892).
SUTTNER, BERTHA VON. *When Thoughts will Soar* (1914).
T. L. H. *Au lendemain de la loi de 3 ans. La guerre contre l'Allemagne. Étude stratégique à l'usage des gens du monde* (1914).
VALLET, LT. A. *L'aviation militaire* (1913).
VAMBERY, ARMINIUS. *La lutte future pour la possession de l'Inde* (1885).
VON DER GOLTZ, BARON COLMAR. *The Nation in Arms* (1906).
WALTER, MAJ. J. *England's Naval and Military Weakness* (1882).
WALTER, MAJ. J. *England's Volunteer Force* (1888).
WILSON, CAPT. C. H. *Offence, not defence* (1907).

X. *Armée anglaise et guerre continentale* (1912).

X, Comdt. *Ce que nous réserve la prochaine guerre* (1893).

Z., Commandant (Pseud.). *Les Guerres navales de demain* (1891).

Zéryn, Comte. *La Débâcle de l'Allemagne dans la prochaine guerre* (1905).

(iii) *1915–64*

Alléhaut, Général. *Être prêts: puissance aérienne, forces de terre; doctrine, organisation, moral* (1935).

Ancona, Gén. A. *Gli aggressivi chimici e la difesa della popolazione civile* (1936). Rome.

Andrews, Marshall. *Disaster Through Air Power* (1950). New York.

Anon. *Die wirtschaftlichen Vorbereitungen der Auslandsstaaten für den Zukunftskrieg* (1926).

Bakeless, John. *Origin of the Next War* (1926).

Bauer, Ludwig. *War Again Tomorrow* (1932). Translated from the German.

Beaton, Leonard, and Maddox, John. *The Spread of Nuclear Weapons* (1962).

Belli de Pino, Anton v. *Der Krieg der Zukunft im Urteil des Auslandes* (1936).

Bergh, Oberst E. van den. *Volk und Heer im Krieg der Zukunft; eine Überschau für jedermann* (1938).

Bircher, Oberstdivisionar Eugen, and Clam, Ernst. *Krieg ohne Gnade; von Tannenberg zur Schlacht der Zukunft* (1937). Zürich.

Bos, C. *Les Hécatombes de la guerre prochaine* (1923).

Brodie, Bernard. *Strategy in the Missile Age* (1959).

Bull, Hedley. *The Control of the Arms Race* (1961).

Burney, Comdr. Sir C. D. *The World, the Air and the Future* (1929).

Campbell, Sir Malcolm. *The Peril from the Air* (1937).

Charlton, Air Comm. L. E. O. *The Menace of the Clouds* (1937).

Charlton, Air Comm. L. E. O. *The Next War* (1937).

Charlton, Air Comm. L. E. O. *War from the Air; Past, present, future* (1935).

Charlton, Air Comm. L. E. O. *War over England* (1936).

Davies, J. Langdon. *Air Raid; the technique of Silent Approach* (1938).

DONINGTON, R. and B. *The Citizen Faces War* (1936).

DORMAN SMITH, COL. E. E. *Infantry in the Next War* (1938).

DOUHET, GIULIO. *The Command of the Air* (1943). Translated from the Italian.

DUCHÉ, ROBERT. *Un plan de guerre contre l'Allemagne; étude stratégique* (1929).

DUPUY, MAJ. RICHARD ERNEST, and ELIOT, MAJ. GEORGE FIELDING. *U.S.A. If War Comes* (1937). New York.

DUTIL, CAPT. L. *Les Chars d'assaut: leur création et leur rôle pendant la Guerre 1915–18* (1919).

FAURE, PIERRE. *Vers un nouveau Charleroi* (1931).

FAURE, PIERRE. *L'avion tuera la guerre* (1935).

FROBENIUS, OBERSTLT. H. *Schwestern der Schicksalstunde* (1915).

FULLER, COL. J. F. C. *The Influence of tanks on Cavalry tactics* (1920).

FULLER, COL. J. F. C. *Tanks in Future Warfare* (1921).

GOLOVINE, GEN. N. N. *Air Strategy* (1936).

GOLOVINE, GEN. N. N. *The Problem of the Pacific* (1922).

GRENFELL, COMDR. RUSSELL. *Sea Power in the Next War* (1938).

GROVES, BRIG.-GEN. P. R. C. *Our Future in the Air* (1935).

GUDERIAN, GEN.-MAJ. H. *Achtung—Panzer!* (1938).

IRWIN, W. *'The Next War': an appeal to common sense* (1921). New York.

ISHIMARU, LT.-COMDR. T. *The Next World War* (1937). Translated from the Japanese.

JUSTROW, OBERSTLT. K. *Der technische Krieg* (1938).

KAHN, HERMAN. *Thinking about the Unthinkable* (1963).

KAHN, HERMAN. *On Thermonuclear War* (1960).

KARIG, WALTER. *War in the Atomic Age?* (1946). New York.

KENNWORTHY, J. M. *Will Civilisation Crash?* (1927).

KINDELÁN, ALFREDO. *La Proxima Guerra* (1945). Madrid.

KISSINGER, HENRY A. *Nuclear Weapons and Foreign Policy* (1957).

KLOTZ, H. *Der neue deutsche Krieg* (1937).

KNORR, KLAUS, and READ, THORNTON. *Limited Strategic War* (1962).

LAPP, RALPH E. *Kill and Overkill* (1962).

LIDDELL HART, B. H. *Paris; or, the Future of War* (1925).

LIDDELL HART, B. H. *Deterrent or Defence* (1960).

LIEPMANN, H. *Death from the Skies* (1937). Translated from the German.

LUDENDORFF, GEN. ERICH. *The Coming War* (1931).

LUDENDORFF, GEN. ERICH. *The Nation at War* (1936).

MAITROT, GÉN. *La Prochaine Guerre* (1921).

MIKSCHE, FERDINAND OTTO. *Unconditional Surrender* (1952).

MIKSCHE, FERDINAND OTTO. *War between Continents* (1948).

MORDACQ, HENRI. *Les Leçons de 1914 et la prochaine guerre* (1934).

MORRETTA, ROCCO. *Come sarà la guerra di domani?* (1934). Rome.

MURPHY, P. *Armadas of the Sky: the Problem of Armaments* (1931).

OSGOOD, ROBERT ENDICOTT. *Limited War* (1957).

PACINOTTI, GIOVANNI. *La Guerra che non prevediamo* (1946). Rome.

PINON, R. *Les problèmes d'aujourd'hui* (1924).

POSSONY, S. T. *To-morrow's War, its Planning, Management and Cost* (1938).

REINHARDT, GEORGE C. *Atomic Weapons in Land Combat* (1953).

RITTER, HAUPT. H. *Der Luftkrieg* (1926).

RITTER, HAUPT. H. *Der Zukunftskrieg und seine Waffen* (1924).

ROGERSON, CAPT. SIDNEY. *Propaganda in the Next War* (1938).

ROUGERON, CAMILLE. *La Prochaine Guerre* (1948).

ROWAN, R. W. *Spy and Counter-Spy* (1928).

SCHUTTEL, MAJ. L. *Fallschirmtruppen und Luftinfanterie* (1938).

SCHWARTE, GEN.-LT. M. *Die Technik im Zukunftskrieg* (1923).

SHEPPARD, MAJ. E. W. *Tanks in the Next War* (1938).

SIKORSKI, GEN. W. *La Guerre moderne* (1935).

SLESSOR, WING COMDR. J. C. *Air Power and Armies* (1936).

SORB, COMDT. (CORNIER, JULES AUGUSTE). *La Revanche de l'Allemagne; la guerre qui vient; l'Angleterre menacée* (1928).

SPAIGHT, J. M. *Air Power in the Next War* (1938).

STERNBERG, F. *Germany and a lightning war* (1939). Translated from the German.

STRACHEY, JOHN. *On the Prevention of War* (1962).

SUETER, REAR-ADML. SIR M. *The Evolution of the Tank* (1937).

THUILLIER, MAJ.-GEN. SIR H. F. *Gas in the Next War* (1939)

VAUTHIER, LT.-COL. *Le Danger aérien et l'avenir du pays* (1930).

VELPRY, LT.-COL. *L'avenir des chars de combat* (1923).

WYNNE, CAPT. G. C. *If Germany Attacks* (1940).

C. *Check List of Imaginary Wars, 1763–1965*

The following list is arranged in chronological order. It gives all titles of imaginary wars so far discovered. The place of publication has been omitted for English works published in London, German works published in Berlin, and French works published in Paris. American publications later published in the United Kingdom are indicated as 'First printed U.S.A.'

1763 ANON. *The Reign of George VI.*

1803 ANON. *The Invasion of England. A farce in three acts.*

1806 BURKE, WILLIAM. *The Armed Briton; or, the invaders vanquished. A play in four acts.*

1841 GEOFFROY, LOUIS. *Napoléon Apocryphe, 1812–32. Histoire de la conquête du Monde et de la Monarchie universelle.*

1851 ANON. *A history of the Sudden and Terrible Invasion of England by the French in . . . May, 1852.*

1854 COEURDEROY, ERNEST. *Hurrah!!! ou la Révolution par les Cosaques.*

1870 RICHARDS, ALFRED BATES. *The Invasion of England.* Printed privately in August 1870.

1871 ANON. (SIR GEORGE TOMKYNS CHESNEY). *The Battle of Dorking: Reminiscences of a Volunteer.* First printed in *Blackwood's Magazine,* May 1871; and subsequently republished in numerous special editions. The literature relating to the *Battle of Dorking* episode is listed below:

1. *Overseas Editions in English*

The Fall of England? The Battle of Dorking: Reminiscences of a Volunteer (New York, 1871).

The German Conquest of England in 1875, and Battle of Dorking; or Reminiscences of a Volunteer (Philadelphia, 1871). This edition was also published in Toronto by Adam, Stevenson & Co. in 1871.

The Battle of Dorking: being an account of the German invasion of England, and capture of London & Woolwich, &c, as told by a Volunteer to his Grandchildren (Toronto; Copp, Clark, 1871).

The Battle of Dorking. Reminiscences of a Volunteer. Reprinted from Blackwood's Magazine for May 1871 (Melbourne, 1871).

Reminiscences of a Volunteer, A.D. 1925. The Battle of Dorking. Abridged version published in the *Otago Witness,* Dunedin, 19 August 1871, pp. 10–11; 26 August 1871, pp. 5–7.

2. *Foreign Translations*

A batalha de Dorking. Episodio do conquista da Inglaterra pela Allemanha em 187–. (Rio de Janeiro, 1871). In this edition the authorship was attributed to Benjamin Disraeli.

La Bataille de Dorking (1871). Preface by Charles Yriarte.

Die Schlacht bei Dorking. Grenzboten, vol. 30, 1871; pp. 870–9; 910–24; 936–47; 796–90.

Engelands Val. 1875–1925 (1871). Deventer.

Englands Ende in der Schlacht bei Dorking (1879) (Hamburg).

Il Racconto di un guardiano di spiaggia (1872) (Rome).

Slaget vid Dorking (1872). Fahlun.

Was England erwartet. Voraussagen eines englischen Militärschriftstellers aus dem Jahre 1871 (1940).

3. *Related Works*

ANON. *After the Battle of Dorking; or, what became of the invaders?* (1871).

ANON. *The Battle of Foxhill* (1871).

ANON. *The Battle of Dorking: a myth* (1871).

The Battle of Berlin. Celebrated Medley written by Frank W. Green, Esq. Music composed and arranged by Carl Bernstein (1871).

The Battle of Dorking. A dream of John Bull's. Written by Frank W. Green, Esq. The music arranged by Carl Bernstein (1871).

ANON. *The Battle of the Ironclads; or, England and her foes in 1879* (1871).

ANON. *Britannia in Council* (1871).

ANON. *The Cruise of the Anti-Torpedo* (1871).

ANON. *The Hens who tried to Crow* (1871).

ANON. *The Suggested Invasion of England by the Germans* (1871). A translation of a facetious German scheme for invasion. See entry under J. M. Trutz-Baumwoll.

ANON. *The Official Despatches and Correspondence relative to the Battle of Dorking, as moved for in the House of Commons. 21st July 1920* (1871).

ANON. *Our Hero: or, who wrote 'The Battle of Dorking'* (1871).

ANON. (HAYWARD, A.). *The Second Armada* (1871).

ANON. (STONE, CHARLES). *What Happened after the Battle of Dorking; or, the Victory of Tunbridge Wells* (1871).

HEMYNG, BRACEBRIDGE. *The Commune in London; or, thirty years hence, a chapter of anticipated history* (1871).

HUNTER, LT.-COL. WILLIAM. *Army Speech by an old Harrovian dedicated to those who have been frightened by the Battle of Dorking* (1871).

LEIGHTON, SIR BALDWYN. *The Lull before Dorking* (1871).

M., J. W. *The Coming Cromwell* (1871).

M., J. W. *The Siege of London. Reminiscences of 'Another Volunteer'* (1871).

MCCAULEY, MOTLEY RANK (Pseud.). *Chapters from Future History* (1871).

MOLTRUHN, M. (Pseud.). *The Other Side at the Battle of Dorking* (1871).

SKETCHLEY, ARTHUR. *Mrs Brown on the Battle of Dorking* (1871).

TRUTZ-BAUMWOLL, J. M. (Pseud.). *Sendschreiben des deutsch-englischen Zukunftspolitikers . . . an S.M. den Deutschen Kaiser* (*Ausserordentliche Beilage zur Allgemeinen Zeitung*, Nr. 154, 3 June 1871).

1871 DANGIN, ÉDOUARD. *La Bataille de Berlin en 1875.*

1873 STAMPF, FR. *La Dernière Bataille* (*Die letzte Schlacht*). Allegedly translated from the German by Edmond Thiaudière.

[1874] MACAULAY, CLARENDON (Adams, Walter Marsham). *The Carving of Turkey.*

1874 VOSS, RICHARD. *Visionen eines deutschen Patrioten.* Zürich.

1875 ANON. *The Battle of Pluck.*

ANON. *Europa's Fate.*

ANON. *La Guerre future.*

1876 ANON. *La France et l'Allemagne au printemps prochain.*

ANON. *The Invasion of 1883.* Glasgow.

ANON. *A Parallel Case; or, the Straits of Dover question. A.D. 2345.* Darlington.

CASSANDRA (Pseud.). *The Channel Tunnel; or, England's ruin.*

1877 ANON. *Fifty Years Hence.*

LA MÈCHE, GÉN. *La Guerre franco-allemande de 1878.*

1878 ANON. *Gortschakoff and Bismarck; or, Europe in 1940.*

1879 ANON. (CHESNEY, SIR GEORGE TOMKYNS) *The New Ordeal.*

DEKHNEWALLAH, A. (Pseud.). *The Great Russian invasion of India.*

1881 BOLAND, HENRI. *La Guerre prochaine entre la France et l'Allemagne.*

LANG-TUNG (Pseud.). *The Decline and Fall of the British Empire.*

SPERBER-NIBORSKI, LEON. *Krieg mit Russland!* Loeban.

1882 A., F. *The Seizure of the Channel Tunnel.*

ANON. *The Channel Tunnel: a poem.*

ANON. *Ireland's War! Parnell victorious.* New York.

ANON. *1900. Garde à vous! De la Sprée à l'Escaut par la Marne.*

ANON. *The Story of the Channel Tunnel.*

ANON. (BUTLER, SIR W. F.). *The Invasion of England.*

THE DEMURE ONE (Pseud.). *The Battle of Boulogne.*

GRIP (Pseud.). *How John Bull lost London.*

GUTHRIE, T. A. *The Seizure of the Channel Tunnel.*

1883 ANON. *The Battle of the Moy; or, how Ireland gained her independence in 1892–1894.*

ANON. *The Battle of Port Said.* Translated as *La Bataille de Port Said,* 1883.

ANON. *La Guerre de 1884.*

ANON. *India in 1983.* Calcutta.

FORTH, C. *The Surprise of the Channel Tunnel.*

1884 DEBANS, CAMILLE. *Les Malheurs de John Bull.*

POSTERITAS (Pseud.). *The Siege of London.*

1885 ANON. *The Battle of Tomorrow.*

ANON. *The Great War and Disastrous Peace of 1885.*

BARILLET-LAGARGOUSSE. *La Guerre finale; histoire fantastique.*

GREER, T. *A Modern Daedalus.*

POSTERITAS (Pseud.). *La Bataille de Londres en 188.* Translation of *The Siege of London.*

X. *La Revanche.*

1886 ANON. *The Great Irish Rebellion of 1886.*

ANON. *Newry Bridge; or, Ireland in 1887.*

ANON. *Openings and Proceedings of the Irish Parliament.*

LESTER, EDWARD. *The Siege of Bodike.*

S., H. W. *Wie wir Indien verloren.* Translated from the English original published at Allahabad, India.

1887 ANON. (CLOWES, W. L., and BURGOYNE, A. H.). *The Great Naval War of 1887.*

ANON. *Der rache Krieg zwischen Frankreich und Deutschland.* Hanover.

ANON. *Plus d'Angleterre.*

ANON. *La Première Bataille.*

CAPTAIN OF THE ROYAL NAVY, A. *The battle off Worthing.*

GOPČEVIČ, SPIRIDION. *The Conquest of Britain in 1888.* Translation *Der grosse Seekrieg im Jahre 1888.* First published in *Internationale Revue über die gesamten Armeen und Flotten,* July–Sept. 1886.

HOPE, LT.-COL. W. *An omitted incident in the 'Great Naval War of 1887'.*

MONFALCONE, PIERRE, and CASTELIN, ANDRÉ. *La Première Bataille Franco-Allemande le 18 Août 18... Réponse a la brochure: Die erste Schlacht im Zukunftskriege par le Général. . . .*

PEDDIE, J. *The Capture of London.*

ROBIDA, ALBERT. *La Guerre au vingtième siècle.*

1888 ANON. *La Bataille de Damvillers.*

ANON. *'Down with England!'* Translation of *Plus d'Angleterre* (1887).

ANON. *Der europäische Coalitionskrieg.* Hanover.

ANON. *Der Krieg in Galizien im Frühjahr 1888.* Minden.

ANON. *Plus encore d'Angleterre; or, repulse of the French.*

ARNOLD-FORSTER, H. O. *In a Conning Tower.*

BARTON, SAMUEL. *The Battle of the Swash; and the capture of Canada.* New York.

BLEIBTREU, KARL. *Die Entscheidungsschlachten des europäischen Krieges, 18...* Leipzig.

1. *Die Schlacht von Bochnia.*
2. *Die Schlacht bei Belfort.*
3. *Die Schlacht bei Châlons.*

LESTER, H. F. *The Taking of Dover.*

ROPE, CHARLES. *Opérations sur les côtes de la Méditerranée et de la Baltique au printemps de 1888.*

1889 ANON. *The Bombardment of Scarbro' by the Russian fleet in 1891.*

ANON. *La Prise de Cherbourg.*

CROMIE, ROBERT. *For England's sake.*

1889/1893 DANRIT, CAPITAINE (DRIANT, E. A.). *La Guerre en forteresse.*

DANRIT, CAPITAINE (DRIANT, E. A.). *La Guerre en rase campagne.*

DANRIT, CAPITAINE (DRIANT, E. A.). *La Guerre en ballon.*

1890 ANON. (WATSON, H. C. M.). *Decline and Fall of the British Empire.*

STOCHASTIC (Pseud.). *The Stricken Nation.* New York.

WALSH, RUPERT. *The Fate of the Triple Alliance.*

1891 FERRÉOL, PIERRE. *La Prise de Londres au XXe siècle.*

GOPČEVIĆ, SPIRIDION. *Comment la France conquit l'Angleterre en 1888.* See entry of 1887.

1892 CLOWES, WILLIAM LAIRD. *The Captain of the 'Mary Rose'.*

COLOMB, REAR-ADML. P., and others. *The Great War of 189–*. Translated as *Der grosse Krieg von 189–* (1894).
LE FAURE, GEORGES. *La Guerre sous l'eau.*
LA FAURE, GEORGES. *Mort aux Anglais!*
SEAFORTH, A. N. (Pseud.). *The Last Great Naval war.*
SOMNOLENT (Pseud.). *Invasion of England in the 19th century.* Madras.
1893 SMITH, J. H. DE VILLIERS. *The Great Southern Revolution.* Cape Town.
1894 ANON. *La France et la Russie contre la Triple Alliance.*
DANRIT, CAPITAINE (DRIANT, E. A.). *La Guerre au vingtième siècle.*
EARDLEY-WILMOT, CAPT. S. *The Next Naval War.*
GARCON, AUGUSTIN (Translator). *Un corsaire anglais.* Condensed version of *The Captain of the 'Mary Rose'* (1893).
LE QUEUX, WILLIAM. *The Great War in England in 1897.*
THE EARL OF MAYO. *The War Cruise of the Aries.* Dublin.
NIGOTE, CHARLES. *La Bataille de la Vesles.*
ROSA, SAMUEL ALBERT. *The Coming Terror; or the Australian Revolution.* Sydney.
1895 ANON. (CLOWES, W. L. and WILSON, BECCLES). *The Siege of Portsmouth.* (*Portsmouth Mail*, June, 1895.)
COVERDALE, SIR HENRY STANDISH (Pseud.). *The Fall of the Great Republic.* Boston, Mass.
1895/1896 DANRIT, CAPITAINE (DRIANT, E. A.). *L'Invasion noire.*
DANYERS, G. *Blood is Thicker than Water.*
EASTWICK, J. *The New Centurion.*
JANE, F. T. *Blake of the 'Rattlesnake'.*
LERMINA, JULES. *La Bataille de Strasbourg.*
MACKAY, KENNETH. *The Yellow Wave; a romance of the Asiatic invasion of Australia.*
X (FAWKES, F. ATTFIELD). *Marmaduke, Emperor of Europe.*
1896 ANSON, CAPT. (Editor?). *The Great Anglo-American War of 1900.*
BURTON, FRANCIS G. *The Naval Engineer and the command of the sea.*
CROMIE, ROBERT. *The Next Crusade.*
DANRIT, CAPITAINE (DRIANT, E. A.). *Le Journal de guerre du Lieutenant von Piefke.*
TRACY, LOUIS. *The Final War.*
1897 ANON. *The Back Door.* Hong Kong.
BJELOMOR, A. *Der Zukuntftskrieg im Jahre 18..* Dresden.

GLEIG, CHARLES. *When All Men Starve.*

GORST, H. E. *Without Bloodshed.*

GRIFFITH, GEORGE. *Briton or Boer?*

HENDOW, Z. S. *The Future Power; or, the great revolution of 190–.*

PALMER, J. H. *The Invasion of New York; or, how Hawaii was annexed.*

TRACY, LOUIS. *An American Emperor.*

1898 DAVENPORT, BENJAMIN RUSH. *Anglo-Saxons Onwards!* Cleveland, Ohio.

GRAVES, C. L., and LUCAS, E. V. *The War of the Wenuses.*

HAMPSON, J. N. *Great Britain vs. France and Russia.* (*National Review*, June 1898.)

MORRIS, J. *What Will Japan Do?*

SHIEL, M. P. *The Yellow Danger.*

TRACY, LOUIS. *The Lost Provinces.*

WELLS, H. G. *The War of the Worlds.*

WILSON, H. W., and WHITE, A. *When War Breaks Out.*

1899 ARGUS (Pseud.). *La Guerra del 190..* Con prefazione di D. Bonamico. Pubblicazione della *Lega Navale Italiana.* Spezia.

GRIFFITH, G. *The Great Pirate Syndicate.*

HILL, HEADON (GRANGER, F. E.). *Spies of the Wight.*

JANE, F. T. *The Violet Flame.*

LE QUEUX, W. *England's Peril.*

STEVENSON, P. L. *How the Jubilee Fleet escaped destruction, and the Battle of Ushant.*

1900 ANON. (MAUDE, COL. F. N.). *The New Battle of Dorking.*

DE NOUSSANNE, HENRI. *La Guerre Anglo-Franco-Russe.* Special number of *Le Monde Illustré*, 10 March.

EISENHART, DR KARL. *Die Abrechnung mit England.* Munich.

ERDMANN, GUSTAV ADOLF. *Wehrlos zur See; eine Flottenphantasie an der Jahrhundertwende.*

X., LIEUTENANT. *La Guerre avec l'Angleterre.*

OFFIN, T. W. *How the Germans took London.*

1901 ANON. *The Sack of London in the Great French war of 1901.*

CAIRNES, CAPT. *The Coming Waterloo.*

1901/2 DANRIT, CAPITAINE (DRIANT, E. A.). *La Guerre fatale France-Angleterre.*

DEMOLDER, EUGÈNE *L'Agonie d'Albion.* (Later translated as: *Albions Todeskampf*, Munich, 1915.)

DOWNEY, E. *London's Peril.*

FORD, WILLIAM WILBRAHAM. *Psyche, 1902.*

PEMBERTON, M. *Pro Patria.*

SHIEL, M. P. *The Lord of the Sea.*

TRACY, LOUIS. *The Invaders.*

1902 CURTIS, ALBERT CHARLES. *A New Trafalgar.*

STABLES, W. G. *The Cruise of the 'Vengeful'.*

1903 ANON. *The Boy Galloper.*

BACKSIGHT FORETHOUGHT (SWINTON, SIR EDWARD). *The defence of Duffers Drift.*

CHILDERS, ERSKINE. *The Riddle of the Sands.*

HILL, H. (GRAINGER, F. E.). *Seaward for the Foe.*

MEHEMED, EMI EFENDI. *Das neue Weltreich.* Leipzig.

UBIQUE (GUGGISBERG, CAPT. F.). *Modern warfare, or, how our soldiers fight.*

1904 CLARKE, A. *Starved into Surrender.*

HALL, G. R. *Black Fortnight; or, the invasion of 1915.*

NIEMANN, A. *Der Weltkrieg—Deutsche Träume.* Translated as *The Coming Conquest of England.*

1905 ANON. (MILLS, E. E.). *The Decline and Fall of the British Empire.*

BARNES, J. *Unpardonable War.*

CLOWES, SIR WILLIAM LAIRD, and BURGOYNE, ALAN H. *Trafalgar Refought.*

CONDOR (Pseud.). *Im Kampf um Südamerika.*

DANRIT, CAPITAINE (DRIANT, E. A.). *L'Invasion jaune.*

IVOI, PAUL, and ROYET, COL. *La Patrie en danger.*

S. *'Sink, burn, destroy.' Der Schlag gegen Deutschland!*

STABLES, G. *The Meteor Flag of England.*

1906 ANON. *Völker Europas . . . ! Der krieg der Zukunft.*

BEOWULF (Pseud.). *Der deutsch-englische Krieg.*

CASSANDRE (Pseud.). *Une guerre franco-allemande.*

GENERAL STAFF (Pseud.). *The Writing on the Wall.*

GENERAL STAFF (Pseud.). *Mene, mene tekel upharsin! Englands Überwältigung durch Deutschland. Von einem englischen Generalstabsoffizier. Autorisierte Übersetzung von einem deutschen Stabsoffizier.* Hanover.

GOY, LUCIEN. *La Bataille de 1915.*

HANSA (HOEPNER, KAPT. A. D.). *Hamburg und Bremen in Gefahr!*

LE QUEUX, WILLIAM. *The Invasion of 1910.*
LE QUEUX, WILLIAM. *Der Einfall der Deutschen in England.*
LE QUEUX, WILLIAM. *Die Invasion von 1910.*
MORITURUS (Pseud.). *Mit deutschen Waffen über Paris nach London.* Hanover.
OLDMEADOW, E. *The North Sea Bubble.*
SEESTERN (GRAUTOFF, F. H.). *'1906'—Der Zusammenbruch der alten Welt.* Leipzig.
VAUX, P. *The Shock of Battle.*
WOOD, W. *The Enemy in our Midst.*

1907 ANON. (BRAMAH, E.). *What Might Have Been: the story of a social war.*
ANON. (KERCHNAWE, H.). *Unser letzter Kampf.* Leipzig.
ANON. *A Second Franco-German War and its consequences for England.* Translation of Cassandre, *Une guerre franco-allemande* (1906).
ASKEW, ALICE, and CLAUDE. *The Sword of Peace.*
BLEIBTREU, KARL. *Die 'Offensiv-Invasion' gegen England.*
BUNDSCHUH. *Die Revolution von 1912.* Leipzig.
COLE, R. W. *The Death Trap.*
DAWSON, A. J. *The Message.*
GRIER, S. C. *The Power of the Keys.*
GRIFFITH, G. *The World Peril of 1910.*
HOPPENSTEDT, JULIUS. *Die Schlacht der Zukunft.*
LE QUEUX, WILLIAM. *L'Invasion de 1910.*
MACPHERSON, J. F. *A Yankee Napoleon.*
MARTIN, RUDOLF EMIL. *Berlin–Bagdad, 1910–1931.* Leipzig.
OPPENHEIM, E. P. *The Secret.*
SCOTT, H. *The Way of War.*
SEESTERN (GRAUTOFF, F. H.). *Armageddon, 190–.* Translation of *'1906' Der Zusammenbruch der alten Welt.*
TERANUS, V. E. (ZAPP, ARTHUR). *Der letzte Krieg; ein Zukunftsbild.*
VAUX, P., and YEXLEY, L. *When the Eagle Flies Seaward.*

1908 AGRICOLA (Pseud.). *How England was Saved.*
ANON. *Luftschiff 13. Ein Zukunftsroman.* Leipzig.
ARGUS (Pseud.). *Die Engländer kommen! Der Ueberfall Hamburgs durch die englische Flotte.* Hamburg.
BURGOYNE, A. H. *The War Inevitable.*

Crabapple, John (Pseud.). *The War of 1908 for the supremacy of the Pacific.* Translated as: *Der Krieg von 1908 um die Vorherrschaft im 'Stillen Ozean'.*

Danrit, Capitaine (Driant, E. A.). *Guerre maritime et sous-marine.*

Giffard, P. *La Guerre infernale.*

Grace, S. *Dennis Martin, traitor.*

Kernahan, C. *The Red Peril.*

Kipling, A. W. *The New Dominion: a tale of tomorrow's wars.*

Mayne, J. D. *The Triumph of Socialism.*

Navarchus (Vaux, P., and Yexley, L.). *The World's Awakening.*

Norton, Roy. *The Vanishing Fleets.*

Parabellum (Grautoff, F. H.) *Banzai!* Leipzig.

Wagebald, Michael. *Europa in Flammen. Der deutsche Zukunftskrieg von 1909.*

Wells, H. G. *The War in the Air.*

1909 Andrew, Stephen. *The Serpent and the Cross.*

Anon. *Provinz Nordmark.*

Bernstorff, Graf von. *Deutschlands Flotte im Kampf.*

Blyth, J. *The Swoop of the Vulture.*

Chester, Lord. *The Great Red Dragon.* Florida.

Curties, Capt. H. *When England Slept.*

Fitzpatrick, Everett Hugh. *The Coming Conflict of Nations.* New York.

Hawke, Napier. *The Invasion that did not Come Off.*

Hookham, Albert E. *Amid the Strife.*

Hoppenstedt, Julius. *Ein neues Wörth. Ein Schlachtenbild der Zukunft.*

Hoppenstedt, Julius. *Une bataille de demain. Exposé critique de l'ouvrage du major Hoppenstedt, 'Die Schlacht der Zukunft'.*

Kirmess, C. H. *The Australian Crisis.*

Martin, Rudolf. *Der Weltkrieg in den Lüften.* Leipzig.

Maurus (Pseud.). *Ave Caesar! Deutsche Luftschiffe im Kampfe um Marokko.* Leipzig.

Parabellum (Grautoff, F. H.). *Banzai!* Translated from the German.

A Patriot (du Maurier, Guy). *An Englishman's Home. A play.*

SLADEN, DOUGLAS. *The Tragedy of the Pyramids.*

TOWNROE, B. S. *A Nation in Arms.*

WILLIAMS, L. *The Great Raid.*

WODEHOUSE, P. G. *The Swoop! or, how Clarence saved England.*

1910 ANON. *The German Invasion of England.*

ANON. *Neerlands doodsstrijd in 1918.* Utrecht.

BELL, COL. CHARLES PERCIVAL LYNDEN. *How Germany Makes War.*

BERESFORD, L. *The Second Rising.*

CUTLIFFE-HYNE, C. J. *Empire of the World.*

DANRIT, CAPITAINE (DRIANT, E. A.). *L'Alerte.*

DUDLEY, CARL HENSON. *And This is War.* New York.

GLENDON, G. *The Emperor of the Air.*

GODFREY, H. *The Man who ended War.*

HALE, COL. LONSDALE. *The Horrors of War in Great Britain.*

KIPLING, ARTHUR WELLESLEY. *The Shadow of Glory, being a history of the Great War of 1910–1911.*

1911 GRIFFITH, G. *The Lord of Labour.*

POLLOCK, LT.-Col. ALSAGER. *Lord Roastem's Campaign in North-Eastern France.*

SCHMIDT-KESTNER, HANS. *Die Gelbe Gefahr.* Wiesbaden.

1912 ANON. *Birkenfeld. Und dann . . .?! Fortsetzung der Schlacht auf dem Birkenfelde in Westfalen 191..! Errettung des deutschen Reichs vom Untergang! Von einem aktiven deutschen General.* See the entry below under Civrieux.

BLYTH, J. *The Peril of Pines Place.*

BRACCIO DI MONTONE, N. (MAUNI, BARON ROGER DE). *La Bataille de la Woevre (1915).*

BREX (TWELLS, J.). *The Civil War of 1915.*

CAMPBELL, SPENCER. *Under the Red Ensign.*

CIVRIEUX, COMMANDANT DE. *La bataille du 'Champ des Bouleaux' 191..* Translated as: *Der Untergang des deutschen Reiches. Die Schlacht auf dem Birkenfeld 191..*

EXZELSIOR (SCHULZE-GALLERA, DR. SIEGMAR). *Michael der Grosse. Eine Kaiserbiographie der Zukunft.* Leipzig.

FAWKES, F. ATTFIELD. *Found—a Man.*

JANSON, GUSTAF. *Pride of War.* Translated from the Swedish.

LAMSZUS, W. *Das Menschenschlachthaus.*

MARK TIME (IRWIN, H. C.). *A Derelict Empire.*

NAVAL OFFICER, A. *Great was the Fall.*

PALMER, WILLIAM. *Under Home Rule.*

ROSNY, J-H. *Bataille.*

SEARCHLIGHT (EARDLEY-WILMOT, REAR-ADML). *The Battle of the North Sea in 1914.*

SOMMERFELD, A. *Frankreichs Ende im Jahre 19??.*

WALLACE, EDGAR. *Private Sellby.*

1913. ANON. *Les Ailes de la victoire.*

ANON. *Le Partage de l'Allemagne.* Written in answer to Sommerfeld, A., above.

AUSTIN, F. BRITTEN. *In Action: Studies in war.*

BLEIBTREU, KARL. *Weltbrand.*

GASTINE, L. *War in Space: a grand romance of aircraft war between France and Germany.* Translated from the French.

GAULOIS, FRANC (Pseud.). *La Fin de la Prusse et le démembrement de l'Allemagne.* Geneva.

HANSEN, V. *Die vierte Waffe.* Leipzig.

HOPPENSTEDT, JULIUS. *Deutschlands Heer in der Entscheidungsschlacht.*

HOPPENSTEDT, JULIUS. *Die Millionenschlacht an der Saar. Ein Beispiel moderner Kriegskunst.*

LAMSZUS, WILHELM. *The Human Slaughter-House.* Translation of *Das Menschenschlachthaus* (1912).

POLLOCK, LT.-COL. ALSAGER. *In the Cockpit of Europe.*

SEWELL, H. *A German Invasion.*

SHIEL, M. P. *The Dragon.*

SOMMERFELD, A. *Le Partage de la France.* See entry under Sommerfeld, A., 1912.

1914 ANON. (BUAT, LT. GÉNÉRAL). *La Concentration allemande. D'après un document trouvé dans un compartiment de chemin de fer.*

ANON. *Der europäische krieg.*

ANON. *Das Resultat des russisch-österreichischen Krieges, 1918.* Cracow.

ANON. (LEHMANN-RUSSBÜLDT, O.). *Die Schöpfung der Vereinigten Staaten von Europa.*

DOYLE, SIR A. C. *Danger. Strand Magazine,* July. Translated as: *Der Tauchbootkrieg. Wie Kapitän Sirius England niederzwang.*

GOUVRIEUX, MARC. *Haut les ailes! Carnet de route d'un officier aviateur pendant la guerre de 19...*

LEONARD, FRANÇOIS. *La Conquête de Londres*. Geneva.

MACHEN, A. *The Bowmen. Evening News*, 20 September.

SAKI (MONRO, H. H.). *When William Came.*

NEWTON, W. D. *The North Afire: a picture of what may be.*

NEWTON, W. D. *War.*

PALMER, FREDERICK. *The Last Shot*. New York.

RAUTENBURG, L. *Der Dreibund an die front!* Dresden.

SOMMERFELD, ADOLF. *'How Germany crushed France'. The story of the greatest conspiracy in history*. Translated from the German. See entry under Sommerfeld, A. 1912.

WELLS, H. G. *The World Set Free.*

Y. *The German Campaign against France.* Reprinted from the *Fortnightly Review*, Sept. 1911. Washington.

1915 ANON. (MÜNCH, PAUL GEORG). *Hindenburgs Einmarsch in London.* Leipzig.

BARNEY, J. STEWART. *L.P.M. The End of the Great War.* New York.

BERNSTORFF, HANS NIKOLAUS ERNST. *Ran an den feind.* Leipzig.

COWEN, L. *'Wake up!': a dream of tomorrow.*

GIESY, JOHN ULRICH. *All for His Country.* New York.

HAINES, D. H. *Clearing the Seas.*

WALLACE, E. *'1925': the Story of a Fatal Peace.*

WALKER, J. BERNARD. *America Fallen! The sequel to the European War.* London and New York.

1916 ANON. (MÜNCH, PAUL GEORG). *Hindenburg's March into London.* Translation of Münch's *Hindenburgs Einmarsch* (1915).

ANON. *Der nächste Weltkrieg. Die Prophezeiung eines neutralen Diplomaten.*

CASSANDRA (Pseud.). *Belgien 1906 überfallen!* Translation of *Une guerre Franco-allemande* (1906).

GOUVRIEUX, MARC. *With Wings Outspread.* Translation of *Haut les ailes* (1914).

MOFFETT, CLEVELAND. *The Conquest of America.* London and New York.

MULLER, JULIUS WASHINGTON. *The Invasion of America.* New York.

WALKER, ROWLAND. *Buckle of Submarine V2.*

1917 ALLEN, R. *Captain Gardiner of the International Police.*

KARTOFFEL, BARON VON (Pseud.). *The Germans in Cork: being the letters of his Excellency, the . . . Military Governor of Cork in the year 1918.*

STEAD, F. HERBERT. *No more War!*

1919 COURNOS, JOHN. *London under the Bolsheviks: a Londoner's dream on returning from Petrograd.*

MOTTA, LUIGI. *The Princess of the Roses.* Translated from the Italian.

NEWTE, H. W. C. *The Red Fury.*

WAGNER, ÉMILE R. *La troisième guerre punique; la revanche de la kultur.*

1920 HAMBROOK, E. C. *The Red Tomorrow.*

SHANKS, E. *The People of the Ruins.*

1921 AUTENRIETH, OTTO. *Der Roman der deutschen Zukunft.* Munich.

DE SAUNIER, BAUDRY. *Comment Paris a été détruit.*

SOLF, MAJ. F. E. *1934: Deutschlands Auferstehung.* Naumburg.

1922 ABEL-MUSGRAVE, DR CURT. *Der Bazillenkrieg.* Frankfurt.

BARBOR, H. R. *Against the Red Sky.*

FECHNER, E. *Die Vernichtung der Westmächte durch den erwachenden Orient.* Naumburg.

GRASSEGGER, W. *Die rächende Stunde.* Naumburg.

GRASSEGGER, W. *Der zweite Weltkrieg.* Naumburg.

LIST, MAJ. SINGLE (Pseud.). *The Battle of Booby's Bluffs.*

RABE, C. *Nie wieder Krieg.* Naumburg.

VAN PEDROE-SAVIDGE, E. *The Flying Submarine.*

1923 ADDISON, H. (OWEN, H. C.). *The Battle of London.*

GRAHAM, P. A. *The Collapse of Homo Sapiens.*

WHARTON, A. *The Man on the Hill.*

X, PROFESSEUR. *La Guerre microbienne; la fin du monde.*

1924 ANON. (FORBES, ALEXANDER). *The Radio Gunner.* Boston, Mass.

BYWATER, H. C. *The Great Pacific war; a history of the American–Japanese campaign of 1931–33.* London and New York.

HUSSINGTREE, MARTIN. *Konyetz.*

MACCLURE, V. *Ultimatum.*

MEILLAC, C. *1935. Roman sur la prochaine guerre franco-allemande.*

1925 CORON, H. *Ten Years Hence?*

EGBERT, H. M. *The Sea Demons.*

Lynch, Bohun. *Menace from the Moon.*

Panhans, Ernst J. *Der schwarzgelbe Weltbund.* Hamburg.

Schoenaich, Gen.-Maj. *Der Krieg im Jahre 1930.*

1926 Alexander, Hans. *Der Völkermord im kommenden Gift-gaskrieg.* Wiesbaden.

Austin, F. Britten. *The war-god walks again.*

Becher, Johannes. $(CHCl{=}CH)_3As$ (*Levisite*)*; oder der einzige gerechte krieg.* Vienna.

Desmond, S. *Ragnarok.*

Grant, I. F. *A Candle in the Hills.*

Halsbury, Earl of. *1944.*

Spanner, E. F. *The Broken Trident.*

Spanner, E. F. *The Naviators.*

1927 Daudet, Léon. *Le Napus.*

Guggenberger, S. *Eurafasia.* Vienna.

Hofbauer, L. *Der Pestkrieg.* Regensburg.

Montague, C. E. *Right off the Map.*

Spanner, E. F. *The Harbour of Death.*

1928 Bentley, N. K. *Drake's Mantle.*

Noyes, P. B. *The Pallid Giant.*

Raxin, Alexander. *Der nächste Massenmord.* Leipzig.

Sadler, A. *Red Ending.*

1929 Edwards, G. (Pendray, G. E.). *The Earth Tube.*

Gibbons, F. P. *The Red Napoleon.* London and New York.

Heyck, Hans. *Deutschland ohne Deutsche.* Leipzig.

Méric, Victor. *La 'Der des Der'.*

Penmare, W. (Nisot, M. E.). *The Man who Could Stop War.*

1930 Anon. *Revolution 1933.*

Blair, Hamish. *1957.* Edinburgh.

Güntsche, Georg. *Panropa.* Cologne.

Jerrold, Douglas. *Storm over Europe.*

Kossak-Raytenau, K. L. *Katastrophe, 1940.*

1931 Alter, Junius. *Nie wieder Krieg . . .?!* Leipzig.

Anon. *La surprise. Überraschung. Traduction de C. Bernart.* Claims to be the translation of a manuscript written in 1931 by an officer in the German army, in which he describes the first weeks of the war he believes to be imminent.

Artus, Louis. *Paix sur la terre.*

BARTZ, KARL. *Krieg—1960.*

BERKELEY, REGINALD. *Cassandra.*

BLAIR, H. *Governor Hardy.*

BLAIR, H. *The Great Gesture.*

BRAUN, F. *Einfall in London.*

GOBSCH, H. *Wahn-Europa, 1934.*

GRAHAM, H. E. (HAMILTON, ERNEST GRAHAM). *The Battle of Dora.*

KLINE, OTIS ADELBERT. *Maza of the Moon.* New York.

LE PRÊTRE, WILLIAM. *The Bolshevik.*

MILES (SOUTHWOLD, S.). *The Gas War of 1940.*

NEWMAN, B. *Armoured Doves.*

ROYET, COL. *La Guerre est déclarée.*

1932 EDMONDS, HARRY. *The Riddle of the Straits.*

GOBSCH, HANS. *Death Rattle.* Translation of *Wahn-Europa* (1931).

GODWIN, G. *Empty Victory.*

HELDERS, MAJ. (KNAUSS, ROBERT). *Luftkrieg—1936. Die Zertrümmerung von Paris.*

HELDERS, MAJ. (KNAUSS, ROBERT). *The War in the Air, 1936.*

IMMANUEL (Pseud.). *Der grosse Zukunftskrieg.*

JONES, E. W. C., and OWEN, F. *Red Rainbow.*

KONDOR (Pseud.). *Gelb gegen Weiss.*

LEERS, JOHANN VON. *Bomben auf Hamburg.* Leipzig.

NITRAM, H. (MARTIN, H.). *Achtung! Ostmarkenrundfunk! Polnische Truppen haben heute Nacht die ostpreussische Grenze überschritten.* Oldenburg.

O'SHEEL, S. *It Never Could Happen; or, the second American revolution.* New York.

1933 BLACK, LADBROKE. *The Poison War.*

CORDAY, MICHEL. *Ciel rose.*

EDMONDS, H. *Red Invader.*

GROSSER, R. F. *Asakafu mobilisiert den Osten.* Bremen.

HERMANN, FRANZ. *Die Erde in Flammen.* Leipzig.

SIBSON, F. H. *Unthinkable.*

STERNE, JULIAN. *The Secret of the Zodiac.*

VIERECK, G. S., and ELDRIDGE, P. *Prince Pax.*

WELLS, H. G. *The Shape of Things to Come.*

WILLIAMS, C. *Shadows of Ecstasy.*

1934 CHRISTIE, D. *The Striking Force.*
CHOMTON, WERNER. *Weltbrand von Morgen.* Stuttgart.
CURTIS, MONICA. *Landslide.*
DALTON, M. *The Black Death.*
DAUDET, LÉON. *Ciel de feu.*
MACILRAITH, F., and CONNOLLY, R. *Invasion from the Air.*
MOSELEY, M. *War upon Women.*
PRESTRE, WILLY. *Tocsins dans la nuit.*
REID, LESLIE. *Cauldron Bubble.*
SPENCER, D. A., and RANDERSON, W. *North Sea Monster.*
TROUBETZKOY, PRINCESS P., and NEVINSON, C. R. W. *Exodus A.D. A Warning to Civilians.*
WHEATLEY, D. *Black August.*
BIALKOWSKI, STANISLAUS. *Krieg im All.* Leipzig.
BROWNE, DOUGLAS G. *The Stolen Boat-Train.*
CONNELL, JOHN. *David go Back.*
CORNWALLIS-WEST, G. *The Woman who Stopped War.*
DETRE, L. *Kampf zweier Welten.* Vienna.
DIVINE, A. D. *They Blocked the Suez Canal.*
1935 OHLINGER, ERNST. *Bomben auf Kohlenstadt.*
POLLARD, L. *Menace.*
STOKES, SIMPSON. *Air-Gods' Parade.*
STUART, FRANCIS. *The Angel of Pity.*
WARD, R. H. *The Sun Shall Rise.*
WRIGHT, S. F. *Prelude in Prague: a story of the war of 1938.*
1936 BARAUDE, H. (TUPINIER, BARON AUGUSTIN JOSEPH). *La Catastrophe.*
BEVERLEY, BARRINGTON. *The Space Raiders.*
BREHPOL, WILHELM. *Vom Ende der Tage.* Essen.
CHANNING, MARK. *The poisoned mountain.*
DETRE, L. *War of Two Worlds.* Translation of *Kampf zweier Welten* (1935).
DEVERDUN, P-L. *Le 'Redoutable'; journal d'un commandant de vedette.*
KOSSAK-RAYTENAU, KARL-LUDWIG. *Lermontow vernichtet die Welt.*
MACLEOD, J. G. *Overture to Cambridge.*
MACPHERSON, IAN. *Wild Harbour.*
O'NEILL, J. *Day of Wrath.*

Phillpotts, E. *The Owl of Athene.*

Tolstoi, Alexei. *The Death Box.* Translated from the Russian.

Tunstall, B. *Eagles Restrained.*

Wright, S. F. *Four Days' War.*

1937 Bialkowski, Stanislaus. *Der Radiumkrieg!* Leipzig.

Campion, Sarah (Coulton, Mary). *Thirty Million Gas Masks.*

Capek, K. *War with the Newts.* Translated from the Czech.

Wright, S. F. *Megiddo's Ridge.*

1938 Cacaud, Michel. *La Guerre des ailes . . . demain.* Toulouse.

Desmond, S. *Chaos.*

Linklater, E. *The Impregnable Women.*

Martin, J. S. *General Manpower.* New York.

Pavlenko, P. *Red Planes fly East.* Translated from the Russian.

Pollard, Capt. A. O. *Air Reprisal.*

Ramseyer, Edwin. *Airmen over the Suburb.* Translated from the French.

Seton, Graham. *According to Plan.*

1939 Cazal, Comdt. *L'Afrique en flammes.*

Cazal, Comdt. *Batailles pour la mer.*

Cazal, Comdt. *La Fin par le pétrole.*

Cazal, Comdt. *La guerre! La guerre!*

Cazal, Comdt. *Maginot-Siegfried.*

Chadwick, Philip George. *The death guard.*

Craig, T. *Plague over London.*

Schubert, A. *Weltenwende durch Gas.*

Shute, N. (Norway, N.S.). *What Happened to the Corbetts.* (American edition: *Ordeal*, New York, 1939.)

Verdun, Comdt. *L'escadron cyclone.*

Verdun, Comdt. *Face à l'ennemi.*

White, A. *Attack on America.* Boston, Mass.

1940 Brown, D., and Serpell, C. *Loss of Eden.*

Nelson, A. D. *America Betrayed.*

Noyes, Alfred. *The Last Man.*

Prasser, Viktoria. *Die Sage von der Zukunftsschlacht am Baum.*

1941 Nathan, Robert. *They Went on Together.*

1942 Boshell, Gordon. *John Brown's body.*

Divine, A. D. *Tunnel from Calais.*

Newman, Bernard. *Secret Weapon.*

SACKVILLE-WEST, V. *Grand Canyon.*
1943 CHAMBERS, WHITMAN. *Invasion!* New York.
HAWKIN, M. *When Adolf came.*
KENT, CLAUDE H. *Armistice or Total Victory?*
RUSSELL, E. F. *Sinister Barrier.*
1944 BEYMER, WILLIAM GILMORE. *12.20 p.m.* New York.
COLLINS, E. *Mariners of Space.*
LESSNER, ERWIN. *Phantom Victory: A Fictional History of the Fourth Reich 1945–60.* New York.
1945 FOWLER, SYDNEY (WRIGHT, SYDNEY FOWLER). *The Adventure of the Blue Room.*
1946 ROSE, F. H. *The Maniac's Dream.*
1947 ENGEL, LEONARD, and PILLER, EMANUEL S. *World Aflame.*
KEPPEL-JONES, ARTHUR. *When Smuts Goes.*
1948 DE CAMP, L. SPRAGUE. *Divide and Rule.* Reading, Pa.
FAULCONBRIDGE, PHILIP (Pseud.). *Commissars over Britain.*
GIBBS, H. *Pawns in Ice.*
GROOM, P. *The Purple Twilight.*
HUBBARD, L. RON. *Final Blackout.* Providence, R.I.
HUXLEY, ALDOUS. *Ape and Essence.*
1949 BARJAVEL, RENÉ. *Le Diable l'emporte.*
BINDER, EANDO. *Lords of Creation.* Philadelphia.
DEMAITRE, EDMUND, and APPLEMAN, MARK J. *The Liberation of Manhattan.* New York.
JAMESON, S. *The Moment of Truth.*
ORWELL, GEORGE (BLAIR, ERIC). *Nineteen Eighty-Four.*
1950 FITZGIBBON, C. *Iron Hoop.*
GOHDE, HERMANN. *Der achte Tag.* Innsbruck.
ROBBAN, RANDOLPH. *Si l'Allemagne avait vaincu.*
SUDDABY, D. *The Star Raiders.*
1951 DUBOIS, THEODORA. *Solution T-25.* New York.
GUERARD, A. J. *Night Journey.*
SMITH, G. O. *Pattern for Conquest.*
1952 CAMERON, BERL. *Cosmic Echelon.*
JONES, RAYMOND, F. *This Island Earth.* Chicago.
KORRODI-WYLER, KARL. *Die drei grossen Weltkriege der Endzeit der christlichen Aera.* Zürich.
MACDONALD, JOHN D. *Ballroom of the Skies.* New York.

REYNOLDS, PHILIP (Pseud.). *When and If.* New York. English edition: *It happened like this* (1952).
SCOTT, W. *The Domesday Story.*
SLATER, H. J. *The Smashed World.*
WARD, JULIAN. *We Died in Bond Street.*
WILLIAMS, I. *Dangerous Waters.*
1953 BERRY, B. *From What Far Star.*
BERRY, B. *The Venom-Seekers.*
BULMER, H. K. *Empire in Chaos.*
BULMER, H. K. *Galactic Intrigue.*
BULMER, H. K. *Space Salvage.*
BULMER, H. K. *The Stars are Ours.*
CAPON, P. *The World at Bay.*
CONKLIN, G. (ed.). *Invaders of Earth.*
DIVINE, DAVID. *Atom at Spithead.*
ELLIOT, L. *Overlord New York.*
ELLIOT, L. *The Third Mutant.*
LANG, GREGOR. *Terra.* New York.
LORRAINE, P. *Dark Boundaries.*
McINTOSH, J. T. (MACGREGOR, J. M.). *World out of Mind.* First printed U.S.A.
MERRIL, J. *Shadow on the Hearth.* First printed U.S.A.
TUCKER, W. *The Long Loud Silence.* First printed U.S.A.
VAN VOGT, A. E. *The House that Stood Still.* First printed U.S.A.
VAN VOGT, A. E. *Slan.* First printed U.S.A.
VONNEGUT, K. *Player Piano.* First printed U.S.A.
WELLARD, J. *Night in Babylon.*
WILLIAMSON, J. *The Humanoids.* First printed U.S.A.
WYNDHAM, J. (HARRIS, J. B.). *The Kraken Wakes.*
1954 BENNETT, M. *The Long Way Back.*
BLACK, DOROTHY. *Candles in the Dark.*
BOUQUET, MARCEL. *Et ce fut la guerre atomique.*
BRADBURY, R. *Fahrenheit 451.* First printed U.S.A.
BURKE, J. *The Echoing Worlds.*
CROWCROFT, P. *The Fallen Sky.*
DEXTER, W. (PRITCHARD, W. T.). *World in Eclipse.*
KUTTNER, HENRY. *Fury.* First printed U.S.A.

Leinster, Murray. *The Forgotten Planet*. New York.

Mackenzie, N. *Invasion from Space.*

Merak, A. J. *Dark Andromeda.*

Rockwell, Carey. *The Revolt on Venus*. New York.

Russell, E. F. *Sentinels from Space.*

Smith, E. E. *Triplanetary*. First printed U.S.A.

Tubb, E. C. *World at Bay.*

Tubb, E. C. *The Stellar Legion.*

Vandel, J. G. *Enemy beyond Pluto*. Translated from the French.

Van Vogt, A. E. *The Weapon Makers*. First printed U.S.A.

Wright, S. Fowler. *Spider's War*. New York.

Wylie, Philip. *Tomorrow!* New York.

1955 Ash, A. *Conditioned for Space.*

Boland, J. *White August.*

Bounds, S. J. *The Moon Raiders.*

Brackett, Leigh. *The Long Tomorrow.*

Burke, J. *Revolt of the Humans.*

Carr, C. *Salamander War.*

Elliott, H. Chandler. *Reprieve from Paradise*. New York.

Elton, J. *The Green Plantations.*

Falkner, J. *Overlords of Andromeda.*

Frazee, Steve. *The Sky Block*. First printed U.S.A.

Jones, Raymond F. *This Island Earth*. First printed U.S.A.

McIntosh, J. T. (J. M. MacGregor). *The Fittest*. New York.

Moore, Ward. *Bring the Jubilee*. First printed U.S.A.

Pangborn, E. *A Mirror for Observers.*

Savage, R. *When the Moon Died.*

Shafer, R. *The Conquered Place*. First printed U.S.A.

Silverberg, Robert. *Revolt on Alpha C.* New York.

1956 Bounds, S. J. *The World Wrecker.*

Frank, Pat. *Forbidden Area*. Philadelphia.

Jones, Raymond F. *The Secret People*. New York.

Kornbluth, C. M. *Christmas Eve*. First printed U.S.A., with title *Not this August.*

Lott, S. Makepeace. *Escape to Venus.*

Simak, C. *Time and Again*. First printed U.S.A.

1957 Adler, Allen A. *Mach 1*. New York.

Banister, Manly. *Conquest of Earth*. New York.

Barlow, J. *One Half of the World.*

Bloch-Michel, J. *The Flight into Egypt.* Translated from the French.

Frank, P. (Hart, H.). *Seven Days to Never.*

Gayle, Harold. *Spawn of the Vortex.* New York.

Kirst, H. H. *Keiner kommt davon; Bericht von der letzten Tagen Europas.* Vienna and Munich.

Mackenzie, N. *The Wrath to Come.*

Mars, A. (Gillespie, A. C.). *Atomic Submarine.*

Moore, C. L. *Doomsday Morning.* New York.

Powys, John Cowper. *Up and Out.*

Randall, Robert. *The Shrouded Planet.* New York.

Richards, G. *Brother Bear.*

Shute, N. (Norway, N. S.). *On the Beach.*

Wheatley, D. *Stranger than Fiction.*

1958 Bryant, P. *Two Hours to Doom.*

Cole, B. *Subi: the Volcano.*

Cooper, E. *The Uncertain Midnight.*

Godwin, Tom. *The Survivors.* Hicksville, N.Y.

Jones, E. *Head in the Sand.*

Jones, Mervin. *On the Last Day.*

Rigg, Robert B. *War—1974.* Harrisburg, Pa.

Russell, E. F. *Wasp.*

1959 Brunner, J. *The Brink.*

Chapkin, P. *Light of Mars.*

Clarkson, Helen. *The Last Day.* New York.

Frank, P. *Alas Babylon!* First printed U.S.A.

Holly, J. Hunter. *Encounter.* New York.

Roshwald, M. *Level 7.*

Russell, E. F. *Next of Kin.*

Van Vogt, A. E. *The War Against the Rull.* First printed U.S.A.

1960 Casewit, Curtis W. *The Peacemakers.* New York.

Chilton, C. *The World in Peril.*

Herbert, F. *The Dragon in the Sea.* First printed U.S.A.

Fitzgibbon, C. *When the Kissing had to Stop.*

Hartley, L. P. *Facial Justice.*

King-Hall, Stephen. *Men of Destiny.*

Lymington, J. *The Giant Stumbles.*

MILLER, W. *A Canticle for Leibowitz*. First printed U.S.A.
POHL, FREDERIK. *Slave Ship*. First printed U.S.A.
GRINNELL, DAVID. *Destiny's Orbit*. New York.
JOHNSON, L. P. V. *In the Time of the Thetans*.
LYMINGTON, J. *The Coming of the Strangers*.
MANTLEY, JOHN. *The 27th Day*.
WILSON, ANGUS. *The Old Men at the Zoo*.
1962 BARRON, D. G. *The Zilov Bombs*.
DICK, PHILIP K. *The Man in the High Castle*. New York.
HOLLY, J. HUNTER. *The Dark Planet*. New York.
MACTYRE, PAUL. *Midge*.
NEWMAN, B. *The Blue Ants*.
ROSHWALD, M. *A Small Armageddon*. First printed U.S.A.
SMITH, EVELYN E. *The Perfect Planet*. New York.
VAN GREENAWAY, PETER. *The Crucified City*.
1963 ANDERSON, PAUL. *After Doomsday*. First printed U.S.A.
BOND, J. HARVEY. *The Other World*. New York.
BURDICK, EUGENE, and WHEELER, HARVEY. *Fail Safe*.
1964 BRADDON, RUSSELL. *The Year of the Angry Rabbit*,
HOUGH, S. B. *Beyond the Eleventh Hour*.
TREW, ANTONY. *Two Hours to Darkness*.
WALLIS, DAVE. *Only Lovers Left Alive*.
1965 BLACKER, IRWIN R. *Chain of Command*.
COMPTON, D. G. *The Quality of Mercy*.
GEORGE, PETER. *Commander 1*.
HALE, MARTIN. *The Fourth Reich*.

INDEX

Persons and Subjects

Books and Periodicals mentioned in Text and Notes